The Quran With Tafsir Ibn Kathir Part 10 of 30: Al Anfal 041 To At Tauba 092

The Quran With Tafsir Ibn Kathir Part 10 of 30: Al Anfal 041 To At Tauba 092

With
Arabic Script, Transliteration of Arabic, Meaning in English and Ibn Kathir's Abridged Tafsir (Explanation)

Chapter 8: Al Anfal 041 To Chapter 9: At Tauba 092

Muhammad Saed Abdul-Rahman
BSc, DipHE

© Muhammad Saed Abdul-Rahman, 2012
ISBN 978-1-86179-855-8

All Rights reserved

British Library Cataloguing in Publication Data. A Catalogue record for this book is available from the British Library

Designed, Typeset and produced by:
MSA Publication Limited, 4 Bello Close, Herne Hill,
London SE24 9BW
United Kingdom

Cover design: Houriyah Abdul-Rahman

TABLE OF CONTENTS

TABLE OF CONTENTS .... **V**
PRELUDE .... **XIII**
    OPENING SERMAN XIII
    OUR MISSION XIV
    BIOGRAPHY OF HAFIZ IBN KATHIR (701 H - 774 H) XIV
        Ibn Kathir's Teachers xiv
        Ibn Kathir's Students xv
        Ibn Kathir's Books xv
        Ibn Kathir's Death xvi

PREFACE .... **XVII**
    ABOUT THIS BOOK XVII
    PERFORMING PROSTRATION WHILE READING THE QUR'AN XVII

PART 10 FULL ARABIC TEXT **1**

INTRODUCTION TO CHAPTER (SURAH) 8: AL-ANFAL (SPOILS OF WAR, BOOTY) **12**
    IBN KATHIR'S INTRODUCTION 12

CHAPTER (SURAH) 8: AL-ANFAL (SPOILS OF WAR, BOOTY), VERSES 041–075 .... **12**
    Surah: 8 Ayah: 41 .... *12*
        Tafsir Ibn Kathir 12
        Ruling on the Spoils of War (Ghanimah and Fai) 12
    Surah: 8 Ayah: 42 .... *16*
        Tafsir Ibn Kathir 16
        Some Details of the Battle of Badr 16
    Surah: 8 Ayah: 43 & Ayah: 44 .... *19*
        Tafsir Ibn Kathir 19
        Allah made each Group look few in the Eye of the Other 19
    Surah: 8 Ayah: 45 & Ayah: 46 .... *21*
        Tafsir Ibn Kathir 21
        Manners of War 21
        The Command for Endurance when the Enemy Engaging 22
    Surah: 8 Ayah: 47, Ayah: 48 & Ayah: 49 .... *22*
        Tafsir Ibn Kathir 23
        The Idolators leave Makkah, heading for Badr 23
        Shaytan makes Evil seem fair and deceives the Idolators 24
        The Position of the Hypocrites in Badr 25
    Surah: 8 Ayah: 50 & Ayah: 51 .... *26*
        Tafsir Ibn Kathir 26
        The Angels smite the Disbelievers upon capturing Their Souls 26
    Surah: 8 Ayah: 52 .... *27*

Tafsir Ibn Kathir	28
Surah: 8 Ayah: 53 & Ayah: 54	*28*
Tafsir Ibn Kathir	29
Surah: 8 Ayah: 55, Ayah: 56 & Ayah: 57	*29*
Tafsir Ibn Kathir	30
Striking Hard against Those Who disbelieve and break the Covenants	30
Surah: 8 Ayah: 58	*30*
Tafsir Ibn Kathir	30
Surah: 8 Ayah: 59 & Ayah: 60	*31*
Tafsir Ibn Kathir	32
Making Preparations for War to strike Fear in the Hearts of the Enemies of Allah	32
Surah: 8 Ayah: 61, Ayah: 62 & Ayah: 63	*35*
Tafsir Ibn Kathir	35
The Command to Facilitate Peace when the Enemy seeks a Peaceful Resolution	35
Reminding the Believers of Allah's Favor of uniting Them	36
Surah: 8 Ayah: 64, Ayah: 65 & Ayah: 66	*37*
Tafsir Ibn Kathir	38
Encouraging Believers to fight in Jihad; the Good News that a Few Muslims can overcome a Superior Enemy Force	38
Surah: 8 Ayah: 67, Ayah: 68 & Ayah: 69	*39*
Tafsir Ibn Kathir	40
Surah: 8 Ayah: 70 & Ayah: 71	*42*
Tafsir Ibn Kathir	42
Pagan Prisoners at Badr were promised better than what They lost, if They become Righteous in the Future	42
Surah: 8 Ayah: 72	*45*
Tafsir Ibn Kathir	46
The Muhajirin and Al-Ansar are the Supporters of One Another	46
The Believers Who did not emigrate did not yet receive the Benefits of Wilayah	47
Surah: 8 Ayah: 73	*48*
Tafsir Ibn Kathir	49
The Disbelievers are Allies of Each Other; the Muslims are not their Allies	49
Surah: 8 Ayah: 74 & Ayah: 75	*49*
Tafsir Ibn Kathir	50
Believers in Truth	50
Inheritance is for Designated Degrees of Relatives	51
CHAPTER (SURAH) 9: AL-BARA'AT (THE IMMUNITY) OR AT-TAWBA (REPENTANCE, DISPENSATION) , VERSES 001-092	**51**
Surah: 9 Ayah: 1 & Ayah: 2	*51*
Tafsir Ibn Kathir	52
Why there is no Basmalah in the Beginning of This Surah	52
Publicizing the Disavowal of the Idolators	52
Surah: 9 Ayah: 3	*53*

Table of Contents

    Tafsir Ibn Kathir 53
        Allah says, this is a declaration, ... 53
Surah: 9 Ayah: 4 .... *55*
    Tafsir Ibn Kathir 55
        Existing Peace Treaties remained valid until the End of Their Term 55
Surah: 9 Ayah: 5 .... *56*
    Tafsir Ibn Kathir 56
        This is the Ayah of the Sword 56
Surah: 9 Ayah: 6 .... *57*
    Tafsir Ibn Kathir 57
        Idolators are granted Safe Passage if They seek It 57
Surah: 9 Ayah: 7 .... *59*
    Tafsir Ibn Kathir 59
        Affirming the Disavowel of the Idolators 59
Surah: 9 Ayah: 8 .... *60*
    Tafsir Ibn Kathir 60
Surah: 9 Ayah: 9, Ayah: 10 & Ayah: 11 .... *60*
    Tafsir Ibn Kathir 61
Surah: 9 Ayah: 12 .... *61*
    Tafsir Ibn Kathir 62
        The Oaths of the Leaders of Disbelief mean nothing to Them 62
Surah: 9 Ayah: 13, Ayah: 14 & Ayah: 15 .... *62*
    Tafsir Ibn Kathir 63
        Encouragement to fight the Disbelievers, and some Benefits of fighting Them 63
Surah: 9 Ayah: 16 .... *64*
    Tafsir Ibn Kathir 64
        Among the Wisdom of Jihad is to test the Muslims 64
Surah: 9 Ayah: 17 & Ayah: 18 .... *65*
    Tafsir Ibn Kathir 65
        It is not for Idolators to maintain the Masjids of Allah 65
        Believers are the True Maintainers of the Masjids 66
Surah: 9 Ayah: 19, Ayah: 20, Ayah: 21 & Ayah: 22 .... *67*
    Tafsir Ibn Kathir 67
        Providing Pilgrims with Water and maintaining the Sacred Masjid are not equal to Faith and Jihad 67
Surah: 9 Ayah: 23 & Ayah: 24 .... *69*
    Tafsir Ibn Kathir 69
        The Prohibition of taking the Idolators as Supporters, even with Relatives 69
Surah: 9 Ayah: 25, Ayah: 26 & Ayah: 27 .... *71*
    Tafsir Ibn Kathir 71
        The Outcome of Victory by Way of the Unseen Aid 71
        The Battle of Hunayn 72
Surah: 9 Ayah: 28 & Ayah: 29 .... *74*
    Tafsir Ibn Kathir 75

Idolators are no longer allowed into Al-Masjid Al-Haram 75
The Order to fight People of the Scriptures until They give the Jizyah............................ 76
Paying Jizyah is a Sign of Kufr and Disgrace 77

Surah: 9 Ayah: 30 & Ayah: 31.. 78
Tafsir Ibn Kathir 79
Fighting the Jews and Christians is legislated because They are Idolators and Disbelievers
.... 79

Surah: 9 Ayah: 32 & Ayah: 33.. 80
Tafsir Ibn Kathir 81
People of the Scriptures try to extinguish the Light of Islam... 81
Islam is the Religion That will dominate over all Other Religions..................................... 81

Surah: 9 Ayah: 34 & Ayah: 35.. 82
Tafsir Ibn Kathir 83
Warning against Corrupt Scholars and Misguided Worshippers 83
Torment of Those Who hoard Gold and Silver 84

Surah: 9 Ayah: 36 86
Tafsir Ibn Kathir 86
The Year consists of Twelve Months 86
The Sacred Months.. 88
Fighting in the Sacred Months.. 89

Surah: 9 Ayah: 37 90
Tafsir Ibn Kathir 91
Admonishing the Preference of Opinion in a Religious Matter 91

Surah: 9 Ayah: 38 & Ayah: 39.. 92
Tafsir Ibn Kathir 92
Admonishing clinging to Life rather than rushing to perform Jihad 92

Surah: 9 Ayah: 40 94
Tafsir Ibn Kathir 94
Allah supports His Prophet 94

Surah: 9 Ayah: 41 95
Tafsir Ibn Kathir 96
Jihad is required in all Conditions.. 96

Surah: 9 Ayah: 42 97
Tafsir Ibn Kathir 98
Why Hypocrites would not join in Jihad 98

Surah: 9 Ayah: 43, Ayah: 44 & Ayah: 45... 98
Tafsir Ibn Kathir 99
Moderately criticizing the Prophet for allowing the Hypocrites to stay behind............... 99

Surah: 9 Ayah: 46 & Ayah: 47.. 100
Tafsir Ibn Kathir 101
Exposing Hypocrites 101

Surah: 9 Ayah: 48 102
Tafsir Ibn Kathir 102
Allah encourages His Prophet against hypocrites, ... 102

Table of Contents

Surah: 9 Ayah: 49 .... *102*
    Tafsir Ibn Kathir 103
Surah: 9 Ayah: 50 & Ayah: 51 .... *104*
    Tafsir Ibn Kathir 104
        Allah emphasizes the enmity that the hypocrites have for the Prophet 104
Surah: 9 Ayah: 52, Ayah: 53 & Ayah: 54 .... *105*
    Tafsir Ibn Kathir 106
Surah: 9 Ayah: 55 .... *106*
    Tafsir Ibn Kathir 107
Surah: 9 Ayah: 56 & Ayah: 57 .... *107*
    Tafsir Ibn Kathir 108
        Exposing Hypocrites' Fright and Fear 108
Surah: 9 Ayah: 58 & Ayah: 59 .... *108*
    Tafsir Ibn Kathir 109
        Hypocrites question the Integrity of the Messenger when distributing Alms 109
Surah: 9 Ayah: 60 .... *111*
    Tafsir Ibn Kathir 111
        Expenditures of Zakah (Alms) 111
        The Fuqara' (Poor) 111
        The Masakin (Needy) 111
        Those employed to collect Alms 112
        The Riqab 113
        Virtue of freeing Slaves 113
        Al-Gharimun (the Indebted) 114
        In the Cause of Allah 115
        Ibn As-Sabil (Wayfarer) 115
Surah: 9 Ayah: 61 .... *116*
    Tafsir Ibn Kathir 116
        Hypocrites annoy the Prophet 116
Surah: 9 Ayah: 62 & Ayah: 63 .... *116*
    Tafsir Ibn Kathir 117
        Hypocrites revert to Lies to please People 117
Surah: 9 Ayah: 64 .... *118*
    Tafsir Ibn Kathir 118
        The Hypocrites fear Public Exposure of Their Secrets 118
Surah: 9 Ayah: 65 & Ayah: 66 .... *118*
    Tafsir Ibn Kathir 119
        The Hypocrites rely on False, Misguided Excuses 119
Surah: 9 Ayah: 67 & Ayah: 68 .... *119*
    Tafsir Ibn Kathir 120
        Other Characteristics of Hypocrites 120
Surah: 9 Ayah: 69 .... *121*
    Tafsir Ibn Kathir 121
Surah: 9 Ayah: 70 .... *122*

Tafsir Ibn Kathir 123
    Advising the Hypocrites to learn a Lesson from Those before Them 123
Surah: 9 Ayah: 71 .... *123*
    Tafsir Ibn Kathir 124
        Qualities of Faithful Believers 124
Surah: 9 Ayah: 72 .... *125*
    Tafsir Ibn Kathir 125
        Good News for the Believers of Eternal Delight 125
Surah: 9 Ayah: 73 & Ayah: 74 .... *128*
    Tafsir Ibn Kathir 128
        The Order for Jihad against the Disbelievers and Hypocrites 128
        Reason behind revealing Ayah 9:74 129
        Hypocrites try to kill the Prophet 130
Surah: 9 Ayah: 75, Ayah: 76, Ayah: 77 & Ayah: 78 .... *132*
    Tafsir Ibn Kathir 133
        Hypocrites seek Wealth but are Stingy with Alms 133
Surah: 9 Ayah: 79 .... *133*
    Tafsir Ibn Kathir 134
        Hypocrites defame Believers Who give the Little Charity They can afford 134
Surah: 9 Ayah: 80 .... *135*
    Tafsir Ibn Kathir 135
        The Prohibition of asking for Forgiveness for Hypocrites 135
Surah: 9 Ayah: 81 & Ayah: 82 .... *136*
    Tafsir Ibn Kathir 137
        Hypocrites rejoice because They remained behind from Tabuk! 137
Surah: 9 Ayah: 83 .... *138*
    Tafsir Ibn Kathir 139
        Hypocrites are barred from participating in Jihad 139
Surah: 9 Ayah: 84 .... *139*
    Tafsir Ibn Kathir 140
        The Prohibition of Prayer for the Funeral of Hypocrites 140
Surah: 9 Ayah: 85 .... *141*
    Tafsir Ibn Kathir 141
Surah: 9 Ayah: 86 & Ayah: 87 .... *141*
    Tafsir Ibn Kathir 141
        Admonishing Those Who did not join the Jihad 141
Surah: 9 Ayah: 88 & Ayah: 89 .... *142*
    Tafsir Ibn Kathir 143
        After Allah mentioned the sins of the hypocrites, He praised the faithful believers and described their reward in the Hereafter, ... 143
Surah: 9 Ayah: 90 .... *143*
    Tafsir Ibn Kathir 143
Surah: 9 Ayah: 91, Ayah: 92 (end of Part 10) & Ayah: 93 .... *143*
    Tafsir Ibn Kathir 144

Table of Contents xi

Legitimate Excuses for staying away from Jihad 144

PRELUDE

Opening Serman

Indeed, all praise is due to Allah. We praise Him and seek His help and forgiveness. We seek refuge with Allah from our soul's evil and our wrong doings. He whom Allah guides, no one can misguide; and he whom He misguides, no one can guide

I bear witness that there is no (true) god except Allah – alone without a partner, and I bear witness that Muhammad (peace and blessings of Allah be upon him) is His 'abd (servant) and messenger.

يَـٰٓأَيُّهَا ٱلَّذِينَ ءَامَنُواْ ٱتَّقُواْ ٱللَّهَ حَقَّ تُقَاتِهِۦ وَلَا تَمُوتُنَّ إِلَّا وَأَنتُم مُّسۡلِمُونَ ۞

O you who believe! Fear Allâh (by doing all that He has ordered and by abstaining from all that He has forbidden) as He should be feared. (Obey Him, be thankful to Him, and remember Him always), and die not except in a state of Islâm (as Muslims with complete submission to Allâh)).

يَـٰٓأَيُّهَا ٱلنَّاسُ ٱتَّقُواْ رَبَّكُمُ ٱلَّذِى خَلَقَكُم مِّن نَّفۡسٍ وَٰحِدَةٍ وَخَلَقَ مِنۡهَا زَوۡجَهَا وَبَثَّ مِنۡهُمَا رِجَالًا كَثِيرًا وَنِسَآءً وَٱتَّقُواْ ٱللَّهَ ٱلَّذِى تَسَآءَلُونَ بِهِۦ وَٱلۡأَرۡحَامَ إِنَّ ٱللَّهَ كَانَ عَلَيۡكُمۡ رَقِيبًا ۞

O mankind! Be dutiful to your Lord, Who created you from a single person (Adam), and from him (Adam) He created his wife (Hawwâ (Eve)) and from them both He created many men and women; and fear Allâh through Whom you demand (your mutual rights), and (do not cut the relations of) the wombs (kinship). Surely, Allâh is Ever an All-Watcher over you.

يُصۡلِحۡ لَكُمۡ أَعۡمَـٰلَكُمۡ وَيَغۡفِرۡ لَكُمۡ ذُنُوبَكُمۡ وَمَن يُطِعِ ٱللَّهَ وَرَسُولَهُۥ فَقَدۡ فَازَ فَوۡزًا عَظِيمًا ۞

He will direct you to do righteous good deeds and will forgive you your sins. And whosoever obeys Allâh and His Messenger (peace be upon him), he has indeed achieved a great achievement (i.e. he will be saved from the Hell-fire and will be admitted to Paradise).

Indeed, the best speech is Allah's Book and the best guidance is Muhammad's () guidance. The worst affairs (of religion) are those innovated (by people), for every such innovation is an act of misguidance leading to the Fire

Our Mission

Our mission is to gather in one place, for the English-speaking public, all relevant information needed to make the Qur'an more understandable and easier to study. This book tries to do this by providing the following:

1. The Arabic Text for those who are able to read Arabic
2. Transliteration of the Arabic text for those who are unable to read the Arabic script. This will give them a sample of the sound of the Qur'an, which they could not otherwise comprehend from reading the English meaning.
3. The meaning of the qur'an (translated by Dr. Muhammad Taqi-ud-Din Al-Hilali, Ph.D. and Dr. Muhammad Muhsin Khan)
4. Explanation (abridged Tafsir) by Ibn Kathir (translated by Safi-ur-Rahman al-Mubarakpuri)

We hope that by doing this an ordinary English-speaker will be able to pick up a copy of this book and study and comprehend The Glorious Qur'an in a way that is acceptable to the understanding of the Rightly-guided Muslim Ummah (Community).

Biography of Hafiz Ibn Kathir (701 H - 774 H)

By the Honored Shaykh `Abdul-Qadir Al-Arna'ut, may Allah protect him.

He is the respected Imam, Abu Al-Fida', `Imad Ad-Din Isma il bin 'Umar bin Kathir Al-Qurashi Al-Busrawi - Busraian in origin; Dimashqi in training, learning and residence.

Ibn Kathir was born in the city of Busra in 701 H. His father was the Friday speaker of the village, but he died while Ibn Kathir was only four years old. Ibn Kathir's brother, Shaykh Abdul-Wahhab, reared him and taught him until he moved to Damascus in 706 H., when he was five years old.

Ibn Kathir's Teachers

Ibn Kathir studied Fiqh - Islamic jurisprudence - with Burhan Ad-Din, Ibrahim bin `Abdur-Rahman Al-Fizari, known as Ibn Al-Firkah (who died in 729 H). Ibn Kathir heard Hadiths from `Isa bin Al-Mutim, Ahmad bin Abi Talib, (Ibn Ash-Shahnah) (who died in 730 H), Ibn Al-Hajjar, (who died in 730 H), and the Hadith narrator of Ash-Sham (modern day Syria and surrounding areas); Baha Ad-Din Al-Qasim bin Muzaffar bin `Asakir (who died in 723 H), and Ibn Ash-Shirdzi, Ishaq bin Yahya Al-Ammuddi, also known as `Afif Ad-Din, the Zahiriyyah Shaykh who died in 725 H, and Muhammad bin Zarrad. He remained with Jamal Ad-Din, Yusuf bin Az-Zaki AlMizzi who died in 724 H, he benefited from his knowledge and also married his daughter. He also read with Shaykh Al-Islam, Taqi Ad-Din Ahmad bin `Abdul-Halim bin `Abdus-Salam bin Taymiyyah who died in 728 H. He also read with the Imam Hafiz and historian Shams Ad-Din, Muhammad bin Ahmad bin Uthman bin Qaymaz Adh-Dhahabi, who died in 748 H. Also, Abu Musa Al-Qarafai, Abu Al-Fath Ad-Dabbusi and

Prelude

'Ali bin `Umar As-Suwani and others who gave him permission to transmit the knowledge he learned with them in Egypt.

In his book, Al-Mu jam Al-Mukhtas, Al-Hafiz Adh-Dhaliabi wrote that Ibn Kathir was, "The Imam, scholar of jurisprudence, skillful scholar of Hadith, renowned Fagih and scholar of Tafsir who wrote several beneficial books."

Further, in Ad-Durar Al-Kdminah, Al-Hafiz Ibn Hajar AlAsqalani said, "Ibn Kathir worked on the subject of the Hadith in the areas of texts and chains of narrators. He had a good memory, his books became popular during his lifetime, and people benefited from them after his death."

Also, the renowned historian Abu Al-Mahasin, Jamal Ad-Din Yusuf bin Sayf Ad-Din (Ibn Taghri Bardi), said in his book, AlManhal As-Safi, "He is the Shaykh, the Imam, the great scholar `Imad Ad-Din Abu Al-Fida'. He learned extensively and was very active in collecting knowledge and writing. He was excellent in the areas of Fiqh, Tafsfr and Hadith. He collected knowledge, authored (books), taught, narrated Hadith and wrote. He had immense knowledge in the fields of Hadith, Tafsir, Fiqh, the Arabic language, and so forth. He gave Fatawa (religious verdicts) and taught until he died, may Allah grant him mercy. He was known for his precision and vast knowledge, and as a scholar of history, Hadith and Tafsir."

Ibn Kathir's Students

Ibn Hajji was one of Ibn Kathir's students, and he described Ibn Kathir: "He had the best memory of the Hadith texts. He also had the most knowledge concerning the narrators and authenticity, his contemporaries and teachers admitted to these qualities. Every time I met him I gained some benefit from him."

Also, Ibn Al-`Imad Al-Hanbali said in his book, Shadhardt Adh-Dhahab, "He is the renowned Hafiz `Imad Ad-Din, whose memory was excellent, whose forgetfulness was miniscule, whose understanding was adequate, and who had good knowledge in the Arabic language." Also, Ibn Habib said about Ibn Kathir, "He heard knowledge and collected it and wrote various books. He brought comfort to the ears with his Fatwas and narrated Hadith and brought benefit to other people. The papers that contained his Fatwas were transmitted to the various (Islamic) provinces. Further, he was known for his precision and encompassing knowledge."

Ibn Kathir's Books

1 - One of the greatest books that Ibn Kathir wrote was his Tafsir of the Noble Qur'an, which is one of the best Tafsir that rely on narrations [of Ahadith, the Tafsir of the Companions, etc.]. The Tafsir by Ibn Kathir was printed many times and several scholars have summarized it.

2- The History Collection known as Al-Biddyah, which was printed in 14 volumes under the name Al-Bidayah wanNihdyah, and contained the stories of the Prophets and previous nations, the Prophet's Seerah (life story) and Islamic history until his time. He also added a book Al-Fitan, about the Signs of the Last Hour.

3- At-Takmil ft Ma`rifat Ath-Thiqat wa Ad-Du'afa wal Majdhil which Ibn Kathir collected from the books of his two Shaykhs Al-Mizzi and Adh-Dhahabi; Al-Kdmal and Mizan Al-Ftiddl. He added several benefits regarding the subject of Al-Jarh and AtT'adil.

4- Al-Hadi was-Sunan ft Ahadith Al-Masdnfd was-Sunan which is also known by, Jami` Al-Masdnfd. In this book, Ibn Kathir collected the narrations of Imams Ahmad bin Hanbal, Al-Bazzar, Abu Ya`la Al-Mawsili, Ibn Abi Shaybah and from the six collections of Hadith: the Two Sahihs [Al-Bukhari and Muslim] and the Four Sunan [Abu Dawud, At-Tirmidhi, AnNasa and Ibn Majah]. Ibn Kathir divided this book according to areas of Fiqh.

5-Tabaqat Ash-Shaf iyah which also contains the virtues of Imam Ash-Shafi.

6- Ibn Kathir wrote references for the Ahadith of Adillat AtTanbfh, from the Shafi school of Fiqh.

7- Ibn Kathir began an explanation of Sahih Al-Bukhari, but he did not finish it.

8- He started writing a large volume on the Ahkam (Laws), but finished only up to the Hajj rituals.

9- He summarized Al-Bayhaqi's 'Al-Madkhal. Many of these books were not printed.

10- He summarized `Ulum Al-Hadith, by Abu `Amr bin AsSalah and called it Mukhtasar `Ulum Al-Hadith. Shaykh Ahmad Shakir, the Egyptian Muhaddith, printed this book along with his commentary on it and called it Al-Ba'th Al-Hathfth fi Sharh Mukhtasar `Ulum Al-Hadith.

11- As-Sfrah An-Nabawiyyah, which is contained in his book Al-Biddyah, and both of these books are in print.

12- A research on Jihad called Al-Ijtihad ft Talabi Al-Jihad, which was printed several times.

Ibn Kathir's Death

Al-Hafiz Ibn Hajar Al-Asgalani said, "Ibn Kathir lost his sight just before his life ended. He died in Damascus in 774 H." May Allah grant mercy upon Ibn Kathir and make him among the residents of His Paradise.

PREFACE

In the name of Allah, Most Gracious, Most Merciful.

About this book

The previous publication of this book included some background information to the chapters of the Qur'an by an Islamic scholar known as Abul Ala Maududi. This information was used to shed more light on the chapters by giving a summery of why each chapter was given its name, It's period of revelation and the circumstances surrounding its revelatiom. However, some Muslims objected to the inclusion of the contributions of Maududi.

In this new publication of Tafsir Ibn Kathir, we have removed all traces of the contribution of Abul Ala Maududi. Personally, I do not know the reasons for the objections to Maududi, but this work concerns only the tafsir of Ibn Kathir, so we have not included anything from Maududi in it. We have also corrected all the typing and formatting errors found in the previous publication. We have not alter the structure of the book. The reader is still able to read the full Arabic Text of the thirty Parts of the Qur'an and follow its meanings in the English language. The transliteration of the Arabic text should also give the reader a taste of the sound of the original Arabic.

May Almighty Allah accept this effort from us, and make it a source of blessings for us in this world and in the next. I bear witness that there is none worthy of worship but Allah and I bear witness that Muhammad (may the peace and blessings of Allah be upon him) is the slave and messenger of Allah.

Performing Prostration While Reading the Qur'an

Question:

Could you please give a list of the Qur'anic verses when a prostration is recommended? What happens if we read these verses and not perform a prostration?

A. Jalil

Answer:

There are 15 verses in the Qur'an that mention prostration before God Almighty as a good action by God-fearing believers. Therefore, it is strongly recommended to perform such a prostration when we read or listen to any of these verses, whether during prayer or in any situation.

Some scholars are of the view that even if one has not performed ablution, one should prostrate oneself. These verses are given here, starting with the Arabic title of the surah which is followed by two numbers, the first indicating the surah, and the second indicating the verse,: Al-Araf 7: 206; Al-Raad 13: 15; Al-Nahl 16: 50; Al-Isra 17: 109; Maryam 19: 58; Al-Hajj 22: 18 & 22: 77; Al-Furqan 25: 60; Al-Naml 27: 26;

Al-Sajdah 32: 15; Saad 38: 25; Fussilat 41: 38; Al-Najm 53: 62; Al-Inshiqaq 84: 21 and Al-Alaq 96: 19.

If you do not perform a prostration when you read or listen to any of these verses, you have done badly because you miss out on the reward of performing a prostration for God. You incur no sin and violate no divine order.

Reference:
http://archive.arabnews.com/?page=5&section=0&article=97811&d=1&m=7&y=2007

The Glorious Qur'an Juz' 10 (Part 10): Chapter (Surah) 8: Al-Anfal (Spoils Of War, Booty) 041 To Chapter (Surah) 9: Al-Bara'at (The Immunity) Or At-Tawba (Repentance, Dispensation) 092

PART 10 FULL ARABIC TEXT

Chapter (Surah) 8: Al-Anfal 041-075

۞ وَٱعْلَمُوٓاْ أَنَّمَا غَنِمْتُم مِّن شَىْءٍ فَأَنَّ لِلَّهِ خُمُسَهُۥ وَلِلرَّسُولِ وَلِذِى ٱلْقُرْبَىٰ وَٱلْيَتَٰمَىٰ وَٱلْمَسَٰكِينِ وَٱبْنِ ٱلسَّبِيلِ إِن كُنتُمْ ءَامَنتُم بِٱللَّهِ وَمَآ أَنزَلْنَا عَلَىٰ عَبْدِنَا يَوْمَ ٱلْفُرْقَانِ يَوْمَ ٱلْتَقَى ٱلْجَمْعَانِ ۗ وَٱللَّهُ عَلَىٰ كُلِّ شَىْءٍ قَدِيرٌ ﴿٤١﴾ إِذْ أَنتُم بِٱلْعُدْوَةِ ٱلدُّنْيَا وَهُم بِٱلْعُدْوَةِ ٱلْقُصْوَىٰ وَٱلرَّكْبُ أَسْفَلَ مِنكُمْ ۚ وَلَوْ تَوَاعَدتُّمْ لَٱخْتَلَفْتُمْ فِى ٱلْمِيعَٰدِ ۙ وَلَٰكِن لِّيَقْضِىَ ٱللَّهُ أَمْرًا كَانَ مَفْعُولًا لِّيَهْلِكَ مَنْ هَلَكَ عَنۢ بَيِّنَةٍ وَيَحْيَىٰ مَنْ حَىَّ عَنۢ بَيِّنَةٍ ۗ وَإِنَّ ٱللَّهَ لَسَمِيعٌ عَلِيمٌ ﴿٤٢﴾ إِذْ يُرِيكَهُمُ ٱللَّهُ فِى مَنَامِكَ قَلِيلًا ۖ وَلَوْ أَرَىٰكَهُمْ كَثِيرًا لَّفَشِلْتُمْ وَلَتَنَٰزَعْتُمْ فِى ٱلْأَمْرِ وَلَٰكِنَّ ٱللَّهَ سَلَّمَ ۗ إِنَّهُۥ عَلِيمٌۢ بِذَاتِ ٱلصُّدُورِ ﴿٤٣﴾ وَإِذْ يُرِيكُمُوهُمْ إِذِ ٱلْتَقَيْتُمْ فِىٓ أَعْيُنِكُمْ قَلِيلًا وَيُقَلِّلُكُمْ فِىٓ أَعْيُنِهِمْ لِيَقْضِىَ ٱللَّهُ أَمْرًا كَانَ مَفْعُولًا ۗ وَإِلَى ٱللَّهِ تُرْجَعُ ٱلْأُمُورُ ﴿٤٤﴾ يَٰٓأَيُّهَا ٱلَّذِينَ ءَامَنُوٓاْ إِذَا لَقِيتُمْ فِئَةً فَٱثْبُتُوا۟ وَٱذْكُرُوا۟ ٱللَّهَ كَثِيرًا لَّعَلَّكُمْ تُفْلِحُونَ ﴿٤٥﴾ وَأَطِيعُوا۟ ٱللَّهَ وَرَسُولَهُۥ وَلَا تَنَٰزَعُوا۟ فَتَفْشَلُوا۟ وَتَذْهَبَ رِيحُكُمْ ۖ وَٱصْبِرُوٓا۟ ۚ إِنَّ ٱللَّهَ مَعَ ٱلصَّٰبِرِينَ ﴿٤٦﴾ وَلَا تَكُونُوا۟ كَٱلَّذِينَ خَرَجُوا۟ مِن دِيَٰرِهِم بَطَرًا وَرِئَآءَ ٱلنَّاسِ وَيَصُدُّونَ عَن سَبِيلِ ٱللَّهِ ۚ وَٱللَّهُ بِمَا يَعْمَلُونَ مُحِيطٌ ﴿٤٧﴾ وَإِذْ زَيَّنَ لَهُمُ ٱلشَّيْطَٰنُ أَعْمَٰلَهُمْ وَقَالَ لَا غَالِبَ لَكُمُ ٱلْيَوْمَ

مِنَ ٱلنَّاسِ وَإِنِّي جَارٌ لَّكُمْ ۖ فَلَمَّا تَرَآءَتِ ٱلْفِئَتَانِ نَكَصَ عَلَىٰ عَقِبَيْهِ وَقَالَ إِنِّي بَرِىٓءٌ مِّنكُمْ إِنِّىٓ أَرَىٰ مَا لَا تَرَوْنَ إِنِّىٓ أَخَافُ ٱللَّهَ ۚ وَٱللَّهُ شَدِيدُ ٱلْعِقَابِ ۝ إِذْ يَقُولُ ٱلْمُنَـٰفِقُونَ وَٱلَّذِينَ فِى قُلُوبِهِم مَّرَضٌ غَرَّ هَـٰٓؤُلَآءِ دِينُهُمْ ۗ وَمَن يَتَوَكَّلْ عَلَى ٱللَّهِ فَإِنَّ ٱللَّهَ عَزِيزٌ حَكِيمٌ ۝ وَلَوْ تَرَىٰٓ إِذْ يَتَوَفَّى ٱلَّذِينَ كَفَرُوا۟ ۙ ٱلْمَلَـٰٓئِكَةُ يَضْرِبُونَ وُجُوهَهُمْ وَأَدْبَـٰرَهُمْ وَذُوقُوا۟ عَذَابَ ٱلْحَرِيقِ ۝ ذَٰلِكَ بِمَا قَدَّمَتْ أَيْدِيكُمْ وَأَنَّ ٱللَّهَ لَيْسَ بِظَلَّـٰمٍ لِّلْعَبِيدِ ۝ كَدَأْبِ ءَالِ فِرْعَوْنَ ۙ وَٱلَّذِينَ مِن قَبْلِهِمْ ۚ كَفَرُوا۟ بِـَٔايَـٰتِ ٱللَّهِ فَأَخَذَهُمُ ٱللَّهُ بِذُنُوبِهِمْ ۗ إِنَّ ٱللَّهَ قَوِىٌّ شَدِيدُ ٱلْعِقَابِ ۝ ذَٰلِكَ بِأَنَّ ٱللَّهَ لَمْ يَكُ مُغَيِّرًا نِّعْمَةً أَنْعَمَهَا عَلَىٰ قَوْمٍ حَتَّىٰ يُغَيِّرُوا۟ مَا بِأَنفُسِهِمْ ۙ وَأَنَّ ٱللَّهَ سَمِيعٌ عَلِيمٌ ۝ كَدَأْبِ ءَالِ فِرْعَوْنَ ۙ وَٱلَّذِينَ مِن قَبْلِهِمْ ۚ كَذَّبُوا۟ بِـَٔايَـٰتِ رَبِّهِمْ فَأَهْلَكْنَـٰهُم بِذُنُوبِهِمْ وَأَغْرَقْنَآ ءَالَ فِرْعَوْنَ ۚ وَكُلٌّ كَانُوا۟ ظَـٰلِمِينَ ۝ إِنَّ شَرَّ ٱلدَّوَآبِّ عِندَ ٱللَّهِ ٱلَّذِينَ كَفَرُوا۟ فَهُمْ لَا يُؤْمِنُونَ ۝ ٱلَّذِينَ عَـٰهَدتَّ مِنْهُمْ ثُمَّ يَنقُضُونَ عَهْدَهُمْ فِى كُلِّ مَرَّةٍ وَهُمْ لَا يَتَّقُونَ ۝ فَإِمَّا تَثْقَفَنَّهُمْ فِى ٱلْحَرْبِ فَشَرِّدْ بِهِم مَّنْ خَلْفَهُمْ لَعَلَّهُمْ يَذَّكَّرُونَ ۝ وَإِمَّا تَخَافَنَّ مِن قَوْمٍ خِيَانَةً فَٱنۢبِذْ إِلَيْهِمْ عَلَىٰ سَوَآءٍ ۚ إِنَّ ٱللَّهَ لَا يُحِبُّ ٱلْخَآئِنِينَ ۝ وَلَا يَحْسَبَنَّ ٱلَّذِينَ كَفَرُوا۟ سَبَقُوٓا۟ ۚ إِنَّهُمْ لَا يُعْجِزُونَ ۝ وَأَعِدُّوا۟ لَهُم مَّا ٱسْتَطَعْتُم مِّن قُوَّةٍ وَمِن رِّبَاطِ ٱلْخَيْلِ تُرْهِبُونَ بِهِۦ عَدُوَّ ٱللَّهِ وَعَدُوَّكُمْ وَءَاخَرِينَ مِن دُونِهِمْ لَا تَعْلَمُونَهُمُ ٱللَّهُ يَعْلَمُهُمْ ۚ وَمَا تُنفِقُوا۟ مِن شَىْءٍ فِى سَبِيلِ ٱللَّهِ يُوَفَّ إِلَيْكُمْ وَأَنتُمْ لَا تُظْلَمُونَ ۝ ۞ وَإِن جَنَحُوا۟ لِلسَّلْمِ فَٱجْنَحْ لَهَا وَتَوَكَّلْ عَلَى ٱللَّهِ ۚ إِنَّهُۥ هُوَ ٱلسَّمِيعُ ٱلْعَلِيمُ ۝ وَإِن يُرِيدُوٓا۟ أَن يَخْدَعُوكَ فَإِنَّ حَسْبَكَ ٱللَّهُ ۚ هُوَ ٱلَّذِىٓ أَيَّدَكَ بِنَصْرِهِۦ

وَبِٱلْمُؤْمِنِينَ ۝ وَأَلَّفَ بَيْنَ قُلُوبِهِمْ ۚ لَوْ أَنفَقْتَ مَا فِى ٱلْأَرْضِ جَمِيعًا مَّآ أَلَّفْتَ بَيْنَ قُلُوبِهِمْ وَلَٰكِنَّ ٱللَّهَ أَلَّفَ بَيْنَهُمْ ۚ إِنَّهُۥ عَزِيزٌ حَكِيمٌ ۝ يَٰٓأَيُّهَا ٱلنَّبِىُّ حَسْبُكَ ٱللَّهُ وَمَنِ ٱتَّبَعَكَ مِنَ ٱلْمُؤْمِنِينَ ۝ يَٰٓأَيُّهَا ٱلنَّبِىُّ حَرِّضِ ٱلْمُؤْمِنِينَ عَلَى ٱلْقِتَالِ ۚ إِن يَكُن مِّنكُمْ عِشْرُونَ صَٰبِرُونَ يَغْلِبُوا۟ مِا۟ئَتَيْنِ ۚ وَإِن يَكُن مِّنكُم مِّا۟ئَةٌ يَغْلِبُوٓا۟ أَلْفًا مِّنَ ٱلَّذِينَ كَفَرُوا۟ بِأَنَّهُمْ قَوْمٌ لَّا يَفْقَهُونَ ۝ ٱلْـَٰٔنَ خَفَّفَ ٱللَّهُ عَنكُمْ وَعَلِمَ أَنَّ فِيكُمْ ضَعْفًا ۚ فَإِن يَكُن مِّنكُم مِّا۟ئَةٌ صَابِرَةٌ يَغْلِبُوا۟ مِا۟ئَتَيْنِ ۚ وَإِن يَكُن مِّنكُمْ أَلْفٌ يَغْلِبُوٓا۟ أَلْفَيْنِ بِإِذْنِ ٱللَّهِ ۗ وَٱللَّهُ مَعَ ٱلصَّٰبِرِينَ ۝ مَا كَانَ لِنَبِىٍّ أَن يَكُونَ لَهُۥٓ أَسْرَىٰ حَتَّىٰ يُثْخِنَ فِى ٱلْأَرْضِ ۚ تُرِيدُونَ عَرَضَ ٱلدُّنْيَا وَٱللَّهُ يُرِيدُ ٱلْآخِرَةَ ۗ وَٱللَّهُ عَزِيزٌ حَكِيمٌ ۝ لَّوْلَا كِتَٰبٌ مِّنَ ٱللَّهِ سَبَقَ لَمَسَّكُمْ فِيمَآ أَخَذْتُمْ عَذَابٌ عَظِيمٌ ۝ فَكُلُوا۟ مِمَّا غَنِمْتُمْ حَلَٰلًا طَيِّبًا ۚ وَٱتَّقُوا۟ ٱللَّهَ ۚ إِنَّ ٱللَّهَ غَفُورٌ رَّحِيمٌ ۝ يَٰٓأَيُّهَا ٱلنَّبِىُّ قُل لِّمَن فِىٓ أَيْدِيكُم مِّنَ ٱلْأَسْرَىٰٓ إِن يَعْلَمِ ٱللَّهُ فِى قُلُوبِكُمْ خَيْرًا يُؤْتِكُمْ خَيْرًا مِّمَّآ أُخِذَ مِنكُمْ وَيَغْفِرْ لَكُمْ ۗ وَٱللَّهُ غَفُورٌ رَّحِيمٌ ۝ وَإِن يُرِيدُوا۟ خِيَانَتَكَ فَقَدْ خَانُوا۟ ٱللَّهَ مِن قَبْلُ فَأَمْكَنَ مِنْهُمْ ۗ وَٱللَّهُ عَلِيمٌ حَكِيمٌ ۝ إِنَّ ٱلَّذِينَ ءَامَنُوا۟ وَهَاجَرُوا۟ وَجَٰهَدُوا۟ بِأَمْوَٰلِهِمْ وَأَنفُسِهِمْ فِى سَبِيلِ ٱللَّهِ وَٱلَّذِينَ ءَاوَوا۟ وَّنَصَرُوٓا۟ أُو۟لَٰٓئِكَ بَعْضُهُمْ أَوْلِيَآءُ بَعْضٍ ۚ وَٱلَّذِينَ ءَامَنُوا۟ وَلَمْ يُهَاجِرُوا۟ مَا لَكُم مِّن وَلَٰيَتِهِم مِّن شَىْءٍ حَتَّىٰ يُهَاجِرُوا۟ ۚ وَإِنِ ٱسْتَنصَرُوكُمْ فِى ٱلدِّينِ فَعَلَيْكُمُ ٱلنَّصْرُ إِلَّا عَلَىٰ قَوْمٍۭ بَيْنَكُمْ وَبَيْنَهُم مِّيثَٰقٌ ۗ وَٱللَّهُ بِمَا تَعْمَلُونَ بَصِيرٌ ۝ وَٱلَّذِينَ كَفَرُوا۟ بَعْضُهُمْ أَوْلِيَآءُ بَعْضٍ ۚ إِلَّا تَفْعَلُوهُ تَكُن فِتْنَةٌ فِى ٱلْأَرْضِ وَفَسَادٌ كَبِيرٌ ۝ وَٱلَّذِينَ ءَامَنُوا۟ وَهَاجَرُوا۟ وَجَٰهَدُوا۟ فِى سَبِيلِ ٱللَّهِ وَٱلَّذِينَ ءَاوَوا۟ وَّنَصَرُوٓا۟ أُو۟لَٰٓئِكَ هُمُ ٱلْمُؤْمِنُونَ حَقًّا ۚ لَّهُم مَّغْفِرَةٌ وَرِزْقٌ

كَرِيمٌ ۝ وَالَّذِينَ ءَامَنُوا مِنۢ بَعْدُ وَهَاجَرُوا وَجَـٰهَدُوا مَعَكُمْ فَأُولَـٰٓئِكَ مِنكُمْ ۚ وَأُولُوا۟ ٱلْأَرْحَامِ بَعْضُهُمْ أَوْلَىٰ بِبَعْضٍ فِى كِتَـٰبِ ٱللَّهِ ۗ إِنَّ ٱللَّهَ بِكُلِّ شَىْءٍ عَلِيمٌۢ ۝

(Al-Anfal 041-075)

Chapter (Surah) 9: At-Tauba 001-092

بَرَآءَةٌ مِّنَ ٱللَّهِ وَرَسُولِهِۦٓ إِلَى ٱلَّذِينَ عَـٰهَدتُّم مِّنَ ٱلْمُشْرِكِينَ ۝ فَسِيحُوا۟ فِى ٱلْأَرْضِ أَرْبَعَةَ أَشْهُرٍ وَٱعْلَمُوٓا۟ أَنَّكُمْ غَيْرُ مُعْجِزِى ٱللَّهِ ۙ وَأَنَّ ٱللَّهَ مُخْزِى ٱلْكَـٰفِرِينَ ۝ وَأَذَٰنٌ مِّنَ ٱللَّهِ وَرَسُولِهِۦٓ إِلَى ٱلنَّاسِ يَوْمَ ٱلْحَجِّ ٱلْأَكْبَرِ أَنَّ ٱللَّهَ بَرِىٓءٌ مِّنَ ٱلْمُشْرِكِينَ ۙ وَرَسُولُهُۥ ۚ فَإِن تُبْتُمْ فَهُوَ خَيْرٌ لَّكُمْ ۖ وَإِن تَوَلَّيْتُمْ فَٱعْلَمُوٓا۟ أَنَّكُمْ غَيْرُ مُعْجِزِى ٱللَّهِ ۗ وَبَشِّرِ ٱلَّذِينَ كَفَرُوا۟ بِعَذَابٍ أَلِيمٍ ۝ إِلَّا ٱلَّذِينَ عَـٰهَدتُّم مِّنَ ٱلْمُشْرِكِينَ ثُمَّ لَمْ يَنقُصُوكُمْ شَيْـًٔا وَلَمْ يُظَـٰهِرُوا۟ عَلَيْكُمْ أَحَدًا فَأَتِمُّوٓا۟ إِلَيْهِمْ عَهْدَهُمْ إِلَىٰ مُدَّتِهِمْ ۚ إِنَّ ٱللَّهَ يُحِبُّ ٱلْمُتَّقِينَ ۝ فَإِذَا ٱنسَلَخَ ٱلْأَشْهُرُ ٱلْحُرُمُ فَٱقْتُلُوا۟ ٱلْمُشْرِكِينَ حَيْثُ وَجَدتُّمُوهُمْ وَخُذُوهُمْ وَٱحْصُرُوهُمْ وَٱقْعُدُوا۟ لَهُمْ كُلَّ مَرْصَدٍ ۚ فَإِن تَابُوا۟ وَأَقَامُوا۟ ٱلصَّلَوٰةَ وَءَاتَوُا۟ ٱلزَّكَوٰةَ فَخَلُّوا۟ سَبِيلَهُمْ ۚ إِنَّ ٱللَّهَ غَفُورٌ رَّحِيمٌ ۝ وَإِنْ أَحَدٌ مِّنَ ٱلْمُشْرِكِينَ ٱسْتَجَارَكَ فَأَجِرْهُ حَتَّىٰ يَسْمَعَ كَلَـٰمَ ٱللَّهِ ثُمَّ أَبْلِغْهُ مَأْمَنَهُۥ ۚ ذَٰلِكَ بِأَنَّهُمْ قَوْمٌ لَّا يَعْلَمُونَ ۝ كَيْفَ يَكُونُ لِلْمُشْرِكِينَ عَهْدٌ عِندَ ٱللَّهِ وَعِندَ رَسُولِهِۦٓ إِلَّا ٱلَّذِينَ عَـٰهَدتُّمْ عِندَ ٱلْمَسْجِدِ ٱلْحَرَامِ ۖ فَمَا ٱسْتَقَـٰمُوا۟ لَكُمْ فَٱسْتَقِيمُوا۟ لَهُمْ ۚ إِنَّ ٱللَّهَ يُحِبُّ ٱلْمُتَّقِينَ ۝ كَيْفَ وَإِن يَظْهَرُوا۟ عَلَيْكُمْ لَا يَرْقُبُوا۟ فِيكُمْ إِلًّا وَلَا ذِمَّةً ۚ يُرْضُونَكُم بِأَفْوَٰهِهِمْ وَتَأْبَىٰ قُلُوبُهُمْ وَأَكْثَرُهُمْ فَـٰسِقُونَ ۝ ٱشْتَرَوْا۟ بِـَٔايَـٰتِ ٱللَّهِ ثَمَنًا قَلِيلًا فَصَدُّوا۟ عَن سَبِيلِهِۦٓ ۚ إِنَّهُمْ سَآءَ مَا كَانُوا۟ يَعْمَلُونَ ۝ لَا يَرْقُبُونَ فِى مُؤْمِنٍ إِلًّا وَلَا ذِمَّةً ۚ وَأُولَـٰٓئِكَ هُمُ ٱلْمُعْتَدُونَ ۝ فَإِن تَابُوا۟

وَأَقَامُوا۟ ٱلصَّلَوٰةَ وَءَاتَوُا۟ ٱلزَّكَوٰةَ فَإِخْوَٰنُكُمْ فِى ٱلدِّينِ ۗ وَنُفَصِّلُ ٱلْءَايَٰتِ لِقَوْمٍ يَعْلَمُونَ ۝ وَإِن نَّكَثُوٓا۟ أَيْمَٰنَهُم مِّنۢ بَعْدِ عَهْدِهِمْ وَطَعَنُوا۟ فِى دِينِكُمْ فَقَٰتِلُوٓا۟ أَئِمَّةَ ٱلْكُفْرِ ۙ إِنَّهُمْ لَآ أَيْمَٰنَ لَهُمْ لَعَلَّهُمْ يَنتَهُونَ ۝ أَلَا تُقَٰتِلُونَ قَوْمًا نَّكَثُوٓا۟ أَيْمَٰنَهُمْ وَهَمُّوا۟ بِإِخْرَاجِ ٱلرَّسُولِ وَهُم بَدَءُوكُمْ أَوَّلَ مَرَّةٍ ۚ أَتَخْشَوْنَهُمْ ۚ فَٱللَّهُ أَحَقُّ أَن تَخْشَوْهُ إِن كُنتُم مُّؤْمِنِينَ ۝ قَٰتِلُوهُمْ يُعَذِّبْهُمُ ٱللَّهُ بِأَيْدِيكُمْ وَيُخْزِهِمْ وَيَنصُرْكُمْ عَلَيْهِمْ وَيَشْفِ صُدُورَ قَوْمٍ مُّؤْمِنِينَ ۝ وَيُذْهِبْ غَيْظَ قُلُوبِهِمْ ۗ وَيَتُوبُ ٱللَّهُ عَلَىٰ مَن يَشَآءُ ۗ وَٱللَّهُ عَلِيمٌ حَكِيمٌ ۝ أَمْ حَسِبْتُمْ أَن تُتْرَكُوا۟ وَلَمَّا يَعْلَمِ ٱللَّهُ ٱلَّذِينَ جَٰهَدُوا۟ مِنكُمْ وَلَمْ يَتَّخِذُوا۟ مِن دُونِ ٱللَّهِ وَلَا رَسُولِهِۦ وَلَا ٱلْمُؤْمِنِينَ وَلِيجَةً ۚ وَٱللَّهُ خَبِيرٌۢ بِمَا تَعْمَلُونَ ۝ مَا كَانَ لِلْمُشْرِكِينَ أَن يَعْمُرُوا۟ مَسَٰجِدَ ٱللَّهِ شَٰهِدِينَ عَلَىٰٓ أَنفُسِهِم بِٱلْكُفْرِ ۚ أُو۟لَٰٓئِكَ حَبِطَتْ أَعْمَٰلُهُمْ وَفِى ٱلنَّارِ هُمْ خَٰلِدُونَ ۝ إِنَّمَا يَعْمُرُ مَسَٰجِدَ ٱللَّهِ مَنْ ءَامَنَ بِٱللَّهِ وَٱلْيَوْمِ ٱلْءَاخِرِ وَأَقَامَ ٱلصَّلَوٰةَ وَءَاتَى ٱلزَّكَوٰةَ وَلَمْ يَخْشَ إِلَّا ٱللَّهَ ۖ فَعَسَىٰٓ أُو۟لَٰٓئِكَ أَن يَكُونُوا۟ مِنَ ٱلْمُهْتَدِينَ ۝ ۞ أَجَعَلْتُمْ سِقَايَةَ ٱلْحَآجِّ وَعِمَارَةَ ٱلْمَسْجِدِ ٱلْحَرَامِ كَمَنْ ءَامَنَ بِٱللَّهِ وَٱلْيَوْمِ ٱلْءَاخِرِ وَجَٰهَدَ فِى سَبِيلِ ٱللَّهِ ۚ لَا يَسْتَوُۥنَ عِندَ ٱللَّهِ ۗ وَٱللَّهُ لَا يَهْدِى ٱلْقَوْمَ ٱلظَّٰلِمِينَ ۝ ٱلَّذِينَ ءَامَنُوا۟ وَهَاجَرُوا۟ وَجَٰهَدُوا۟ فِى سَبِيلِ ٱللَّهِ بِأَمْوَٰلِهِمْ وَأَنفُسِهِمْ أَعْظَمُ دَرَجَةً عِندَ ٱللَّهِ ۚ وَأُو۟لَٰٓئِكَ هُمُ ٱلْفَآئِزُونَ ۝ يُبَشِّرُهُمْ رَبُّهُم بِرَحْمَةٍ مِّنْهُ وَرِضْوَٰنٍ وَجَنَّٰتٍ لَّهُمْ فِيهَا نَعِيمٌ مُّقِيمٌ ۝ خَٰلِدِينَ فِيهَآ أَبَدًا ۚ إِنَّ ٱللَّهَ عِندَهُۥٓ أَجْرٌ عَظِيمٌ ۝ يَٰٓأَيُّهَا ٱلَّذِينَ ءَامَنُوا۟ لَا تَتَّخِذُوٓا۟ ءَابَآءَكُمْ وَإِخْوَٰنَكُمْ أَوْلِيَآءَ إِنِ ٱسْتَحَبُّوا۟ ٱلْكُفْرَ عَلَى ٱلْإِيمَٰنِ ۚ وَمَن يَتَوَلَّهُم مِّنكُمْ فَأُو۟لَٰٓئِكَ هُمُ ٱلظَّٰلِمُونَ ۝ قُلْ إِن كَانَ ءَابَآؤُكُمْ وَأَبْنَآؤُكُمْ وَإِخْوَٰنُكُمْ وَأَزْوَٰجُكُمْ وَعَشِيرَتُكُمْ وَأَمْوَٰلٌ ٱقْتَرَفْتُمُوهَا

وَتِجَٰرَةٌ تَخْشَوْنَ كَسَادَهَا وَمَسَٰكِنُ تَرْضَوْنَهَآ أَحَبَّ إِلَيْكُم مِّنَ ٱللَّهِ وَرَسُولِهِۦ وَجِهَادٍ فِى سَبِيلِهِۦ فَتَرَبَّصُواْ حَتَّىٰ يَأْتِىَ ٱللَّهُ بِأَمْرِهِۦ ۗ وَٱللَّهُ لَا يَهْدِى ٱلْقَوْمَ ٱلْفَٰسِقِينَ ﴿٢٤﴾ لَقَدْ نَصَرَكُمُ ٱللَّهُ فِى مَوَاطِنَ كَثِيرَةٍ ۙ وَيَوْمَ حُنَيْنٍ ۙ إِذْ أَعْجَبَتْكُمْ كَثْرَتُكُمْ فَلَمْ تُغْنِ عَنكُمْ شَيْـًٔا وَضَاقَتْ عَلَيْكُمُ ٱلْأَرْضُ بِمَا رَحُبَتْ ثُمَّ وَلَّيْتُم مُّدْبِرِينَ ﴿٢٥﴾ ثُمَّ أَنزَلَ ٱللَّهُ سَكِينَتَهُۥ عَلَىٰ رَسُولِهِۦ وَعَلَى ٱلْمُؤْمِنِينَ وَأَنزَلَ جُنُودًا لَّمْ تَرَوْهَا وَعَذَّبَ ٱلَّذِينَ كَفَرُواْ ۚ وَذَٰلِكَ جَزَآءُ ٱلْكَٰفِرِينَ ﴿٢٦﴾ ثُمَّ يَتُوبُ ٱللَّهُ مِنۢ بَعْدِ ذَٰلِكَ عَلَىٰ مَن يَشَآءُ ۗ وَٱللَّهُ غَفُورٌ رَّحِيمٌ ﴿٢٧﴾ يَٰٓأَيُّهَا ٱلَّذِينَ ءَامَنُوٓاْ إِنَّمَا ٱلْمُشْرِكُونَ نَجَسٌ فَلَا يَقْرَبُواْ ٱلْمَسْجِدَ ٱلْحَرَامَ بَعْدَ عَامِهِمْ هَٰذَا ۚ وَإِنْ خِفْتُمْ عَيْلَةً فَسَوْفَ يُغْنِيكُمُ ٱللَّهُ مِن فَضْلِهِۦٓ إِن شَآءَ ۚ إِنَّ ٱللَّهَ عَلِيمٌ حَكِيمٌ ﴿٢٨﴾ قَٰتِلُواْ ٱلَّذِينَ لَا يُؤْمِنُونَ بِٱللَّهِ وَلَا بِٱلْيَوْمِ ٱلْءَاخِرِ وَلَا يُحَرِّمُونَ مَا حَرَّمَ ٱللَّهُ وَرَسُولُهُۥ وَلَا يَدِينُونَ دِينَ ٱلْحَقِّ مِنَ ٱلَّذِينَ أُوتُواْ ٱلْكِتَٰبَ حَتَّىٰ يُعْطُواْ ٱلْجِزْيَةَ عَن يَدٍ وَهُمْ صَٰغِرُونَ ﴿٢٩﴾ وَقَالَتِ ٱلْيَهُودُ عُزَيْرٌ ٱبْنُ ٱللَّهِ وَقَالَتِ ٱلنَّصَٰرَى ٱلْمَسِيحُ ٱبْنُ ٱللَّهِ ۖ ذَٰلِكَ قَوْلُهُم بِأَفْوَٰهِهِمْ ۖ يُضَٰهِـُٔونَ قَوْلَ ٱلَّذِينَ كَفَرُواْ مِن قَبْلُ ۚ قَٰتَلَهُمُ ٱللَّهُ ۚ أَنَّىٰ يُؤْفَكُونَ ﴿٣٠﴾ ٱتَّخَذُوٓاْ أَحْبَارَهُمْ وَرُهْبَٰنَهُمْ أَرْبَابًا مِّن دُونِ ٱللَّهِ وَٱلْمَسِيحَ ٱبْنَ مَرْيَمَ وَمَآ أُمِرُوٓاْ إِلَّا لِيَعْبُدُوٓاْ إِلَٰهًا وَٰحِدًا ۖ لَّآ إِلَٰهَ إِلَّا هُوَ ۚ سُبْحَٰنَهُۥ عَمَّا يُشْرِكُونَ ﴿٣١﴾ يُرِيدُونَ أَن يُطْفِـُٔواْ نُورَ ٱللَّهِ بِأَفْوَٰهِهِمْ وَيَأْبَى ٱللَّهُ إِلَّآ أَن يُتِمَّ نُورَهُۥ وَلَوْ كَرِهَ ٱلْكَٰفِرُونَ ﴿٣٢﴾ هُوَ ٱلَّذِىٓ أَرْسَلَ رَسُولَهُۥ بِٱلْهُدَىٰ وَدِينِ ٱلْحَقِّ لِيُظْهِرَهُۥ عَلَى ٱلدِّينِ كُلِّهِۦ وَلَوْ كَرِهَ ٱلْمُشْرِكُونَ ﴿٣٣﴾ ۞ يَٰٓأَيُّهَا ٱلَّذِينَ ءَامَنُوٓاْ إِنَّ كَثِيرًا مِّنَ ٱلْأَحْبَارِ وَٱلرُّهْبَانِ لَيَأْكُلُونَ أَمْوَٰلَ ٱلنَّاسِ بِٱلْبَٰطِلِ وَيَصُدُّونَ عَن سَبِيلِ ٱللَّهِ ۗ وَٱلَّذِينَ

يَكْنِزُونَ ٱلذَّهَبَ وَٱلْفِضَّةَ وَلَا يُنفِقُونَهَا فِى سَبِيلِ ٱللَّهِ فَبَشِّرْهُم بِعَذَابٍ أَلِيمٍ ۝ يَوْمَ يُحْمَىٰ عَلَيْهَا فِى نَارِ جَهَنَّمَ فَتُكْوَىٰ بِهَا جِبَاهُهُمْ وَجُنُوبُهُمْ وَظُهُورُهُمْ ۖ هَٰذَا مَا كَنَزْتُمْ لِأَنفُسِكُمْ فَذُوقُوا۟ مَا كُنتُمْ تَكْنِزُونَ ۝ إِنَّ عِدَّةَ ٱلشُّهُورِ عِندَ ٱللَّهِ ٱثْنَا عَشَرَ شَهْرًا فِى كِتَٰبِ ٱللَّهِ يَوْمَ خَلَقَ ٱلسَّمَٰوَٰتِ وَٱلْأَرْضَ مِنْهَآ أَرْبَعَةٌ حُرُمٌ ۚ ذَٰلِكَ ٱلدِّينُ ٱلْقَيِّمُ ۚ فَلَا تَظْلِمُوا۟ فِيهِنَّ أَنفُسَكُمْ ۚ وَقَٰتِلُوا۟ ٱلْمُشْرِكِينَ كَآفَّةً كَمَا يُقَٰتِلُونَكُمْ كَآفَّةً ۚ وَٱعْلَمُوٓا۟ أَنَّ ٱللَّهَ مَعَ ٱلْمُتَّقِينَ ۝ إِنَّمَا ٱلنَّسِىٓءُ زِيَادَةٌ فِى ٱلْكُفْرِ ۖ يُضَلُّ بِهِ ٱلَّذِينَ كَفَرُوا۟ يُحِلُّونَهُۥ عَامًا وَيُحَرِّمُونَهُۥ عَامًا لِّيُوَاطِـُٔوا۟ عِدَّةَ مَا حَرَّمَ ٱللَّهُ فَيُحِلُّوا۟ مَا حَرَّمَ ٱللَّهُ ۚ زُيِّنَ لَهُمْ سُوٓءُ أَعْمَٰلِهِمْ ۗ وَٱللَّهُ لَا يَهْدِى ٱلْقَوْمَ ٱلْكَٰفِرِينَ ۝ يَٰٓأَيُّهَا ٱلَّذِينَ ءَامَنُوا۟ مَا لَكُمْ إِذَا قِيلَ لَكُمُ ٱنفِرُوا۟ فِى سَبِيلِ ٱللَّهِ ٱثَّاقَلْتُمْ إِلَى ٱلْأَرْضِ ۚ أَرَضِيتُم بِٱلْحَيَوٰةِ ٱلدُّنْيَا مِنَ ٱلْءَاخِرَةِ ۚ فَمَا مَتَٰعُ ٱلْحَيَوٰةِ ٱلدُّنْيَا فِى ٱلْءَاخِرَةِ إِلَّا قَلِيلٌ ۝ إِلَّا تَنفِرُوا۟ يُعَذِّبْكُمْ عَذَابًا أَلِيمًا وَيَسْتَبْدِلْ قَوْمًا غَيْرَكُمْ وَلَا تَضُرُّوهُ شَيْـًٔا ۗ وَٱللَّهُ عَلَىٰ كُلِّ شَىْءٍ قَدِيرٌ ۝ إِلَّا تَنصُرُوهُ فَقَدْ نَصَرَهُ ٱللَّهُ إِذْ أَخْرَجَهُ ٱلَّذِينَ كَفَرُوا۟ ثَانِىَ ٱثْنَيْنِ إِذْ هُمَا فِى ٱلْغَارِ إِذْ يَقُولُ لِصَٰحِبِهِۦ لَا تَحْزَنْ إِنَّ ٱللَّهَ مَعَنَا ۖ فَأَنزَلَ ٱللَّهُ سَكِينَتَهُۥ عَلَيْهِ وَأَيَّدَهُۥ بِجُنُودٍ لَّمْ تَرَوْهَا وَجَعَلَ كَلِمَةَ ٱلَّذِينَ كَفَرُوا۟ ٱلسُّفْلَىٰ ۗ وَكَلِمَةُ ٱللَّهِ هِىَ ٱلْعُلْيَا ۗ وَٱللَّهُ عَزِيزٌ حَكِيمٌ ۝ ٱنفِرُوا۟ خِفَافًا وَثِقَالًا وَجَٰهِدُوا۟ بِأَمْوَٰلِكُمْ وَأَنفُسِكُمْ فِى سَبِيلِ ٱللَّهِ ۚ ذَٰلِكُمْ خَيْرٌ لَّكُمْ إِن كُنتُمْ تَعْلَمُونَ ۝ لَوْ كَانَ عَرَضًا قَرِيبًا وَسَفَرًا قَاصِدًا لَّٱتَّبَعُوكَ وَلَٰكِنۢ بَعُدَتْ عَلَيْهِمُ ٱلشُّقَّةُ ۚ وَسَيَحْلِفُونَ بِٱللَّهِ لَوِ ٱسْتَطَعْنَا لَخَرَجْنَا مَعَكُمْ يُهْلِكُونَ أَنفُسَهُمْ وَٱللَّهُ يَعْلَمُ إِنَّهُمْ لَكَٰذِبُونَ ۝ عَفَا ٱللَّهُ عَنكَ لِمَ أَذِنتَ لَهُمْ حَتَّىٰ يَتَبَيَّنَ لَكَ ٱلَّذِينَ صَدَقُوا۟ وَتَعْلَمَ ٱلْكَٰذِبِينَ

لَا يَسْتَـٔذِنُكَ ٱلَّذِينَ يُؤْمِنُونَ بِٱللَّهِ وَٱلْيَوْمِ ٱلْـَٔاخِرِ أَن يُجَـٰهِدُوا۟ بِأَمْوَٰلِهِمْ وَأَنفُسِهِمْ ۗ وَٱللَّهُ عَلِيمٌۢ بِٱلْمُتَّقِينَ ﴿٤٤﴾ إِنَّمَا يَسْتَـٔذِنُكَ ٱلَّذِينَ لَا يُؤْمِنُونَ بِٱللَّهِ وَٱلْيَوْمِ ٱلْـَٔاخِرِ وَٱرْتَابَتْ قُلُوبُهُمْ فَهُمْ فِى رَيْبِهِمْ يَتَرَدَّدُونَ ﴿٤٥﴾ ۞ وَلَوْ أَرَادُوا۟ ٱلْخُرُوجَ لَأَعَدُّوا۟ لَهُۥ عُدَّةًۭ وَلَـٰكِن كَرِهَ ٱللَّهُ ٱنۢبِعَاثَهُمْ فَثَبَّطَهُمْ وَقِيلَ ٱقْعُدُوا۟ مَعَ ٱلْقَـٰعِدِينَ ﴿٤٦﴾ لَوْ خَرَجُوا۟ فِيكُم مَّا زَادُوكُمْ إِلَّا خَبَالًۭا وَلَأَوْضَعُوا۟ خِلَـٰلَكُمْ يَبْغُونَكُمُ ٱلْفِتْنَةَ وَفِيكُمْ سَمَّـٰعُونَ لَهُمْ ۗ وَٱللَّهُ عَلِيمٌۢ بِٱلظَّـٰلِمِينَ ﴿٤٧﴾ لَقَدِ ٱبْتَغَوُا۟ ٱلْفِتْنَةَ مِن قَبْلُ وَقَلَّبُوا۟ لَكَ ٱلْأُمُورَ حَتَّىٰ جَآءَ ٱلْحَقُّ وَظَهَرَ أَمْرُ ٱللَّهِ وَهُمْ كَـٰرِهُونَ ﴿٤٨﴾ وَمِنْهُم مَّن يَقُولُ ٱئْذَن لِّى وَلَا تَفْتِنِّىٓ ۚ أَلَا فِى ٱلْفِتْنَةِ سَقَطُوا۟ ۗ وَإِنَّ جَهَنَّمَ لَمُحِيطَةٌۢ بِٱلْكَـٰفِرِينَ ﴿٤٩﴾ إِن تُصِبْكَ حَسَنَةٌۭ تَسُؤْهُمْ ۖ وَإِن تُصِبْكَ مُصِيبَةٌۭ يَقُولُوا۟ قَدْ أَخَذْنَآ أَمْرَنَا مِن قَبْلُ وَيَتَوَلَّوا۟ وَّهُمْ فَرِحُونَ ﴿٥٠﴾ قُل لَّن يُصِيبَنَآ إِلَّا مَا كَتَبَ ٱللَّهُ لَنَا هُوَ مَوْلَىٰنَا ۚ وَعَلَى ٱللَّهِ فَلْيَتَوَكَّلِ ٱلْمُؤْمِنُونَ ﴿٥١﴾ قُلْ هَلْ تَرَبَّصُونَ بِنَآ إِلَّآ إِحْدَى ٱلْحُسْنَيَيْنِ ۖ وَنَحْنُ نَتَرَبَّصُ بِكُمْ أَن يُصِيبَكُمُ ٱللَّهُ بِعَذَابٍۢ مِّنْ عِندِهِۦٓ أَوْ بِأَيْدِينَا ۖ فَتَرَبَّصُوٓا۟ إِنَّا مَعَكُم مُّتَرَبِّصُونَ ﴿٥٢﴾ قُلْ أَنفِقُوا۟ طَوْعًا أَوْ كَرْهًۭا لَّن يُتَقَبَّلَ مِنكُمْ ۖ إِنَّكُمْ كُنتُمْ قَوْمًۭا فَـٰسِقِينَ ﴿٥٣﴾ وَمَا مَنَعَهُمْ أَن تُقْبَلَ مِنْهُمْ نَفَقَـٰتُهُمْ إِلَّآ أَنَّهُمْ كَفَرُوا۟ بِٱللَّهِ وَبِرَسُولِهِۦ وَلَا يَأْتُونَ ٱلصَّلَوٰةَ إِلَّا وَهُمْ كُسَالَىٰ وَلَا يُنفِقُونَ إِلَّا وَهُمْ كَـٰرِهُونَ ﴿٥٤﴾ فَلَا تُعْجِبْكَ أَمْوَٰلُهُمْ وَلَآ أَوْلَـٰدُهُمْ ۚ إِنَّمَا يُرِيدُ ٱللَّهُ لِيُعَذِّبَهُم بِهَا فِى ٱلْحَيَوٰةِ ٱلدُّنْيَا وَتَزْهَقَ أَنفُسُهُمْ وَهُمْ كَـٰفِرُونَ ﴿٥٥﴾ وَيَحْلِفُونَ بِٱللَّهِ إِنَّهُمْ لَمِنكُمْ وَمَا هُم مِّنكُمْ وَلَـٰكِنَّهُمْ قَوْمٌۭ يَفْرَقُونَ ﴿٥٦﴾ لَوْ يَجِدُونَ مَلْجَـًٔا أَوْ مَغَـٰرَٰتٍ أَوْ مُدَّخَلًۭا لَّوَلَّوْا۟ إِلَيْهِ وَهُمْ يَجْمَحُونَ ﴿٥٧﴾ وَمِنْهُم مَّن يَلْمِزُكَ فِى ٱلصَّدَقَـٰتِ فَإِنْ أُعْطُوا۟ مِنْهَا رَضُوا۟ وَإِن لَّمْ

يُعْطَوْا۟ مِنْهَآ إِذَا هُمْ يَسْخَطُونَ ۝ وَلَوْ أَنَّهُمْ رَضُوا۟ مَآ ءَاتَىٰهُمُ ٱللَّهُ وَرَسُولُهُۥ وَقَالُوا۟ حَسْبُنَا ٱللَّهُ سَيُؤْتِينَا ٱللَّهُ مِن فَضْلِهِۦ وَرَسُولُهُۥٓ إِنَّآ إِلَى ٱللَّهِ رَٰغِبُونَ ۝ ۞ إِنَّمَا ٱلصَّدَقَٰتُ لِلْفُقَرَآءِ وَٱلْمَسَٰكِينِ وَٱلْعَٰمِلِينَ عَلَيْهَا وَٱلْمُؤَلَّفَةِ قُلُوبُهُمْ وَفِى ٱلرِّقَابِ وَٱلْغَٰرِمِينَ وَفِى سَبِيلِ ٱللَّهِ وَٱبْنِ ٱلسَّبِيلِ ۖ فَرِيضَةً مِّنَ ٱللَّهِ ۗ وَٱللَّهُ عَلِيمٌ حَكِيمٌ ۝ وَمِنْهُمُ ٱلَّذِينَ يُؤْذُونَ ٱلنَّبِىَّ وَيَقُولُونَ هُوَ أُذُنٌ ۚ قُلْ أُذُنُ خَيْرٍ لَّكُمْ يُؤْمِنُ بِٱللَّهِ وَيُؤْمِنُ لِلْمُؤْمِنِينَ وَرَحْمَةٌ لِّلَّذِينَ ءَامَنُوا۟ مِنكُمْ ۚ وَٱلَّذِينَ يُؤْذُونَ رَسُولَ ٱللَّهِ لَهُمْ عَذَابٌ أَلِيمٌ ۝ يَحْلِفُونَ بِٱللَّهِ لَكُمْ لِيُرْضُوكُمْ وَٱللَّهُ وَرَسُولُهُۥٓ أَحَقُّ أَن يُرْضُوهُ إِن كَانُوا۟ مُؤْمِنِينَ ۝ أَلَمْ يَعْلَمُوٓا۟ أَنَّهُۥ مَن يُحَادِدِ ٱللَّهَ وَرَسُولَهُۥ فَأَنَّ لَهُۥ نَارَ جَهَنَّمَ خَٰلِدًا فِيهَا ۚ ذَٰلِكَ ٱلْخِزْىُ ٱلْعَظِيمُ ۝ يَحْذَرُ ٱلْمُنَٰفِقُونَ أَن تُنَزَّلَ عَلَيْهِمْ سُورَةٌ تُنَبِّئُهُم بِمَا فِى قُلُوبِهِمْ ۚ قُلِ ٱسْتَهْزِءُوٓا۟ إِنَّ ٱللَّهَ مُخْرِجٌ مَّا تَحْذَرُونَ ۝ وَلَئِن سَأَلْتَهُمْ لَيَقُولُنَّ إِنَّمَا كُنَّا نَخُوضُ وَنَلْعَبُ ۚ قُلْ أَبِٱللَّهِ وَءَايَٰتِهِۦ وَرَسُولِهِۦ كُنتُمْ تَسْتَهْزِءُونَ ۝ لَا تَعْتَذِرُوا۟ قَدْ كَفَرْتُم بَعْدَ إِيمَٰنِكُمْ ۚ إِن نَّعْفُ عَن طَآئِفَةٍ مِّنكُمْ نُعَذِّبْ طَآئِفَةًۢ بِأَنَّهُمْ كَانُوا۟ مُجْرِمِينَ ۝ ٱلْمُنَٰفِقُونَ وَٱلْمُنَٰفِقَٰتُ بَعْضُهُم مِّنۢ بَعْضٍ ۚ يَأْمُرُونَ بِٱلْمُنكَرِ وَيَنْهَوْنَ عَنِ ٱلْمَعْرُوفِ وَيَقْبِضُونَ أَيْدِيَهُمْ ۚ نَسُوا۟ ٱللَّهَ فَنَسِيَهُمْ ۗ إِنَّ ٱلْمُنَٰفِقِينَ هُمُ ٱلْفَٰسِقُونَ ۝ وَعَدَ ٱللَّهُ ٱلْمُنَٰفِقِينَ وَٱلْمُنَٰفِقَٰتِ وَٱلْكُفَّارَ نَارَ جَهَنَّمَ خَٰلِدِينَ فِيهَا ۚ هِىَ حَسْبُهُمْ ۚ وَلَعَنَهُمُ ٱللَّهُ ۖ وَلَهُمْ عَذَابٌ مُّقِيمٌ ۝ كَٱلَّذِينَ مِن قَبْلِكُمْ كَانُوٓا۟ أَشَدَّ مِنكُمْ قُوَّةً وَأَكْثَرَ أَمْوَٰلًا وَأَوْلَٰدًا فَٱسْتَمْتَعُوا۟ بِخَلَٰقِهِمْ فَٱسْتَمْتَعْتُم بِخَلَٰقِكُمْ كَمَا ٱسْتَمْتَعَ ٱلَّذِينَ مِن قَبْلِكُم بِخَلَٰقِهِمْ وَخُضْتُمْ كَٱلَّذِى خَاضُوٓا۟ ۚ أُو۟لَٰٓئِكَ حَبِطَتْ أَعْمَٰلُهُمْ فِى ٱلدُّنْيَا وَٱلْءَاخِرَةِ ۖ وَأُو۟لَٰٓئِكَ هُمُ ٱلْخَٰسِرُونَ ۝ أَلَمْ يَأْتِهِمْ نَبَأُ ٱلَّذِينَ مِن قَبْلِهِمْ قَوْمِ

نُوحٍ وَعَادٍ وَثَمُودَ وَقَوْمِ إِبْرَٰهِيمَ وَأَصْحَٰبِ مَدْيَنَ وَٱلْمُؤْتَفِكَٰتِ ۚ أَتَتْهُمْ رُسُلُهُم بِٱلْبَيِّنَٰتِ ۖ فَمَا كَانَ ٱللَّهُ لِيَظْلِمَهُمْ وَلَٰكِن كَانُوٓا۟ أَنفُسَهُمْ يَظْلِمُونَ ۝٧٠ وَٱلْمُؤْمِنُونَ وَٱلْمُؤْمِنَٰتُ بَعْضُهُمْ أَوْلِيَآءُ بَعْضٍ ۚ يَأْمُرُونَ بِٱلْمَعْرُوفِ وَيَنْهَوْنَ عَنِ ٱلْمُنكَرِ وَيُقِيمُونَ ٱلصَّلَوٰةَ وَيُؤْتُونَ ٱلزَّكَوٰةَ وَيُطِيعُونَ ٱللَّهَ وَرَسُولَهُۥٓ ۚ أُو۟لَٰٓئِكَ سَيَرْحَمُهُمُ ٱللَّهُ ۗ إِنَّ ٱللَّهَ عَزِيزٌ حَكِيمٌ ۝٧١ وَعَدَ ٱللَّهُ ٱلْمُؤْمِنِينَ وَٱلْمُؤْمِنَٰتِ جَنَّٰتٍ تَجْرِى مِن تَحْتِهَا ٱلْأَنْهَٰرُ خَٰلِدِينَ فِيهَا وَمَسَٰكِنَ طَيِّبَةً فِى جَنَّٰتِ عَدْنٍ ۚ وَرِضْوَٰنٌ مِّنَ ٱللَّهِ أَكْبَرُ ۚ ذَٰلِكَ هُوَ ٱلْفَوْزُ ٱلْعَظِيمُ ۝٧٢ يَٰٓأَيُّهَا ٱلنَّبِىُّ جَٰهِدِ ٱلْكُفَّارَ وَٱلْمُنَٰفِقِينَ وَٱغْلُظْ عَلَيْهِمْ ۚ وَمَأْوَىٰهُمْ جَهَنَّمُ ۖ وَبِئْسَ ٱلْمَصِيرُ ۝٧٣ يَحْلِفُونَ بِٱللَّهِ مَا قَالُوا۟ وَلَقَدْ قَالُوا۟ كَلِمَةَ ٱلْكُفْرِ وَكَفَرُوا۟ بَعْدَ إِسْلَٰمِهِمْ وَهَمُّوا۟ بِمَا لَمْ يَنَالُوا۟ ۚ وَمَا نَقَمُوٓا۟ إِلَّآ أَنْ أَغْنَىٰهُمُ ٱللَّهُ وَرَسُولُهُۥ مِن فَضْلِهِۦ ۚ فَإِن يَتُوبُوا۟ يَكُ خَيْرًا لَّهُمْ ۖ وَإِن يَتَوَلَّوْا۟ يُعَذِّبْهُمُ ٱللَّهُ عَذَابًا أَلِيمًا فِى ٱلدُّنْيَا وَٱلْآخِرَةِ ۚ وَمَا لَهُمْ فِى ٱلْأَرْضِ مِن وَلِىٍّ وَلَا نَصِيرٍ ۝٧٤ وَمِنْهُم مَّنْ عَٰهَدَ ٱللَّهَ لَئِنْ ءَاتَىٰنَا مِن فَضْلِهِۦ لَنَصَّدَّقَنَّ وَلَنَكُونَنَّ مِنَ ٱلصَّٰلِحِينَ ۝٧٥ فَلَمَّآ ءَاتَىٰهُم مِّن فَضْلِهِۦ بَخِلُوا۟ بِهِۦ وَتَوَلَّوا۟ وَّهُم مُّعْرِضُونَ ۝٧٦ فَأَعْقَبَهُمْ نِفَاقًا فِى قُلُوبِهِمْ إِلَىٰ يَوْمِ يَلْقَوْنَهُۥ بِمَآ أَخْلَفُوا۟ ٱللَّهَ مَا وَعَدُوهُ وَبِمَا كَانُوا۟ يَكْذِبُونَ ۝٧٧ أَلَمْ يَعْلَمُوٓا۟ أَنَّ ٱللَّهَ يَعْلَمُ سِرَّهُمْ وَنَجْوَىٰهُمْ وَأَنَّ ٱللَّهَ عَلَّٰمُ ٱلْغُيُوبِ ۝٧٨ ٱلَّذِينَ يَلْمِزُونَ ٱلْمُطَّوِّعِينَ مِنَ ٱلْمُؤْمِنِينَ فِى ٱلصَّدَقَٰتِ وَٱلَّذِينَ لَا يَجِدُونَ إِلَّا جُهْدَهُمْ فَيَسْخَرُونَ مِنْهُمْ ۙ سَخِرَ ٱللَّهُ مِنْهُمْ وَلَهُمْ عَذَابٌ أَلِيمٌ ۝٧٩ ٱسْتَغْفِرْ لَهُمْ أَوْ لَا تَسْتَغْفِرْ لَهُمْ إِن تَسْتَغْفِرْ لَهُمْ سَبْعِينَ مَرَّةً فَلَن يَغْفِرَ ٱللَّهُ لَهُمْ ۚ ذَٰلِكَ بِأَنَّهُمْ كَفَرُوا۟ بِٱللَّهِ وَرَسُولِهِۦ ۗ وَٱللَّهُ لَا يَهْدِى ٱلْقَوْمَ ٱلْفَٰسِقِينَ ۝٨٠ فَرِحَ ٱلْمُخَلَّفُونَ بِمَقْعَدِهِمْ خِلَٰفَ رَسُولِ ٱللَّهِ وَكَرِهُوٓا۟

أن تجَاهِدُوا بِأَمْوَالِهِمْ وَأَنفُسِهِمْ فِي سَبِيلِ ٱللَّهِ وَقَالُوا۟ لَا تَنفِرُوا۟ فِى ٱلْحَرِّ ۗ قُلْ نَارُ جَهَنَّمَ أَشَدُّ حَرًّا ۚ لَّوْ كَانُوا۟ يَفْقَهُونَ ۝ فَلْيَضْحَكُوا۟ قَلِيلًا وَلْيَبْكُوا۟ كَثِيرًا جَزَآءًۢ بِمَا كَانُوا۟ يَكْسِبُونَ ۝ فَإِن رَّجَعَكَ ٱللَّهُ إِلَىٰ طَآئِفَةٍ مِّنْهُمْ فَٱسْتَـْٔذَنُوكَ لِلْخُرُوجِ فَقُل لَّن تَخْرُجُوا۟ مَعِىَ أَبَدًا وَلَن تُقَـٰتِلُوا۟ مَعِىَ عَدُوًّا ۖ إِنَّكُمْ رَضِيتُم بِٱلْقُعُودِ أَوَّلَ مَرَّةٍ فَٱقْعُدُوا۟ مَعَ ٱلْخَـٰلِفِينَ ۝ وَلَا تُصَلِّ عَلَىٰٓ أَحَدٍ مِّنْهُم مَّاتَ أَبَدًا وَلَا تَقُمْ عَلَىٰ قَبْرِهِۦٓ ۖ إِنَّهُمْ كَفَرُوا۟ بِٱللَّهِ وَرَسُولِهِۦ وَمَاتُوا۟ وَهُمْ فَـٰسِقُونَ ۝ وَلَا تُعْجِبْكَ أَمْوَٰلُهُمْ وَأَوْلَـٰدُهُمْ ۚ إِنَّمَا يُرِيدُ ٱللَّهُ أَن يُعَذِّبَهُم بِهَا فِى ٱلدُّنْيَا وَتَزْهَقَ أَنفُسُهُمْ وَهُمْ كَـٰفِرُونَ ۝ وَإِذَآ أُنزِلَتْ سُورَةٌ أَنْ ءَامِنُوا۟ بِٱللَّهِ وَجَـٰهِدُوا۟ مَعَ رَسُولِهِ ٱسْتَـْٔذَنَكَ أُو۟لُوا۟ ٱلطَّوْلِ مِنْهُمْ وَقَالُوا۟ ذَرْنَا نَكُن مَّعَ ٱلْقَـٰعِدِينَ ۝ رَضُوا۟ بِأَن يَكُونُوا۟ مَعَ ٱلْخَوَالِفِ وَطُبِعَ عَلَىٰ قُلُوبِهِمْ فَهُمْ لَا يَفْقَهُونَ ۝ لَـٰكِنِ ٱلرَّسُولُ وَٱلَّذِينَ ءَامَنُوا۟ مَعَهُۥ جَـٰهَدُوا۟ بِأَمْوَٰلِهِمْ وَأَنفُسِهِمْ ۚ وَأُو۟لَـٰٓئِكَ لَهُمُ ٱلْخَيْرَٰتُ ۖ وَأُو۟لَـٰٓئِكَ هُمُ ٱلْمُفْلِحُونَ ۝ أَعَدَّ ٱللَّهُ لَهُمْ جَنَّـٰتٍ تَجْرِى مِن تَحْتِهَا ٱلْأَنْهَـٰرُ خَـٰلِدِينَ فِيهَا ۚ ذَٰلِكَ ٱلْفَوْزُ ٱلْعَظِيمُ ۝ وَجَآءَ ٱلْمُعَذِّرُونَ مِنَ ٱلْأَعْرَابِ لِيُؤْذَنَ لَهُمْ وَقَعَدَ ٱلَّذِينَ كَذَبُوا۟ ٱللَّهَ وَرَسُولَهُۥ ۚ سَيُصِيبُ ٱلَّذِينَ كَفَرُوا۟ مِنْهُمْ عَذَابٌ أَلِيمٌ ۝ لَّيْسَ عَلَى ٱلضُّعَفَآءِ وَلَا عَلَى ٱلْمَرْضَىٰ وَلَا عَلَى ٱلَّذِينَ لَا يَجِدُونَ مَا يُنفِقُونَ حَرَجٌ إِذَا نَصَحُوا۟ لِلَّهِ وَرَسُولِهِۦ ۚ مَا عَلَى ٱلْمُحْسِنِينَ مِن سَبِيلٍ ۚ وَٱللَّهُ غَفُورٌ رَّحِيمٌ ۝ وَلَا عَلَى ٱلَّذِينَ إِذَا مَآ أَتَوْكَ لِتَحْمِلَهُمْ قُلْتَ لَآ أَجِدُ مَآ أَحْمِلُكُمْ عَلَيْهِ تَوَلَّوا۟ وَّأَعْيُنُهُمْ تَفِيضُ مِنَ ٱلدَّمْعِ حَزَنًا أَلَّا يَجِدُوا۟ مَا يُنفِقُونَ ۝

(At-Tauba 001-092)

INTRODUCTION TO CHAPTER (SURAH) 8: AL-ANFAL (SPOILS OF WAR, BOOTY)

Ibn Kathir's Introduction

There are seventy-five Ayat in this Surah. The word count of this Surah is one thousand, six hundred and thirty-one words and its letters number five thousand, two hundred and ninety-four.

CHAPTER (SURAH) 8: AL-ANFAL (SPOILS OF WAR, BOOTY), VERSES 041–075

Surah: 8 Ayah: 41

﴿ ۞ وَٱعْلَمُوٓا۟ أَنَّمَا غَنِمْتُم مِّن شَىْءٍ فَأَنَّ لِلَّهِ خُمُسَهُۥ وَلِلرَّسُولِ وَلِذِى ٱلْقُرْبَىٰ وَٱلْيَتَـٰمَىٰ وَٱلْمَسَـٰكِينِ وَٱبْنِ ٱلسَّبِيلِ إِن كُنتُمْ ءَامَنتُم بِٱللَّهِ وَمَآ أَنزَلْنَا عَلَىٰ عَبْدِنَا يَوْمَ ٱلْفُرْقَانِ يَوْمَ ٱلْتَقَى ٱلْجَمْعَانِ ۗ وَٱللَّهُ عَلَىٰ كُلِّ شَىْءٍ قَدِيرٌ ﴾

41. And know that whatever of war-booty that you may gain, verily one-fifth (/5th) of it is assigned to Allâh, and to the Messenger, and to the near relatives (of the Messenger (Muhammad (peace be upon him))) (and also) the orphans, Al-Masâkin (the poor) and the wayfarer, if you have believed in Allâh and in that which We sent down to Our slave (Muhammad (peace be upon him)) on the Day of criterion (between right and wrong), the Day when the two forces met (the battle of Badr); And Allâh is Able to do all things.

Transliteration

41. WaiAAlamoo annama ghanimtum min shay-in faanna lillahi khumusahu walilrrasooli walithee alqurba waalyatama waalmasakeeni waibni alssabeeli in kuntum amantum biAllahi wama anzalna AAala AAabdina yawma alfurqani yawma iltaqa aljamAAani waAllahu AAala kulli shay-in qadeerun

Tafsir Ibn Kathir

Ruling on the Spoils of War (Ghanimah and Fai)

Allah explains the spoils of war in detail, as He has specifically allowed it for this honorable Ummah over all others. We should mention that the `Ghanimah' refers to war spoils captured from the disbelievers, using armies and instruments of war. As for `Fai', it refers to the property of the disbelievers that they forfeit in return for peace, what they leave behind when they die and have no one to inherit from them, and the Jizyah (tribute tax) and Khiraj (property tax). Allah said,

Chapter 8: Al-Anfal (Spoils of War, Booty), Verses 041-075

(And know that whatever of war booty that you may gain, verily, one-fifth of it is assigned to Allah) indicating that the one-fifth should be reserved and paid in full (to Muslim leaders) whether it was little or substantial, even a yarn and needle.

(And whosoever deceives (his companions over the booty), he shall bring forth on the Day of Resurrection that which he took (illegally). Then every person shall be paid in full what he has earned, and they shall not be dealt with unjustly.) (3:161)

Allah's statement,

(verily, one-fifth of it is assigned to Allah, and to the Messenger,) was explained by Ibn `Abbas, as Ad-Dahhak reported from him, "Whenever the Messenger of Allah sent an army, he used to divide the war booty they collected into five shares, reserving one-fifth and divided it into five shares." Then he recited;

(And know that whatever of war booty that you may gain, verily, one-fifth of it is assigned to Allah, and to the Messenger,)

Ibn Abbas said, "Allah's statement,

(verily, one-fifth of it is assigned to Allah) is inclusive (of the Messenger's share), just as the following Ayah is inclusive (of Allah owning whatever is on the earth also),

(To Allah belongs all that is in the heavens and on the earth)(2:284)." So He addressed the share of Allah and the share of His Messenger in the same statement.

Ibrahim An-Nakha`i, Al-Hasan bin Muhammad bin Al-Hanifiyyah, Al-Hasan Al-Basri, Ash-Sha`bi, `Ata' bin Abi Rabah, `Abdullah bin Buraydah, Qatadah, Mughirah and several others, all said that the share designated for Allah and the Messenger is one and the same. Supporting this is what Imam Al-Hafiz Abu Bakr Al-Bayhaqi recorded, with a Sahih chain of narrators, that `Abdullah bin Shaqiq said that a man from Bilqin said, "I came to the Prophet when he was in Wadi Al-Qura inspecting a horse. I asked, `O Allah's Messenger! What about the Ghanimah' He said,

«لله خُمُسُهَا وَأَرْبَعَةُ أَخْمَاسِهَا لِلْجَيْشِ»

(Allah's share is one fifth and four-fifths are for the army.)

I asked, `None of them has more right to it than anyone else' He said,

«لَا، وَلَا السَّهْمُ تَسْتَخْرِجُهُ مِنْ جَنْبِكَ لَيْسَ أَنْتَ أَحَقَّ بِهِ مِنْ أَخِيكَ الْمُسْلِمِ»

(No. Even if you remove an arrow that pierced your flank, you have no more right to it than your Muslim brother.)"

Imam Ahmad recorded that Al-Miqdam bin Ma`dikarib Al-Kindi sat with `Ubadah bin As-Samit, Abu Ad-Darda' and Al-Harith bin Mu`awiyah Al-Kindi, may Allah be pleased with them, reminding each other of the statements of the Messenger of Allah . Abu Ad-Darda' said to `Ubadah, "O `Ubadah! What about the words of the Messenger of Allah during such and such battle, about the fifth (of the war booty)" `Ubadah said, "The Messenger of Allah led them in prayer, facing a camel from the war booty. When he finished the prayer, he stood up, held pelt of a camel between his fingers and said,

«إِنَّ هَذِهِ مِنْ غَنَائِمِكُمْ وَإِنَّهُ لَيْسَ لِي فِيهَا إِلَّا نَصِيبِي مَعَكُمْ إِلَّا الْخُمُسَ، وَالْخُمُسُ مَرْدُودٌ عَلَيْكُمْ، فَأَدُّوا الْخَيْطَ وَالْمَخِيطَ، وَأَكْبَرَ مِنْ ذَلِكَ وَأَصْغَرَ، وَلَا تَغُلُّوا فَإِنَّ الْغُلُولَ نَارٌ وَعَارٌ عَلَى أَصْحَابِهِ فِي الدُّنْيَا وَالْآخِرَةِ، وَجَاهِدُوا النَّاسَ فِي اللهِ الْقَرِيبَ وَالْبَعِيدَ، وَلَا تُبَالُوا فِي اللهِ لَوْمَةَ لَائِمٍ، وَأَقِيمُوا حُدُودَ اللهِ فِي الْحَضَرِ وَالسَّفَرِ، وَجَاهِدُوا فِي سَبِيلِ اللهِ، فَإِنَّ الْجِهَادَ بَابٌ مِنْ أَبْوَابِ الْجَنَّةِ عَظِيمٌ، يُنْجِي بِهِ اللهُ مِنَ الْهَمِّ وَالْغَمِّ»

(This is also a part of the war booty you earned. Verily, I have no share in it, except my own share, the fifth designated to me. Even that fifth will be given to you (indicating the Prophet's generosity). Therefore, surrender even the needle and the thread, and whatever is bigger or smaller than that (from the war spoils). Do not cheat with any of it, for stealing from the war booty before its distribution is Fire and a shame on its people in this life and the Hereafter. Perform Jihad against the people in Allah's cause, whether they are near or far, and do not fear the blame of the blamers, as long as you are in Allah's cause. Establish Allah's rules while in your area and while traveling. Perform Jihad in Allah's cause, for Jihad is a tremendous door leading to Paradise. Through it, Allah saves (one) from sadness and grief.)"

This is a tremendous Hadith, but I did not find it in any of the six collections of Hadith through this chain of narration. However, Imam Ahmad, Abu Dawud and An-Nasa'i recorded a Hadith from `Amr bin Shu`ayb, from his father, from his grandfather `Abdullah bin `Amr, from the Messenger of Allah , and this narration is similar to the one above, and a version from `Amr bin `Anbasah was recorded by Abu Dawud and An-Nasa'i. The Prophet used to choose some types of the war booty for himself; a servant, a horse, or a sword, according to the reports from Muhammad bin Sirin, `Amir Ash-Sha`bi and many scholars. For instance, Imam Ahmad and At-Tirmidhi -- who graded it Hasan -- recorded from Ibn `Abbas that the Messenger of Allah chose a sword called `Dhul-Fiqar' on the day of Badr. `A'ishah narrated that Safiyyah was among the captured women, and the Prophet chose (and married) her (upon his own choice and before distribution of war booty), as Abu Dawud narrated in the Sunan. As for the share of the Prophet's relatives, it is paid to Bani Hashim and Bani Al-Muttalib, because the children of Al-Muttalib supported Bani Hashim in Jahiliyyah after Islam.

They also went to the mountain pass of Abu Talib in support of the Messenger of Allah and to protect him (when the Quraysh boycotted Muslims for three years). Those who were Muslims (from Bani Al-Muttalib) did all this in obedience to Allah and His Messenger, while the disbelievers among them did so in support of their tribe and in obedience to Abu Talib, the Messenger's uncle.

Allah said next,

(the orphans), in reference to Muslim orphans,

(and the wayfarer), the traveler and those who intend to travel for a distance during which shortening the prayer is legislated, but do not have resources to spend from. We will explain this subject in Surah Bara'h (9:60), Allah willing, and our reliance and trust is in Him alone.

Allah said,

(If you have believed in Allah and in that which We sent down to Our servant)

Allah says, 'Adhere to what We legislated for you, such as the ruling about one-fifth of the war spoils, if you truly believe in Allah, the Last Day and what We have revealed to Our Messenger.' In the Two Sahihs, it is recorded that `Abdullah bin `Abbas said, - while narrating the lengthy Hadith about the delegation of Bani Abdul Qays - that the Messenger of Allah said to them,

«وَآمُرُكُمْ بِأَرْبَعٍ، وَأَنْهَاكُمْ عَنْ أَرْبَعٍ. آمُرُكُمْ بِالْإِيمَانِ بِاللهِ ثُمَّ قَالَ: هَلْ تَدْرُونَ مَا الْإِيمَانُ بِاللهِ؟ شَهَادَةُ أَنْ لَا إِلَهَ إِلَّا اللهُ، وَأَنَّ مُحَمَّدًا رَسُولُ اللهِ، وَإِقَامُ الصَّلَاةِ وَإِيتَاءُ الزَّكَاةِ، وَأَنْ تُؤَدُّوا الْخُمُسَ مِنَ الْمَغْنَمِ»

I command you with four and forbid four from you. I command you to believe in Allah. Do you know what it means to believe in Allah Testifying that there is no deity worthy of worship except Allah and that Muhammad is the Messenger of Allah, establishing the prayer, giving Zakah and honestly surrendering one-fifth of the war spoils.)

Therefore, the Messenger listed surrendering one-fifth of the war booty as part of faith. This is why Al-Bukhari wrote a chapter in his Sahih entitled, "Chapter: Paying the Khumus (one-fifth) is Part of Faith." He then narrated the above Hadith from Ibn `Abbas. Allah said next,

(on the Day of Criterion, the Day when the two forces met; and Allah is Able to do all things.) Allah is making His favors and compassion towards His creation known, when He distinguished between truth and falsehood in the battle of Badr. That day was called, `Al-Furqan', because Allah raised the word of faith above the word of falsehood, He made His religion apparent and supported His Prophet and his group.

`Ali bin Abi Talhah and Al-`Awfi reported that Ibn `Abbas said, "Badr is YawmAl-Furqan; during it, Allah separated between truth and falsehood." Al-Hakim collected this statement. Similar statements were reported from Mujahid, Miqsam, `Ubaydullah bin `Abdullah, Ad-Dahhak, Qatadah, Muqatil bin Hayyan and several others.

Surah: 8 Ayah: 42

﴿ إِذْ أَنتُم بِٱلْعُدْوَةِ ٱلدُّنْيَا وَهُم بِٱلْعُدْوَةِ ٱلْقُصْوَىٰ وَٱلرَّكْبُ أَسْفَلَ مِنكُمْ وَلَوْ تَوَاعَدتُّمْ لَٱخْتَلَفْتُمْ فِى ٱلْمِيعَٰدِ وَلَٰكِن لِّيَقْضِىَ ٱللَّهُ أَمْرًا كَانَ مَفْعُولًا لِّيَهْلِكَ مَنْ هَلَكَ عَنۢ بَيِّنَةٍ وَيَحْيَىٰ مَنْ حَىَّ عَنۢ بَيِّنَةٍ ۗ وَإِنَّ ٱللَّهَ لَسَمِيعٌ عَلِيمٌ ﴾

42. (And remember) when you (the Muslim army) were on the near side of the valley, and they on the farther side, and the caravan on the ground lower than you. Even if you had made a mutual appointment to meet, you would certainly have failed in the appointment, but (you met) that Allâh might accomplish a matter already ordained (in His Knowledge), so that those who were to be destroyed (for their rejecting the Faith) might be destroyed after a clear evidence, and those who were to live (i.e. believers) might live after a clear evidence. And surely, Allâh is All-Hearer, All-Knower.

Transliteration

42. Ith antum bialAAudwati alddunya wahum bialAAudwati alquswa waalrrakbu asfala minkum walaw tawaAAadtum laikhtalaftum fee almeeAAadi walakin liyaqdiya Allahu amran kana mafAAoolan liyahlika man halaka AAan bayyinatin wayahya man hayya AAan bayyinatin wa-inna Allaha lasameeAAun AAaleemun

Tafsir Ibn Kathir

Some Details of the Battle of Badr

Allah describes Yawm Al-Furqan, (i.e. the day of Badr),

((And remember) when you (the Muslim army) were on the near side of the valley,) camping in the closest entrance of the valley towards Al-Madinah,

(and they), the idolators, who were camped,

(on the farther side), from Al-Madinah, towards Makkah.

(and the caravan), that was under the command of Abu Sufyan, with the wealth that it contained,

(on the ground lower than you), closer to the sea,

(even if you had made a mutual appointment to meet,) you and the idolators,

Chapter 8: Al-Anfal (Spoils of War, Booty), Verses 041-075

(you would certainly have failed in the appointment)

Muhammad bin Ishaq said, "Yahya bin `Abbad bin `Abdullah bin Az-Zubayr narrated to me from his father about this Ayah "Had there been an appointed meeting set between you and them and you came to know of their superior numbers and your few forces, you would not have met them,

(but (you met) that Allah might accomplish a matter already ordained,) Allah had decreed that He would bring glory to Islam and its people, while disgracing Shirk and its people. You (the companions) had no knowledge this would happen, but it was out of Allah's compassion that He did that." In a Hadith, Ka`b bin Malik said, "The Messenger of Allah and the Muslims marched to intercept the Quraysh caravan, but Allah made them meet their (armed) enemy without appointment." Muhammad bin Ishaq said that Yazid bin Ruwman narrated to him that `Urwah bin Az-Zubayr said, "Upon approaching Badr, the Messenger of Allah sent `Ali bin Abi Talib, Sa`d bin Abi Waqqas, Az-Zubayr bin Al-`Awwam and several other Companions to spy the pagans. They captured two boys, a servant of Bani Sa`id bin Al-`As and a servant of Bani Al-Hajjaj, while they were bringing water for Quraysh. So they brought them to the Messenger of Allah , but found him praying. The Companions started interrogating the boys, asking them to whom they belonged. Both of them said that they were employees bringing water for Quraysh (army). The Componions were upset with that answer, since they thought that the boys belonged to Abu Sufyan (who was commanding the caravan). So they beat the two boys vehemently, who said finally that they belonged to Abu Sufyan. Thereupon companions left them alone. When the Prophet ended the prayer, he said,

»إِذَا صَدَّقَاكُمْ ضَرَبْتُمُوهُمَا، وَإِذَا كَذَّبَاكُمْ تَرَكْتُمُوهُمَا، صَدَقَا وَاللهِ إِنَّهُمَا لِقُرَيْشٍ، أَخْبِرَانِي عَنْ قُرَيْشٍ«

(When they tell you the truth you beat them, but when they lie you let them go They have said the truth, by Allah! They belong to the Quraysh. (addressing to the boys He said:) Tell me the news about Quraysh.)

The two boys said, `They are behind this hill that you see, on the far side of the valley.' The Messenger of Allah asked,

»كَمِ الْقَوْمُ؟«

(How many are they)

They said, `They are many.' He asked,

»مَا عُدَّتُهُمْ؟«

(How many) They said, `We do not know the precise number.' He asked,

«كَمْ يَنْحَرُونَ كُلَّ يَوْمٍ؟»

(How many camels do they slaughter every day)

They said, `Nine or ten a day.' The Messenger of Allah said,

«الْقَوْمُ مَا بَيْنَ التِّسْعِمِائَةِ إِلَى الْأَلْفِ»

(They are between nine-hundred and a thousand.) He asked again,

«فَمَنْ فِيهِمْ مِنْ أَشْرَافِ قُرَيْشٍ؟»

(Which chiefs of Quraysh are accompanying the army) They said, `Utbah bin Rabi`ah, Shaybah bin Rabi`ah, Abu Al-Bakhtari bin Hisham, Hakim bin Hizam, Nawfal bin Khuwaylid, Al-Harith bin `Amir bin Nawfal, Tu`aymah bin Adi bin Nawfal, An-Nadr bin Al-Harith, Zam`ah bin Al-Aswad, Abu Jahl bin Hisham, Umayyah bin Khalaf, Nabih and Munabbih sons of Al-Hajjaj, Suhayl bin `Amr and `Amr bin `Abd Wadd.' The Messenger of Allah said to the people,

«هَذِهِ مَكَّةُ قَدْ أَلْقَتْ إِلَيْكُمْ أَفْلَاذَ كَبِدِهَا»

(This is Makkah! She has brought you her most precious sons (its chiefs)!)"

Allah said,

(So that those who were to be destroyed might be destroyed after a clear evidence.) (8:42)

Muhammad bin Ishaq commented, "So that those who disbelieve do so after witnessing clear evidence, proof and lessons, and those who believe do so after witnessing the same." This is a sound explanation. Allah says, He made you meet your enemy in one area without appointment, so that He gives you victory over them.' This way, `He will raise the word of truth above falsehood, so that the matter is made clear, the proof unequivocal and the evidence plain. Then there will be no more plea or doubt for anyone. Then, those destined to destruction by persisting in disbelief do so with evidence, aware that they are misguided and that proof has been established against them,

(and those who were to live might live), those who wish to believe do so,

(after a clear evidence), and proof. Verily, faith is the life of the heart, as Allah said,

(Is he who was dead (without faith by ignorance and disbelief) and We gave him life (by knowledge and faith) and set for him a light (of belief) whereby he can walk among men ...) (6:122).

Allah said next,

(And surely, Allah is All-Hearer), of your invocation, humility and requests for His help,

(All-Knower) meaning; about you, and you deserve victory over your rebellious, disbelieving enemies.

Surah: 8 Ayah: 43 & Ayah: 44

﴿ إِذْ يُرِيكَهُمُ ٱللَّهُ فِى مَنَامِكَ قَلِيلًا ۖ وَلَوْ أَرَاكَهُمْ كَثِيرًا لَّفَشِلْتُمْ وَلَتَنَازَعْتُمْ فِى ٱلْأَمْرِ وَلَـٰكِنَّ ٱللَّهَ سَلَّمَ ۗ إِنَّهُۥ عَلِيمٌۢ بِذَاتِ ٱلصُّدُورِ ﴾

43. (And remember) when Allâh showed them to you as few in your (i.e. Muhammad's peace be upon him) dream; if He had shown them to you as many, you would surely have been discouraged, and you would surely have disputed in making a decision. But Allâh saved (you). Certainly, He is the All-Knower of what is in the breasts.

﴿ وَإِذْ يُرِيكُمُوهُمْ إِذِ ٱلْتَقَيْتُمْ فِىٓ أَعْيُنِكُمْ قَلِيلًا وَيُقَلِّلُكُمْ فِىٓ أَعْيُنِهِمْ لِيَقْضِىَ ٱللَّهُ أَمْرًا كَانَ مَفْعُولًا ۗ وَإِلَى ٱللَّهِ تُرْجَعُ ٱلْأُمُورُ ﴾

44. And (remember) when you met (the army of the disbelievers on the Day of the battle of Badr), He showed them to you as few in your eyes and He made you appear as few in their eyes, so that Allâh might accomplish a matter already ordained (in His Knowledge), and to Allâh return all matters (for decision).

Transliteration

43. Ith yureekahumu Allahu fee manamika qaleelan walaw arakahum katheeran lafashiltum walatanazaAAtum fee al-amri walakinna Allaha sallama innahu AAaleemun bithati alssudoori 44. Wa-ith yureekumoohum ithi iltaqaytum fee aAAyunikum qaleelan wayuqallilukum fee aAAyunihim liyaqdiya Allahu amran kana mafAAoolan wa-ila Allahi turjaAAu al-omooru

Tafsir Ibn Kathir

Allah made each Group look few in the Eye of the Other

Mujahid said, "In a dream, Allah showed the Prophet the enemy as few. The Prophet conveyed this news to his Companions and their resolve strengthened." Similar was said by Ibn Ishaq and several others. Allah said,

(If He had shown them to you as many, you would surely, have been discouraged,) you would have cowardly abstained from meeting them and fell in dispute among yourselves,

(But Allah saved), from all this, when He made you see them as few,

(Certainly, He is the All-Knower of that is in the breasts.) (8:43).

Allah knows what the heart and the inner-self conceal,

(Allah knows the fraud of the eyes, and all that the breasts conceal) (40:19).

Allah's statement,

(And (remember) when you met, He showed them to you as few in your eyes) demonstrates Allah's compassion towards the believers. Allah made them see few disbelievers in their eyes, so that they would be encouraged and feel eager to meet them. Abu Ishaq As-Subai`i said, that Abu `Ubaydah said that `Abdullah bin Mas`ud said, "They were made to seem few in our eyes during Badr, so that I said to a man who was next to me, `Do you think they are seventy' He said, `Rather, they are a hundred.' However, when we captured one of them, we asked him and he said, `We were a thousand.'" Ibn Abi Hatim and Ibn Jarir recorded it. Allah said next,

(and He made you appear as few in their eyes,) Allah said,

(And (remember) when you met. He showed them to you...), He encouraged each of the two groups against the other, according to `Ikrimah, as recorded by Ibn Abi Hatim. This statement has a Sahih chain of narrators. Muhammad bin Ishaq said that Yahya bin `Abbad bin `Abdullah bin Az-Zubayr narrated to him that his father said about Allah's statement,

(so that Allah might accomplish a matter already ordained,) "In order for the war to start between them, so that He would have revenge against those whom He decided to have revenge (pagans), and grant and complete His favor upon those He decided to grant favor to, His supporters." The meaning of this, is that Allah encouraged each group against the other and made them look few in each other's eyes, so that they were eager to meet them. This occurred before the battle started, but when it started and Allah supported the believers with a thousand angels in succession, the disbelieving group saw the believers double their number. Allah said,

(There has already been a sign for you (O Jews) in the two armies that met (in combat, the battle of Badr). One was fighting in the cause of Allah, and as for the other, (they) were disbelievers. They (disbelievers) saw them (believers) with their own eyes twice their number. And Allah supports with His aid whom He wills. Verily, in this is a lesson for those who understand.) (3:13)

This is how we combine these two Ayat, and certainly, each one of them is true, all the thanks are due to Allah and all the favors are from Him.

Surah: 8 Ayah: 45 & Ayah: 46

﴿ يَٰٓأَيُّهَا ٱلَّذِينَ ءَامَنُوٓاْ إِذَا لَقِيتُمْ فِئَةً فَٱثْبُتُواْ وَٱذْكُرُواْ ٱللَّهَ كَثِيرًا لَّعَلَّكُمْ تُفْلِحُونَ ﴾

45. O you who believe! When you meet (an enemy) force, take a firm stand against them and remember the Name of Allâh much (both with tongue and mind), so that you may be successful.

﴿ وَأَطِيعُواْ ٱللَّهَ وَرَسُولَهُۥ وَلَا تَنَٰزَعُواْ فَتَفْشَلُواْ وَتَذْهَبَ رِيحُكُمْ ۖ وَٱصْبِرُوٓاْ ۚ إِنَّ ٱللَّهَ مَعَ ٱلصَّٰبِرِينَ ﴾

46. And obey Allâh and His Messenger, and do not dispute (with one another) lest you lose courage and your strength depart, and be patient. Surely, Allâh is with those who are As-Sâbirin (the patient).

Transliteration

45. Ya ayyuha allatheena amanoo itha laqeetum fi-atan faothbutoo waothkuroo Allaha katheeran laAAallakum tuflihoona 46. WaateeAAoo Allaha warasoolahu wala tanazaAAoo fatafshaloo watathhaba reehukum waisbiroo inna Allaha maAAa alssabireena

Tafsir Ibn Kathir

Manners of War

Allah instructs His faithful servants in the manners of fighting and methods of courage when meeting the enemy in battle,

(O you who believe! When you meet (an enemy) force, take a firm stand against them) In the Two Sahihs, it is recorded that `Abdullah bin Abi Awfa said that during one battle, Allah's Messenger waited until the sun declined, then stood among the people and said,

«يَا أَيُّهَا النَّاسُ لَا تَتَمَنَّوْا لِقَاءَ الْعَدُوِّ، وَاسْأَلُوا اللهَ الْعَافِيَةَ فَإِذَا لَقِيتُمُوهُمْ فَاصْبِرُوا وَاعْلَمُوا أَنَّ الْجَنَّةَ تَحْتَ ظِلَالِ السُّيُوفِ»

(O people! Do not wish to face the enemy (in a battle) and ask Allah to save you (from calamities). But if you should face the enemy, then be patient and let it be known to you that Paradise is under the shadows of the swords.)

He then stood and said,

«اللَّهُمَّ مُنْزِلَ الْكِتَابِ، وَمُجْرِيَ السَّحَابِ، وَهَازِمَ الْأَحْزَابِ، اهْزِمْهُمْ وَانْصُرْنَا عَلَيْهِم»

(O Allah! Revealer of the (Holy) Book, Mover of the clouds, and Defeater of the Confederates, defeat them and grant us victory over them.)

The Command for Endurance when the Enemy Engaging

Allah commands endurance upon meeting the enemy in battle and ordains patience while fighting them. Muslims are not allowed to run or shy away, or show cowardice in battle. They are commanded to remember Allah while in that condition and never neglect His remembrance. They should rather invoke Him for support, trust in Him and seek victory over their enemies from Him. They are required to obey Allah and His Messenger in such circumstances adhering to what He commanded them, and abstaining from what He forbade them. They are required to avoid disputing with each other, for this might lead to their defeat and failure,

(lest your strength departs), so that your strength, endurance and courage do not depart from you,

(and be patient. Surely, Allah is with the patients.)

In their courage, and obedience to Allah and His Messenger, the Companions reached a level never seen before by any nation or generation before them, or any nation that will ever come. Through the blessing of the Messenger and their obedience to what he commanded, the Companions were able to open the hearts, as well as, the various eastern and western parts of the world in a rather short time. This occurred even though they were few, compared to the armies of the various nations at that time. For example, the Romans, Persians, Turks, Slavs, Berbers, Ethiopians, Sudanese tribes, the Copts and the rest of the Children of Adam. They defeated all of these nations, until Allah's Word became the highest and His religion became dominant above all religions. The Islamic state spread over the eastern and western parts of the world in less than thirty years. May Allah grant them His pleasure, as well as, be pleased with them all, and may He gather us among them, for He is the Most Generous, and Giving.

Surah: 8 Ayah: 47, Ayah: 48 & Ayah: 49

﴿ وَلَا تَكُونُوا كَالَّذِينَ خَرَجُوا مِن دِيَـٰرِهِم بَطَرًا وَرِئَآءَ ٱلنَّاسِ وَيَصُدُّونَ عَن سَبِيلِ ٱللَّهِ وَٱللَّهُ بِمَا يَعۡمَلُونَ مُحِيطٌ ﴿٤٧﴾

47. And be not like those who come out of their homes boastfully and to be seen of men, and hinder (men) from the Path of Allâh; and Allâh is Muhîtun (encircling and thoroughly comprehending) all that they do.

Chapter 8: Al-Anfal (Spoils of War, Booty), Verses 041-075

﴿ وَإِذْ زَيَّنَ لَهُمُ ٱلشَّيْطَـٰنُ أَعْمَـٰلَهُمْ وَقَالَ لَا غَالِبَ لَكُمُ ٱلْيَوْمَ مِنَ ٱلنَّاسِ وَإِنِّى جَارٌ لَّكُمْ ۖ فَلَمَّا تَرَآءَتِ ٱلْفِئَتَانِ نَكَصَ عَلَىٰ عَقِبَيْهِ وَقَالَ إِنِّى بَرِىٓءٌ مِّنكُمْ إِنِّىٓ أَرَىٰ مَا لَا تَرَوْنَ إِنِّىٓ أَخَافُ ٱللَّهَ ۚ وَٱللَّهُ شَدِيدُ ٱلْعِقَابِ ﴾

48. And (remember) when Shaitân (Satan) made their (evil) deeds seem fair to them and said, "No one of mankind can overcome you this Day (of the battle of Badr) and verily, I am your neighbor (for each and every help)." But when the two forces came in sight of each other, he ran away and said "Verily, I have nothing to do with you. Verily! I see what you see not. Verily! I fear Allâh for Allâh is Severe in punishment."

﴿ إِذْ يَقُولُ ٱلْمُنَـٰفِقُونَ وَٱلَّذِينَ فِى قُلُوبِهِم مَّرَضٌ غَرَّ هَـٰٓؤُلَآءِ دِينُهُمْ ۗ وَمَن يَتَوَكَّلْ عَلَى ٱللَّهِ فَإِنَّ ٱللَّهَ عَزِيزٌ حَكِيمٌ ﴾

49. When the hypocrites and those in whose hearts was a disease (of disbelief) said: "These people (Muslims) are deceived by their religion." But whoever puts his trust in Allâh, then surely, Allâh is All-Mighty, All-Wise.

Transliteration

47. Wala takoonoo kaallatheena kharajoo min diyarihim bataran wari-aa alnnasi wayasuddoona AAan sabeeli Allahi waAllahu bima yaAAmaloona muheetun 48. Wa-ith zayyana lahumu alshshaytanu aAAmalahum waqala la ghaliba lakumu alyawma mina alnnasi wa-innee jarun lakum falamma taraati alfi-atani nakasa AAala AAaqibayhi waqala innee baree-on minkum innee ara ma la tarawna innee akhafu Allaha waAllahu shadeedu alAAiqabi 49. Ith yaqoolu almunafiqoona waallatheena fee quloobihim maradun gharra haola-i deenuhum waman yatawakkal AAala Allahi fa-inna Allaha AAazeezun hakeemun

Tafsir Ibn Kathir

The Idolators leave Makkah, heading for Badr

After Allah commanded the believers to fight in His cause sincerely and to be mindful of Him, He commanded not to imitate the idolators, who went out of their homes

(boastfully) to suppress the truth,

(and to be seen of men), boasting arrogantly with people. When Abu Jahl was told that the caravan escaped safely, so they should return to Makkah, he commented, "No, by Allah! We will not go back until we proceed to the well of Badr, slaughter camels, drink alcohol and female singers sing to us. This way, the Arabs will always talk about our stance and what we did on that day." However, all of this came back to haunt Abu Jahl, because when they proceeded to the well of Badr, they brought themselves to death; and in the aftermath of Badr, they were thrown in the well of Badr, dead, disgraced, humiliated, despised and miserable in an everlasting, eternal torment. This is why Allah said here,

(and Allah is Muhit (encompassing and thoroughly comprehending) all that they do.) He knows how and what they came for, and this is why He made them taste the worst punishment. Ibn `Abbas, Mujahid, Qatadah, Ad-Dahhak and As-Suddi commented on Allah's statement,

(And be not like those who come out of their homes boastfully and to be seen of men,) "They were the idolators who fought against the Messenger of Allah at Badr." Muhammad bin Ka`b said, "When the Quraysh left Makkah towards Badr, they brought female singers and drums along. Allah revealed this verse,

(And be not like those who come out of their homes boastfully and to be seen of men, and hinder (men) from the path of Allah; and Allah is Muhit (encompassing and thoroughly comprehending) all that they do.)

Shaytan makes Evil seem fair and deceives the Idolators

Allah said next,

(And (remember) when Shaytan made their (evil) deeds seem fair to them and said, "No one of mankind can overcome you today and verily, I am your neighbor.")

Shaytan, may Allah curse him, made the idolators' purpose for marching seem fair to them. He made them think that no other people could defeat them that day. He also ruled out the possibility that their enemies, the tribe of Bani Bakr, would attack Makkah, saying, "I am your neighbor." Shaytan appeared to them in the shape of Suraqah bin Malik bin Ju`shum, the chief of Bani Mudlij, so that, as Allah described them,

(He (Shaytan) makes promises to them, and arouses in them false desires; and Shaytan's promises are nothing but deceptions)(4:120).

Ibn Jurayj said that Ibn `Abbas commented on this Ayah, (8:48) "On the day of Badr, Shaytan, as well as, his flag holder and soldiers, accompanied the idolators. He whispered to the hearts of the idolators, `None can defeat you today! I am your neighbor.' When they met the Muslims and Shaytan witnessed the angels coming to their aid,

(he ran away), he went away in flight while proclaiming,

(Verily, I see what you see not.)"

`Ali bin Abi Talhah said, that Ibn `Abbas said about this Ayah,

("No one of mankind can overcome you today and verily, I am your neighbor')

"Shaytan, as well as, his devil army and flag holders, came on the day of Badr in the shape of a Suraqah bin Malik bin Ju`shum, man from Bani Mudlij, Shaytan said to the idolators, `None will defeat you this day, and I will help you.' When the two armies stood face to face, the Messenger of Allah took a handful of sand and threw it at the faces of the idolators, causing them to retreat. Jibril, peace be upon him, came towards Shaytan, but when Shaytan, while holding the hand of a Mushrik man, saw him, he withdrew his hand and ran away with his soldiers. That man asked him, `O Suraqah! You claimed that you are our neighbor' He said,

(Verily, I see what you see not. Verily, I fear Allah for Allah is severe in punishment)

Shaytan said this when he saw the angels."

The Position of the Hypocrites in Badr

Allah said next,

(When the hypocrites and those in whose hearts was a disease (of disbelief) said: "These people (Muslims) are deceived by their religion.")

`Ali bin Abi Talhah said that Ibn `Abbas commented, "When the two armies drew closer to each other, Allah made the Muslims look few in the eyes of the idolators and the idolators look few in the eyes of the Muslims. The idolators said,

(These people (Muslims) are deceived by their religion.) because they thought that Muslims were so few. They believed, without doubt, that they would defeat the Muslims. Allah said,

(But whoever puts his trust in Allah, then surely, Allah is All-Mighty, All-Wise.) Qatadah commented, "They saw a group of believers who came in defense of Allah's religion. We were informed that when he saw Muhammad and his Companions, Abu Jahl said, `By Allah! After this day, they will never worship Allah!' He said this in viciousness and transgression." `Amir Ash-Sha`bi said, "Some people from Makkah were considering embracing Islam, but when they went with the idolators to Badr and saw how few the Muslims were, they said,

(These people (Muslims) are deceived by their religion.)

Allah said next,

(But whoever puts his trust in Allah), and relies on His grace,

(then surely, Allah is All-Mighty), and verily, those who take His side (in the dispute) are never overwhelmed, for His side is mighty, powerful and His authority is All-Great,

(All-Wise) in all His actions, for He places everything in its rightful place, giving victory to those who deserve it and defeat to those who deserve it.

Surah: 8 Ayah: 50 & Ayah: 51

﴿ وَلَوْ تَرَىٰٓ إِذْ يَتَوَفَّى ٱلَّذِينَ كَفَرُوا۟ ٱلْمَلَـٰٓئِكَةُ يَضْرِبُونَ وُجُوهَهُمْ وَأَدْبَـٰرَهُمْ وَذُوقُوا۟ عَذَابَ ٱلْحَرِيقِ ۝ ﴾

50. And if you could see when the angels take away the souls of those who disbelieve (at death); they smite their faces and their backs, (saying): "Taste the punishment of the blazing Fire."

﴿ ذَٰلِكَ بِمَا قَدَّمَتْ أَيْدِيكُمْ وَأَنَّ ٱللَّهَ لَيْسَ بِظَلَّـٰمٍ لِّلْعَبِيدِ ۝ ﴾

51. "This is because of that which your hands had forwarded. And verily, Allâh is not unjust to His slaves."

Transliteration

50. Walaw tara ith yatawaffa allatheena kafaroo almala-ikatu yadriboona wujoohahum waadbarahum wathooqoo AAathaba alhareeqi 51. Thalika bima qaddamat aydeekum waanna Allaha laysa bithallamin lilAAabeedi

Tafsir Ibn Kathir

The Angels smite the Disbelievers upon capturing Their Souls

Allah says, if you witnessed the angels capturing the souls of the disbelievers, you would witness a tremendous, terrible, momentous and awful matter,

(they smite their faces and their backs), saying to them,

("Taste the punishment of the blazing Fire.")

Ibn Jurayj said that Mujahid said that,

(and their backs), refers to their back sides, as happened on the day of Badr. Ibn Jurayj also reported from Ibn `Abbas, "When the idolators faced the Muslims (in Badr), the Muslims smote their faces with swords. When they gave flight, the angels smote their rear ends."

Although these Ayat are describing Badr, they are general in the case of every disbeliever. This is why Allah did not make His statement here restrictive to the disbelievers at Badr,

(And if you could see when the angels take away the souls of those who disbelieve (at death); they smite their faces and their backs,)

In Surat Al-Qital (or Muhammad chapter 47) there is a similar Ayah, as well as in Surat Al-An`am,

(And if you could but see when the wrongdoers are in the agonies of death, while the angels are stretching forth their hands (saying): "Deliver your souls!") (6:93)

The angels stretch their hands and smite the disbelievers by Allah's command, since their souls refuse to leave their bodies, so they are taken out by force. This occurs when the angels give them the news of torment and Allah's anger. There is a Hadith narrated from Al-Bara' that when the angel of death attends the disbeliever at the time of death, he comes to him in a terrifying and disgusting shape, saying, "Get out, O wicked soul, to fierce hot wind, boiling water and a shadow of black smoke." The disbeliever's soul then scatters throughout his body, but the angels retrieve it, just as a needle is retrieved from wet wool. In this case, veins and nerve cells will be still attached to the soul. Allah states here that angels bring news of the torment of the Fire to the disbelievers. Allah said next,

(This is because of that which your hands forwarded.) meaning, this punishment is the recompense of the evil deeds that you have committed in the life of the world. This is your reckoning from Allah for your deeds,

(And verily, Allah is not unjust to His servants.)

Certainly, Allah does not wrong any of His creatures, for He is the Just, who never puts anything in an inappropriate place. Honored, Glorified, Exalted and Praised be He, the All-Rich, Worthy of all praise. Muslim recorded that Abu Dharr said that the Messenger of Allah said;

«إِنَّ اللهَ تَعَالَى يَقُولُ: يَا عِبَادِي إِنِّي حَرَّمْتُ الظُّلْمَ عَلَى نَفْسِي وَجَعَلْتُهُ بَيْنَكُمْ مُحَرَّمًا فَلَا تَظَالَمُوا، يَا عِبَادِي إِنَّمَا هِيَ أَعْمَالُكُمْ أُحْصِيهَا لَكُمْ فَمَنْ وَجَدَ خَيْرًا فَلْيَحْمَدِ اللهَ وَمَنْ وَجَدَ غَيْرَ ذَلِكَ فَلَا يَلُومَنَّ إِلَّا نَفْسَه»

(Allah, the Exalted, said, `O My servants! I have prohibited injustice for Myself, and made it prohibited to you between each other. Therefore, do not commit injustice against each other. O My servants! It is your deeds that I am keeping count of, so whoever found something good, let him praise Allah for it. Whoever found other than that, has only himself to blame.)

Surah: 8 Ayah: 52

﴿كَدَأْبِ ءَالِ فِرْعَوْنَ ۙ وَٱلَّذِينَ مِن قَبْلِهِمْ ۚ كَفَرُوا۟ بِـَٔايَـٰتِ ٱللَّهِ فَأَخَذَهُمُ ٱللَّهُ بِذُنُوبِهِمْ ۗ إِنَّ ٱللَّهَ قَوِىٌّ شَدِيدُ ٱلْعِقَابِ۝﴾

52. Similar to the behavior of the people of Fir'aun (Pharaoh), and of those before them - they rejected the Ayât (proofs, verses, etc.) of Allâh, so Allâh punished them for their sins. Verily, Allâh is All-Strong, Severe in punishment.

Transliteration

52. Kada/bi ali firAAawna waallatheena min qablihim kafaroo bi-ayati Allahi faakhathahumu Allahu bithunoobihim inna Allaha qawiyyun shadeedu alAAiqabi

Tafsir Ibn Kathir

Allah says, `The behavior of these rebellious disbelievers against what I sent you with, O Muhammad, is similar to the behavior of earlier disbelieving nations. So We behaved with them according to Our Da'b, that is, Our behavior (or custom) and way, as We did with them with what We often do and decide concerning their likes, the denying people of Fir`awn and the earlier nations who rejected the Messengers and disbelieved in Our Ayat,'

(so Allah punished them for their sins.)

Because of their sins, Allah destroyed them

(Verily, Allah is All-Strong, severe in punishment.)

none can resist Him or escape His grasp.

Surah: 8 Ayah: 53 & Ayah: 54

﴿ ذَٰلِكَ بِأَنَّ ٱللَّهَ لَمْ يَكُ مُغَيِّرًا نِّعْمَةً أَنْعَمَهَا عَلَىٰ قَوْمٍ حَتَّىٰ يُغَيِّرُوا۟ مَا بِأَنفُسِهِمْ وَأَنَّ ٱللَّهَ سَمِيعٌ عَلِيمٌ ﴾

53. That is so because Allâh will never change a grace which He has bestowed on a people until they change what is in their own selves. And verily, Allâh is All-Hearer, All-Knower.

﴿ كَدَأْبِ ءَالِ فِرْعَوْنَ وَٱلَّذِينَ مِن قَبْلِهِمْ كَذَّبُوا۟ بِـَٔايَـٰتِ رَبِّهِمْ فَأَهْلَكْنَـٰهُم بِذُنُوبِهِمْ وَأَغْرَقْنَآ ءَالَ فِرْعَوْنَ وَكُلٌّ كَانُوا۟ ظَـٰلِمِينَ ﴾

54. Similar to the behavior of the people of Fir'aun (Pharaoh), and those before them. They belied the Ayât (proofs, evidences, verses, lessons, signs, revelations, etc.), of their Lord, so We destroyed them for their sins, and We drowned the people of Fir'aun (Pharaoh) for they were all Zâlimûn (polytheists and wrong-doers).

Transliteration

53. Thalika bi-anna Allaha lam yaku mughayyiran niAAmatan anAAamaha AAala qawmin hatta yughayyiroo ma bi-anfusihim waanna Allaha sameeAAun AAaleemun
54. Kada/bi ali firAAawna waallatheena min qablihim kaththaboo bi-ayati rabbihim faahlaknahum bithunoobihim waaghraqna ala firAAawna wakullun kanoo thalimeena

Tafsir Ibn Kathir

Allah affirms His perfect justice and fairness in His decisions, for He decided that He will not change a bounty that He has granted someone, except on account of an evil that they committed. Allah said in another Ayah,

(Verily, Allah will not change the (good) condition of a people as long as they do not change their state (of goodness) themselves. But when Allah wills a people's punishment, there can be no turning it back, and they will find besides Him no protector.) (13:11)

Allah said next,

(Similar to the behavior of the people of Fir`awn,) meaning, He punished Fir`awn and his kind, those who denied His Ayat. Allah destroyed them because of their sins, and took away the favors that He granted them, such as gardens, springs, plants, treasures and pleasant dwellings, as well as all of the delights that they enjoyed. Allah did not wrong them, but it is they who wronged themselves.

Surah: 8 Ayah: 55, Ayah: 56 & Ayah: 57

﴿ إِنَّ شَرَّ ٱلدَّوَابِّ عِندَ ٱللَّهِ ٱلَّذِينَ كَفَرُواْ فَهُمْ لَا يُؤْمِنُونَ ۝ ﴾

55. Verily, The worst of moving (living) creatures before Allâh are those who disbelieve, - so they shall not believe.

﴿ ٱلَّذِينَ عَٰهَدتَّ مِنْهُمْ ثُمَّ يَنقُضُونَ عَهْدَهُمْ فِى كُلِّ مَرَّةٍ وَهُمْ لَا يَتَّقُونَ ۝ ﴾

56. They are those with whom you made a covenant, but they break their covenant every time and they do not fear Allâh.

﴿ فَإِمَّا تَثْقَفَنَّهُمْ فِى ٱلْحَرْبِ فَشَرِّدْ بِهِم مَّنْ خَلْفَهُمْ لَعَلَّهُمْ يَذَّكَّرُونَ ۝ ﴾

57. So if you gain the mastery over them in war, punish them severely in order to disperse those who are behind them, so that they may learn a lesson.

Transliteration

55. Inna sharra alddawabbi AAinda Allahi allatheena kafaroo fahum la yu/minoona 56. Allatheena AAahadta minhum thumma yanqudoona AAahdahum fee kulli marratin wahum la yattaqoona 57. Fa-imma tathqafannahum fee alharbi fasharrid bihim man khalfahum laAAallahum yaththakkaroona

Tafsir Ibn Kathir

Striking Hard against Those Who disbelieve and break the Covenants

Allah states here that the worst moving creatures on the face of the earth are those who disbelieve, who do not embrace the faith, and break promises whenever they make a covenant, even when they vow to keep them,

(and they do not have Taqwa) meaning they do not fear Allah regarding any of the sins they commit.

(So if you gain the mastery over them in war), if you defeat them and have victory over them in war,

(then disperse those who are behind them,) by severely punishing (the captured people) according to Ibn `Abbas, Al-Hasan Al-Basri, Ad-Dahhak, As-Suddi, `Ata' Al-Khurasani and Ibn `Uyaynah. This Ayah commands punishing them harshly and inflicting casualties on them. This way, other enemies, Arabs and non-Arabs, will be afraid and take a lesson from their end,

(so that they may learn a lesson.)

As-Suddi commented, "They might be careful not to break treaties, so that they do not meet the same end."

Surah: 8 Ayah: 58

﴿ وَإِمَّا تَخَافَنَّ مِن قَوْمٍ خِيَانَةً فَٱنبِذْ إِلَيْهِمْ عَلَىٰ سَوَآءٍ إِنَّ ٱللَّهَ لَا يُحِبُّ ٱلْخَآئِنِينَ ﴾

58. If you (O Muhammad (peace be upon him)) fear treachery from any people throw back (their covenant) to them (so as to be) on equal terms (that there will be no more covenant between you and them). Certainly Allâh likes not the treacherous.

Transliteration

58. Wa-imma takhafanna min qawmin khiyanatan fainbith ilayhim AAala sawa-in inna Allaha la yuhibbu alkha-ineena

Tafsir Ibn Kathir

Allah says to His Prophet ,

(If you fear from any people), with whom you have a treaty of peace,

(treachery), and betrayal of peace treaties and agreements that you have conducted with them,

(then throw back (their covenant) to them), meaning their treaty of peace.

Chapter 8: Al-Anfal (Spoils of War, Booty), Verses 041-075

(on equal terms), informing them that you are severing the treaty. This way, you will be on equal terms, in that, you and they will be aware that a state of war exists between you and that the bilateral peace treaty is null and void,

(Certainly Allah likes not the treacherous.) This even includes treachery against the disbelievers. Imam Ahmad recorded that Salim bin `Amir said, "Mu`awiyah was leading an army in Roman lands, at a time the bilateral peace treaty was valid. He wanted to go closer to their forces so that when the treaty of peace ended, he could invade them. An old man riding on his animal said, `Allahu Akbar (Allah is the Great), Allahu Akbar! Be honest and stay away from betrayal.' The Messenger of Allah said,

«وَمَنْ كَانَ بَيْنَهُ وَبَيْنَ قَوْمٍ عَهْدٌ فَلَا يَحُلَّنَّ عُقْدَةً وَلَا يَشُدَّهَا حَتَّى يَنْقَضِيَ أَمَدُهَا، أَوْ يَنْبُذَ إِلَيْهِمْ عَلَى سَوَاءٍ»

(Whoever has a treaty of peace with a people, then he should not untie any part of it or tie it harder until the treaty reaches its appointed term. Or, he should declare the treaty null and void so that they are both on equal terms.) When Mu`awiyah was informed of the Prophet's statement, he retreated. They found that man to be `Amr bin `Anbasah, may Allah be pleased with him." This Hadith was also collected by Abu Dawud At-Tayalisi, Abu Dawud, At-Tirmidhi, An-Nasa'i and Ibn Hibban in his Sahih. At-Tirmidhi said, "Hasan Sahih."

Surah: 8 Ayah: 59 & Ayah: 60

﴿ وَلَا تَحْسَبَنَّ ٱلَّذِينَ كَفَرُوا۟ سَبَقُوٓا۟ إِنَّهُمْ لَا يُعْجِزُونَ ۝ ﴾

59. And let not those who disbelieve think that they can outstrip (escape from the punishment). Verily, they will never be able to save themselves (from Allâh's Punishment).

﴿ وَأَعِدُّوا۟ لَهُم مَّا ٱسْتَطَعْتُم مِّن قُوَّةٍ وَمِن رِّبَاطِ ٱلْخَيْلِ تُرْهِبُونَ بِهِۦ عَدُوَّ ٱللَّهِ وَعَدُوَّكُمْ وَءَاخَرِينَ مِن دُونِهِمْ لَا تَعْلَمُونَهُمُ ٱللَّهُ يَعْلَمُهُمْ ۚ وَمَا تُنفِقُوا۟ مِن شَىْءٍ فِى سَبِيلِ ٱللَّهِ يُوَفَّ إِلَيْكُمْ وَأَنتُمْ لَا تُظْلَمُونَ ۝ ﴾

60. And make ready against them all you can of power, including steeds of war (tanks, planes, missiles, artillery) to threaten the enemy of Allâh and your enemy, and others besides whom, you may not know but whom Allâh does know. And whatever you shall spend in the Cause of Allâh shall be repaid unto you, and you shall not be treated unjustly.

Transliteration

59. Wala yahsabanna allatheena kafaroo sabaqoo innahum la yuAAjizoona 60. WaaAAiddoo lahum ma istataAAtum min quwwatin wamin ribati alkhayli turhiboona

bihi AAaduwwa Allahi waAAaduwwakum waakhareena min doonihim la taAAlamoonahumu Allahu yaAAlamuhum wama tunfiqoo min shay-in fee sabeeli Allahi yuwaffa ilaykum waantum la tuthlamoona

Tafsir Ibn Kathir

Making Preparations for War to strike Fear in the Hearts of the Enemies of Allah

Allah says to His Prophet , in this Ayah,

(those who disbelieve think that they can outstrip), Do not think that such disbelievers have escaped Us or that We are unable to grasp them. Rather, they are under the power of Our ability and in the grasp of Our will; they will never escape Us.' Allah also said,

(Or think those who do evil deeds that they can outstrip Us (escape Our punishment) Evil is that which they judge!) (29:4),

(Consider not that the disbelievers can escape in the land. Their abode shall be the Fire, and worst indeed is that destination.) (24:57), and,

(Let not the free disposal (and affluence) of the disbelievers throughout the land deceive you. A brief enjoyment; then their ultimate abode is Hell; and worst indeed is that place for rest.) (3:196-197)

Allah commands Muslims to prepare for war against disbelievers, as much as possible, according to affordability and availability. Allah said,

(And make ready against them all you can) whatever you can muster,

(of power, including steeds of war). Imam Ahmad recorded that `Uqbah bin `Amir said that he heard the Messenger of Allah saying, while standing on the Minbar;

﴿وَأَعِدُّواْ لَهُم مَّا اسْتَطَعْتُم مِّن قُوَّةٍ﴾

(And make ready against them all you can of power,)

«أَلَا إِنَّ الْقُوَّةَ الرَّمْيُ أَلَا إِنَّ الْقُوَّةَ الرَّمْيُ»

(Verily, Power is shooting! Power is shooting.)

Muslim collected this Hadith.

Imam Malik recorded that Abu Hurayrah said, "The Messenger of Allah said,

«الْخَيْلُ لِثَلَاثَةٍ، لِرَجُلٍ أَجْرٌ، وَلِرَجُلٍ سِتْرٌ، وَعَلَى رَجُلٍ وِزْرٌ، فَأَمَّا الَّذِي لَهُ أَجْرٌ، فَرَجُلٌ رَبَطَهَا فِي سَبِيلِ اللهِ فَأَطَالَ لَهَا فِي مَرْجٍ أَوْ رَوْضَةٍ، فَمَا أَصَابَتْ فِي طِيَلِهَا ذَلِكَ مِنَ الْمَرْجِ أَوِ الرَّوْضَةِ، كَانَتْ لَهُ حَسَنَاتٍ وَلَوْ أَنَّهَا قَطَعَتْ طِيَلَهَا، فَاسْتَنَّتْ شَرَفًا أَوْ شَرَفَيْنِ كَانَتْ آثَارُهَا وَأَرْوَاثُهَا حَسَنَاتٍ لَهُ، وَلَوْ أَنَّهَا مَرَّتْ بِنَهَرٍ فَشَرِبَتْ مِنْهُ وَلَمْ يُرِدْ أَنْ يَسْقِيَ بِهِ، كَانَ ذَلِكَ حَسَنَاتٍ لَهُ، فَهِيَ لِذَلِكَ الرَّجُلِ أَجْرٌ، وَرَجُلٌ رَبَطَهَا تَغَنِّيًا وَتَعَفُّفًا، وَلَمْ يَنْسَ حَقَّ اللهِ فِي رِقَابِهَا وَلَا ظُهُورِهَا فَهِيَ لَهُ سِتْرٌ، وَرَجُلٌ رَبَطَهَا فَخْرًا وَرِيَاءً وَنِوَاءً، فَهِيَ عَلَى ذَلِكَ وِزْرٌ»

(Horses are kept for one of three purposes; for some people they are a source of reward, for some others they are a means of shelter, and for some others they are a source of sin. The one for whom they are a source of reward, is he who keeps a horse for Allah's cause (Jihad) tying it with a long tether on a meadow or in a garden. The result is that whatever it eats from the area of the meadow or the garden where it is tied, will be counted as good deeds for his benefit; and if it should break its rope and jump over one or two hillocks then all its dung and its footmarks will be written as good deeds for him. If it passes by a river and drinks water from it, even though he had no intention of watering it, then he will get the reward for its drinking. Therefore, this type of horse is a source of good deeds for him. As for the man who tied his horse maintaining self - sufficiency and abstinence from begging, all the while not forgetting Allah's right concerning the neck and back of his horse, then it is a means of shelter for him. And a man who tied a horse for the sake of pride, pretense and showing enmity for Muslims, then this type of horse is a source of sins.)

When Allah's Messenger was asked about donkeys, he replied,

«مَا أَنْزَلَ اللهُ عَلَيَّ فِيهَا شَيْئًا إِلَّا هَذِهِ الْآيَةَ الْجَامِعَةَ الْفَاذَّةَ»

(Nothing has been revealed to me from Allah about them except these unique, comprehensive Ayat:

(Then anyone who does an atom's weight of good, shall see it. And anyone who does an atom's weight of evil, shall see it.)) (99:7-8)"

Al-Bukhari and Muslim collected this Hadith, this is the wording of Al-Bukhari. Imam Ahmad recorded that `Abdullah bin Mas`ud said that the Prophet said,

«الْخَيْلُ ثَلَاثَةٌ: فَفَرَسٌ لِلرَّحْمَنِ، وَفَرَسٌ لِلشَّيْطَانِ، وَفَرَسٌ لِلْإِنْسَانِ، فَأَمَّا فَرَسُ الرَّحْمَنِ فَالَّذِي يُرْبَطُ فِي سَبِيلِ اللهِ، فَعَلَفُهُ وَرَوْثُهُ وَبَوْلُهُ وَذَكَرَ مَا شَاءَ اللهُ وَأَمَّا فَرَسُ الشَّيْطَانِ، فَالَّذِي يُقَامَرُ أَوْ يُرَاهَنُ عَلَيْهَا، وَأَمَّا فَرَسُ الْإِنْسَانِ، فَالْفَرَسُ يَرْبِطُهَا الْإِنْسَانُ يَلْتَمِسُ بَطْنَهَا، فَهِيَ لَهُ سِتْرٌ مِنَ الْفَقْرِ»

(There are three reasons why horses are kept: A horse that is kept for Ar-Rahman (the Most Beneficent), a horse kept for Shaytan and a horse kept for the man. As for the horse kept for Ar-Rahman, it is the horse that is being kept for the cause of Allah (for Jihad), and as such, its food, dung and urine, etc., (he made mention of many things). As for the horse that is for Shaytan, it is one that is being used for gambling. As for the horse that is for man, it is the horse that one tethers, seeking its benefit. For him, this horse will be a shield against poverty.) oAl-Bukhari recorded that `Urwah bin Abi Al-Ja`d Al-Bariqi said that the Messenger of Allah said,

«الْخَيْلُ مَعْقُودٌ فِي نَوَاصِيهَا الْخَيْرُ إِلَى يَوْمِ الْقِيَامَةِ، الْأَجْرُ وَالْمَغْنَمُ»

(Good will remain in the forelocks of horses until the Day of Resurrection, (that is) reward, and the spoils of war.)

Allah said next,

(to threaten), or to strike fear,

(the enemy of Allah and your enemy), the disbelievers,

(and others besides them), such as Bani Qurayzah, according to Mujahid, or persians, according to As-Suddi.

Muqatil bin Hayyan and `Abdur-Rahman bin Zayd bin Aslam said that this Ayah refers to hypocrites, as supported by Allah's statement,

(And among the bedouins around you, some are hypocrites, and so are some among the people of Al-Madinah who persist in hypocrisy; you know them not, We know them.)(9:101).

Allah said next,

(And whatever you shall spend in the cause of Allah shall be repaid to you, and you shall not be treated unjustly.)

Allah says, whatever you spend on Jihad will be repaid to you in full.

We also mentioned Allah's statement,

(The parable of those who spend their wealth in the way of Allah, is that of a grain (of corn); it grows seven ears, and each ear has a hundred grains. Allah gives manifold increase to whom He wills. And Allah is All-Sufficient for His creatures' needs, All-Knower.) (2:261)

Surah: 8 Ayah: 61, Ayah: 62 & Ayah: 63

﴿ ۞ وَإِن جَنَحُوا۟ لِلسَّلْمِ فَٱجْنَحْ لَهَا وَتَوَكَّلْ عَلَى ٱللَّهِ إِنَّهُۥ هُوَ ٱلسَّمِيعُ ٱلْعَلِيمُ ۝ ﴾

61. But if they incline to peace, you also incline to it, and (put your) trust in Allâh. Verily, He is the All-Hearer, the All-Knower.

﴿ وَإِن يُرِيدُوٓا۟ أَن يَخْدَعُوكَ فَإِنَّ حَسْبَكَ ٱللَّهُ هُوَ ٱلَّذِىٓ أَيَّدَكَ بِنَصْرِهِۦ وَبِٱلْمُؤْمِنِينَ ۝ ﴾

62. And if they intend to deceive you, then verily, Allâh is All-Sufficient for you. He it is Who has supported you with His Help and with the believers.

﴿ وَأَلَّفَ بَيْنَ قُلُوبِهِمْ لَوْ أَنفَقْتَ مَا فِى ٱلْأَرْضِ جَمِيعًا مَّآ أَلَّفْتَ بَيْنَ قُلُوبِهِمْ وَلَـٰكِنَّ ٱللَّهَ أَلَّفَ بَيْنَهُمْ إِنَّهُۥ عَزِيزٌ حَكِيمٌ ۝ ﴾

63. And He has united their (i.e. believers') hearts. If you had spent all that is in the earth, you could not have united their hearts, but Allâh has united them. Certainly He is All-Mighty, All-Wise.

Transliteration

61. Wa-in janahoo lilssalmi faijnah laha watawakkal AAala Allahi innahu huwa alssameeAAu alAAaleemu   62. Wa-in yureedoo an yakhdaAAooka fa-inna hasbaka Allahu huwa allathee ayyadaka binasrihi wabialmu/mineena   63. Waallafa bayna quloobihim law anfaqta ma fee al-ardi jameeAAan ma allafta bayna quloobihim walakinna Allaha allafa baynahum innahu AAazeezun hakeemun

Tafsir Ibn Kathir

The Command to Facilitate Peace when the Enemy seeks a Peaceful Resolution

Allah says, if you fear betrayal from a clan of people, then sever the peace treaty with them, so that you both are on equal terms. If they continue being hostile and opposing you, then fight them,

(But if they incline), and seek,

(to peace), if they resort to reconciliation, and seek a treaty of non-hostility,

(you also incline to it), and accept offers of peace from them. This is why when the pagans inclined to peace in the year of Hudaybiyah and sought cessation of hostilities for nine years, between them and the Messenger of Allah he accepted this from them, as well as, accepting other terms of peace they brought forth. `Abdullah bin Al-Imam Ahmad recorded that `Ali bin Abi Talib said that the Messenger of Allah said,

«إِنَّهُ سَيَكُونُ بَعْدِي اخْتِلَافٌ أَوْ أَمْرٌ فَإِنِ اسْتَطَعْتَ أَنْ يَكُونَ السِّلْمَ فَافْعَل»

(There will be disputes after me, so if you have a way to end them in peace, then do so.)

Allah said next,

(and trust in Allah.) Allah says, conduct a peace treaty with those who incline to peace, and trust in Allah. Verily, Allah will suffice for you and aid you even if they resort to peace as a trick, so that they gather and reorganize their forces,

(then verily, Allah is All-Sufficient for you).

Reminding the Believers of Allah's Favor of uniting Them

Allah mentioned His favor on the Prophet , in that He aided him with believers, the Muhajirin and the Ansar,

(He it is Who has supported you with His help and with the believers. And He has united their hearts.)

The Ayah says, `it is Allah who gathered the believers' hearts, believing, obeying, aiding and supporting you -- O Muhammad,'

(If you had spent all that is in the earth, you could not have united their hearts.) because of the enmity and hatred that existed between them. Before Islam, there were many wars between the Ansar tribes of Aws and Khazraj, and there were many causes to stir unrest between them. However, Allah ended all that evil with the light of faith,

(And remember Allah's favor on you, for you were enemies one to another, but He united your hearts, so that, by His grace, you became brethren, and you were on the brink of a pit of Fire, and He saved you from it. Thus Allah makes His Ayat clear to you, that you may be guided.) (3:103)

In the Two Sahihs, it is recorded that when the Messenger of Allah gave a speech to the Ansar about the division of war booty collected in the battle of Hunayn, he said to them,

«يَا مَعْشَرَ الْأَنْصَارِ أَلَمْ أَجِدْكُمْ ضُلَّالًا فَهَدَاكُمُ اللهُ بِي، وَعَالَةً فَأَغْنَاكُمُ اللهُ بِي، وَكُنْتُمْ مُتَفَرِّقِينَ فَأَلَّفَكُمُ اللهُ بِي»

(O Ansar! Did I not find you misguided and Allah guided you by me, poor and Allah enriched you by me, and divided and Allah united you by me) Every question the Prophet asked them, they said, "Truly, the favor is from Allah and His Messenger." Allah said,

(But Allah has united them. Certainly He is All-Mighty, All-Wise.)

He is the Most Formidable, and the hopes of those who have trust in Him, never end unanswered; Allah is All-Wise in all of His decisions and actions.

Surah: 8 Ayah: 64, Ayah: 65 & Ayah: 66

﴿ يَٰٓأَيُّهَا ٱلنَّبِىُّ حَسْبُكَ ٱللَّهُ وَمَنِ ٱتَّبَعَكَ مِنَ ٱلْمُؤْمِنِينَ ۝ ﴾

64. O Prophet (Muhammad (peace be upon him))! Allâh is Sufficient for you and for the believers who follow you.

﴿ يَٰٓأَيُّهَا ٱلنَّبِىُّ حَرِّضِ ٱلْمُؤْمِنِينَ عَلَى ٱلْقِتَالِ إِن يَكُن مِّنكُمْ عِشْرُونَ صَٰبِرُونَ يَغْلِبُوا۟ مِا۟ئَتَيْنِ وَإِن يَكُن مِّنكُم مِّا۟ئَةٌ يَغْلِبُوٓا۟ أَلْفًا مِّنَ ٱلَّذِينَ كَفَرُوا۟ بِأَنَّهُمْ قَوْمٌ لَّا يَفْقَهُونَ ۝ ﴾

65. O Prophet (Muhammad (peace be upon him))! Urge the believers to fight. If there are twenty steadfast persons amongst you, they will overcome two hundreds, and if there be a hundred steadfast persons they will overcome a thousand of those who disbelieve, because they (the disbelievers) are people who do not understand.

﴿ ٱلْـَٰٔنَ خَفَّفَ ٱللَّهُ عَنكُمْ وَعَلِمَ أَنَّ فِيكُمْ ضَعْفًا ۚ فَإِن يَكُن مِّنكُم مِّا۟ئَةٌ صَابِرَةٌ يَغْلِبُوا۟ مِا۟ئَتَيْنِ وَإِن يَكُن مِّنكُمْ أَلْفٌ يَغْلِبُوٓا۟ أَلْفَيْنِ بِإِذْنِ ٱللَّهِ ۗ وَٱللَّهُ مَعَ ٱلصَّٰبِرِينَ ۝ ﴾

66. Now Allâh has lightened your (task), for He knows that there is weakness in you. So if there are of you a hundred steadfast persons, they shall overcome two hundreds, and if there are a thousand of you, they shall overcome two thousand with the Leave of Allâh. And Allâh is with As-Sâbirin (the patient).

Transliteration

64. Ya ayyuha alnnabiyyu hasbuka Allahu wamani ittabaAAaka mina almu/mineena
65. Ya ayyuha alnnabiyyu harridi almu/mineena AAala alqitali in yakun minkum AAishroona sabiroona yaghliboo mi-atayni wa-in yakun minkum mi-atun yaghliboo alfan mina allatheena kafaroo bi-annahum qawmun la yafqahoona   66. Al-ana khaffafa Allahu AAankum waAAalima anna feekum daAAfan fa-in yakun minkum mi-

atun sabiratun yaghliboo mi-atayni wa-in yakun minkum alfun yaghliboo alfayni bi-ithni Allahi waAllahu maAAa alssabireena

Tafsir Ibn Kathir

Encouraging Believers to fight in Jihad; the Good News that a Few Muslims can overcome a Superior Enemy Force

Allah encourages His Prophet and the believers to fight and struggle against the enemy, and wage war against their forces. Allah affirms that He will suffice, aid, support, and help the believers against their enemies, even if their enemies are numerous and have sufficient supplies, while the believers are few. Allah said,

(O Prophet! Urge the believers to fight), encouraged and called them to fight. The Messenger of Allah used to encourage the Companions to fight when they faced the enemy. On the day of Badr when the idolators came with their forces and supplies, he said to his Companions,

«قُومُوا إِلَى جَنَّةٍ عَرْضُهَا السَّمَوَاتُ وَالْأَرْضُ»

(Get ready and march forth towards a Paradise as wide as the heavens and earth.)

`Umayr bin Al-Humam said, "As wide as the heavens and earth" The Messenger said,

«نَعَم»

(Yes) `Umayr said, "Excellent! Excellent!" The Messenger asked him,

«مَا يَحْمِلُكَ عَلَى قَوْلِكَ: بَخٍ بَخٍ»

(What makes you say, `Excellent! Excellent!') He said, "The hope that I might be one of its dwellers." The Prophet said,

«فَإِنَّكَ مِنْ أَهْلِهَا»

(You are one of its people.) Umayr went ahead, broke the scabbard of his sword, took some dates and started eating from them. He then threw the dates from his hand, saying, "Verily, if I lived until I finished eating these dates, then it is indeed a long life." He went ahead, fought and was killed, may Allah be pleased with him.

Allah said next, commanding the believers and conveying good news to them,

(If there are twenty steadfast persons among you, they will overcome two hundred, and if there be a hundred steadfast persons, they will overcome a thousand of those who disbelieve.)

The Ayah says, one Muslim should endure ten disbelievers. Allah abrogated this part later on, but the good news remained. `Abdullah bin Al-Mubarak said that Jarir bin Hazim narrated to them that, Az-Zubayr bin Al-Khirrit narrated to him, from `Ikrimah, from Ibn `Abbas, "When this verse was revealed,

(If there are twenty steadfast persons among you, they will overcome two hundred...) it became difficult for the Muslims, when Allah commanded that one Muslim is required to endure ten idolators. Soon after, this matter was made easy,

(Now Allah has lightened your (task)), until,

(they shall overcome two hundred. ..)

Allah lowered the number (of adversaries that Muslims are required to endure), and thus, made the required patience less, compatible to the decrease in numbers." Al-Bukhari recorded a similar narration from Ibn Al-Mubarak. Muhammad bin Ishaq recorded that Ibn `Abbas said, "When this Ayah was revealed, it was difficult for the Muslims, for they thought it was burdensome since twenty should fight two hundred, and a hundred against a thousand. Allah made this ruling easy for them and abrogated this Ayah with another Ayah,

(Now Allah has lightened your (task), for He knows that there is weakness in you...)

Thereafter, if Muslims were half as many as their enemy, they were not allowed to run away from them. If the Muslims were fewer than that, they were not obligated to fight the disbelievers and thus allowed to avoid hostilities."

Surah: 8 Ayah: 67, Ayah: 68 & Ayah: 69

﴿ مَا كَانَ لِنَبِيٍّ أَن يَكُونَ لَهُۥٓ أَسۡرَىٰ حَتَّىٰ يُثۡخِنَ فِي ٱلۡأَرۡضِۚ تُرِيدُونَ عَرَضَ ٱلدُّنۡيَا وَٱللَّهُ يُرِيدُ ٱلۡأٓخِرَةَۗ وَٱللَّهُ عَزِيزٌ حَكِيمٌ ۝ ﴾

67. It is not for a Prophet that he should have prisoners of war (and free them with ransom) until he had made a great slaughter (among his enemies) in the land. You desire the good of this world (i.e. the money of ransom for freeing the captives), but Allâh desires (for you) the Hereafter. And Allâh is All-Mighty, All-Wise.

﴿ لَّوۡلَا كِتَٰبٌ مِّنَ ٱللَّهِ سَبَقَ لَمَسَّكُمۡ فِيمَآ أَخَذۡتُمۡ عَذَابٌ عَظِيمٌ ۝ ﴾

68. Were it not a previous ordainment from Allâh, a severe torment would have touched you for what you took.

﴿ فَكُلُواْ مِمَّا غَنِمۡتُمۡ حَلَٰلٗا طَيِّبٗاۚ وَٱتَّقُواْ ٱللَّهَۚ إِنَّ ٱللَّهَ غَفُورٞ رَّحِيمٞ ۝ ﴾

69. So enjoy what you have gotten of booty in war, lawful and good, and be afraid of Allâh. Certainly, Allâh is Oft-Forgiving, Most Merciful.

Transliteration

67. Ma kana linabiyyin an yakoona lahu asra hatta yuthkhina fee al-ardi tureedoona AAarada alddunya waAllahu yureedu al-akhirata waAllahu AAazeezun hakeemun 68. Lawla kitabun mina Allahi sabaqa lamassakum feema akhathtum AAathabun AAatheemun 69. Fakuloo mimma ghanimtum halalan tayyiban waittaqoo Allaha inna Allaha ghafoorun raheemun

Tafsir Ibn Kathir

Imam Ahmad recorded that Anas said, "The Prophet asked the people for their opinion about the prisoners of war of Badr, saying,

«إِنَّ اللهَ قَدْ أَمْكَنَكُمْ مِنْهُم»

(Allah has made you prevail above them.) `Umar bin Al-Khattab stood up and said, `O Allah's Messenger! Cut off their necks,' but the Prophet turned away from him. The Messenger of Allah again asked,

«يَاأَيُّهَا النَّاسُ إِنَّ اللهَ قَدْ أَمْكَنَكُمْ مِنْهُمْ وَإِنَّمَا هُمْ إِخْوَانُكُمْ بِالْأَمْس»

(O people! Allah has made you prevail over them, and only yesterday, they were your brothers.) `Umar again stood up and said, `O Allah's Messenger! Cut off their necks.' The Prophet ignored him and asked the same question again and he repeated the same answer. Abu Bakr As-Siddiq stood up and said, `O Allah's Messenger! I think you should pardon them and set them free in return for ransom.' Thereupon the grief on the face of Allah's Messenger vanished. He pardoned them and accepted ransom for their release. Allah, the Exalted and Most Honored, revealed this verse,

(Were it not a previous ordainment from Allah, a severe torment would have touched you for what you took)."

`Ali bin Abi Talhah narrated that Ibn `Abbas said about Allah's statement,

(Were it not a previous ordainment from Allah...),

"In the Preserved Book, that war spoils and prisoners of war will be made allowed for you,

(would have touched you for what you took), because of the captives.

(a severe torment.) Allah, the Exalted said next,

(So enjoy what you have gotten of booty in war, lawful and good)." eAl-`Awfi also reported this statement from Ibn `Abbas. A similar statement was collected from Abu Hurayrah, Ibn Mas`ud, Sa`id bin Jubayr, `Ata', Al-Hasan Al-Basri, Qatadah and Al-A`mash. They all stated that,

Chapter 8: Al-Anfal (Spoils of War, Booty), Verses 041-075

(Were it not a previous ordainment from Allah. .) refers to allowing the spoils of war for this Ummah.

Supporting this view is what the Two Sahihs recorded that Jabir bin `Abdullah said that the Messenger of Allah said,

«أُعْطِيتُ خَمْسًا لَمْ يُعْطَهُنَّ أَحَدٌ مِنَ الْأَنْبِيَاءِ قَبْلِي: نُصِرْتُ بِالرُّعْبِ مَسِيرَةَ شَهْرٍ، وَجُعِلَتْ لِيَ الْأَرْضُ مَسْجِدًا وَطَهُورًا، وَأُحِلَّتْ لِيَ الْغَنَائِمُ وَلَمْ تَحِلَّ لِأَحَدٍ قَبْلِي، وَأُعْطِيتُ الشَّفَاعَةَ، وَكَانَ النَّبِيُّ يُبْعَثُ إِلَى قَوْمِهِ، وَبُعِثْتُ إِلَى النَّاسِ عَامَّةً»

(I have been given five things which were not given to any Prophet before me. (They are:) Allah made me victorious by awe, (by His frightening my enemies) for a distance of one month's journey. The earth has been made a place for praying and a purifier for me. The booty has been made lawful for me, yet it was not lawful for anyone else before me. I have been given the right of intercession (on the Day of Resurrection). Every Prophet used to be sent to his people only, but I have been sent to all mankind.)

Al-A`mash narrated that Abu Salih said that Abu Hurayrah said that the Messenger of Allah said,

«لَمْ تَحِلَّ الْغَنَائِمُ لِسُودِ الرُّؤُوسِ غَيْرَنَا»

(War booty was never allowed for any among mankind except us.) (Abu Hurayrah said;) This is why Allah the Most High said,

(So enjoy what you have gotten of booty in war, lawful and good.)

The Muslims then took the ransom for their captives. In his Sunan, Imam Abu Dawud recorded that Ibn `Abbas said that the Messenger of Allah fixed four hundred (Dirhams) in ransom from the people of Jahiliyyah in the aftermath of Badr. The majority of the scholars say that the matter of prisoners of war is up to the Imam. If he decides, he can have them killed, such as in the case of Bani Qurayzah. If he decides, he can accept a ransom for them, as in the case of the prisoners of Badr, or exchange them for Muslim prisoners. The Messenger exchanged a woman and her daughter who were captured by Salamah bin Al-Akwa`, for exchange of some Muslims who were captured by the idolators, or if he decides he can take the prisoner as a captives.

Surah: 8 Ayah: 70 & Ayah: 71

﴿ يَـٰٓأَيُّهَا ٱلنَّبِىُّ قُل لِّمَن فِىٓ أَيْدِيكُم مِّنَ ٱلْأَسْرَىٰٓ إِن يَعْلَمِ ٱللَّهُ فِى قُلُوبِكُمْ خَيْرًا يُؤْتِكُمْ خَيْرًا مِّمَّآ أُخِذَ مِنكُمْ وَيَغْفِرْ لَكُمْ وَٱللَّهُ غَفُورٌ رَّحِيمٌ ﴾

70. O Prophet! Say to the captives that are in your hands: "If Allâh knows any good in your hearts, He will give you something better than what has been taken from you, and He will forgive you, and Allâh is Oft-Forgiving, Most Merciful."

﴿ وَإِن يُرِيدُواْ خِيَانَتَكَ فَقَدْ خَانُواْ ٱللَّهَ مِن قَبْلُ فَأَمْكَنَ مِنْهُمْ وَٱللَّهُ عَلِيمٌ حَكِيمٌ ﴾

71. But if they intend to betray you (O Muhammad (peace be upon him)) they indeed betrayed Allâh before. So He gave (you) power over them. And Allâh is All-Knower, All-Wise.

Transliteration

70. Ya ayyuha alnnabiyyu qul liman fee aydeekum mina al-asra in yaAAlami Allahu fee quloobikum khayran yu/tikum khayran mimma okhitha minkum wayaghfir lakum waAllahu ghafoorun raheemun 71. Wa-in yureedoo khiyanataka faqad khanoo Allaha min qablu faamkana minhum waAllahu AAaleemun hakeemun

Tafsir Ibn Kathir

Pagan Prisoners at Badr were promised better than what They lost, if They become Righteous in the Future

Muhammad bin Ishaq reported that `Abdullah bin `Abbas said that before the battle of Badr, the Messenger of Allah said,

«إِنِّي قَدْ عَرَفْتُ أَنَّ أُنَاسًا مِنْ بَنِي هَاشِمٍ وَغَيْرِهِمْ قَدْ أُخْرِجُوا كَرْهًا لَا حَاجَةَ لَهُمْ بِقِتَالِنَا فَمَنْ لَقِيَ مِنْكُمْ أَحَدًا مِنْهُمْ أَيْ مِنْ بَنِي هَاشِمٍ فَلَا يَقْتُلْهُ، وَمَنْ لَقِيَ أَبَا الْبُخْتَرِي بْنَ هِشَامٍ مُسْتَكْرِهًا»

(I have come to know that some people from Bani Hashim and others were forced to accompany the pagans, although they had no desire to fight us. Therefore, whoever meets any of them (Bani Hashim), do not kill him. Whoever meets Abu Al-Bukhtari bin Hisham, should not kill him. Whoever meets Al-`Abbas bin `Abdul-Muttalib, let him not kill him, for he was forced to come (with the pagan army).) Abu Hudhayfah bin `Utbah said, "Shall we kill our fathers, children, brothers and tribesmen (from Quraysh), and leave Al-`Abbas By Allah! If I meet him, I will kill him with the sword." When this reached the Messenger of Allah , he said to `Umar bin Al-Khattab,

Chapter 8: Al-Anfal (Spoils of War, Booty), Verses 041-075

«يَا أَبَا حَفْصٍ»

(O Abu Hafs!), and `Umar said, "By Allah that was the first time that the Messenger of Allah called me Abu Hafs."

«أَيُضْرَبُ وَجْهُ عَمِّ رَسُولِ اللهِ بِالسَّيْفِ»

(Will the face of the Messenger of Allah's's uncle be struck with the sword) `Umar said, "O Allah's Messenger! Give me permission to cut off his neck (meaning Abu Hudhayfah) for he has fallen into hypocrisy, by Allah!" Ever since that happened, Abu Hudhayfah used to say, "By Allah! I do not feel safe from this statement coming back to haunt me, and I will continue to fear its repercussions, unless Allah, the Exalted, forgives me for it through martyrdom." Abu Hudhayfah was martyred during the battle of Al-Yamamah, may Allah be pleased with him.

Ibn `Abbas said, "On the eve after Badr, the Messenger of Allah spent the first part of the night awake, while the prisoners were bound. His Companions said to him, `O Allah's Messenger! Why do you not sleep' Al-`Abbas had been captured by a man from Al-Ansar, and the Messenger of Allah said to them,

«سَمِعْتُ أَنِينَ عَمِّي الْعَبَّاسِ فِي وِثَاقِهِ فَأَطْلِقُوه»

(I heard the cries of pain from my uncle Al-`Abbas, because of his shackles, so untie him.) When his uncle stopped crying from pain, Allah's Messenger went to sleep." In his Sahih, Al-Bukhari recorded a Hadith from Musa bin `Uqbah who said that Ibn Shihab said that Anas bin Malik said that some men from Al-Ansar said to the Messenger of Allah , "O Allah's Messenger! Give us permission and we will set free our maternal cousin Al-`Abbas without taking ransom from him." He said,

«لَا وَاللهِ لَا تَذَرُونَ مِنْهُ دِرْهَمًا»

(No, by Allah! Do not leave any Dirham of it.) And from Yunus Bikkir, from Muhammad bin Ishaq, from Yazid bin Ruwman, from `Urwah, from Az-Zuhri that several people said to him, "The Quraysh sent to the Messenger of Allah concerning ransoming their prisoners, and each tribe paid what was required for their prisoners. Al-`Abbas said, `O Allah's Messenger! I became a Muslims before.' The Messenger of Allah said,

«اللهُ أَعْلَمُ بِإِسْلَامِكَ فَإِنْ يَكُنْ كَمَا تَقُولُ فَإِنَّ اللهَ يُجْزِيكَ وَأَمَّا ظَاهِرُكَ فَقَدْ كَانَ عَلَيْنَا فَافْتَدِ نَفْسَكَ وَابْنَيْ أَخِيكَ نَوْفَلَ بْنَ الْحَارِثِ بْنِ عَبْدِالْمُطَّلِبِ

$$\text{وَعَقِيلَ بْنَ أَبِي طَالِبِ بْنِ عَبْدِالْمُطَّلِبِ، وَحَلِيفَكَ عُتْبَةَ بْنَ عَمْرٍو أَخِي بَنِي الْحَارِثِ بْنِ فِهْرٍ}$$

(Allah knows if you are Muslim! If what you are claiming is true, then Allah will compensate you. As for your outward appearance, it was against us. Therefore, ransom yourself, as well as, your nephews Nawfal bin Al-Harith bin `Abdul-Muttalib and `Aqil bin Abu Talib bin `Abdul-Muttalib, and also your ally `Utbah bin `Amr, from Bani Al-Harith bin Fihr.) Al-`Abbas said, `I do not have that (money), O Allah's Messenger!' The Messenger said,

$$\text{«فَأَيْنَ الْمَالُ الَّذِي دَفَنْتَهُ أَنْتَ وَأُمُّ الْفَضْلِ فَقُلْتَ لَهَا: إِنْ أَصَبْتُ فِي سَفَرِي هَذَا، فَهَذَا الْمَالُ الَّذِي دَفَنْتُهُ لِبَنِي الْفَضْلِ وَعَبْدِاللهِ وَقُثَمٍ؟»}$$

(What about the wealth that you and Umm Al-Fadl buried, and you said to her, `If I am killed in this battle, then this money that I buried is for my children Al-Fadl, `Abdullah and Quthm) Al-`Abbas said, `By Allah, O Allah's Messenger! I know that you are Allah's Messenger, for this is a thing that none except Umm Al-Fadl and I knew. However, O Allah's Messenger! Could you count towards my ransom the twenty Uwqiyah (pertaining to a weight) that you took from me (in the battle)' The Messenger of Allah said,

$$\text{«لَا ذَاكَ شَيْءٌ أَعْطَانَا اللهُ تَعَالَى مِنْكَ»}$$

(No, for that was money that Allah made as war spoils for us from you).

So Al-`Abbas ransomed himself, his two nephews and an ally, and Allah revealed this verse,

(O Prophet! Say to the captives that are in your hands: "If Allah knows any good in your hearts, He will give you something better than what has been taken from you, and He will forgive you, and Allah is Oft-Forgiving, Most Merciful.") (8:70) Al-`Abbas commented, `After I became Muslim, Allah gave me twenty servants in place of the twenty Uwqiyah I lost. And I hope for Allah's forgiveness."

Al-Hafiz Abu Bakr Al-Bayhaqi recorded, that Anas bin Malik said, "The Prophet was brought some wealth from Bahrain and said;

$$\text{«انْثُرُوهُ فِي مَسْجِدِي»}$$

(Distribute it in my Masjid) and it was the biggest amount of goods Allah's Messenger had ever received. He left for prayer and did not even look at the goods. After

Chapter 8: Al-Anfal (Spoils of War, Booty), Verses 041-075

finishing the prayer, he sat by those goods and gave some of it to everybody he saw. Al-`Abbas came to him and said, `O Allah's Messenger! give me (something) too, because I gave ransom for myself and `Aqil. ' Allah's Messenger told him to take. So he stuffed his garment with it and tried to carry it away but he failed to do so. He said, `Order someone to help me in lifting it.' The Prophet refused. He then said to the Prophet , `Will you please help me to lift it' Allah's Messenger refused. Then Al-`Abbas dropped some of it and lifted it on his shoulders and went away. Allah's Messenger kept on watching him till he disappeared from his sight and was astonished at his greediness. Allah's Messenger did not get up until the last coin was distributed." Al-Bukhari also collected this Hadith in several places of his Sahih with an abridged chain, in a manner indicating his approral of it.

Allah said,

(But if they intend to betray you, they indeed betrayed Allah before) meaning,

(But if they intend to betray you) in contradiction to what they declare to you by words.

(they indeed betrayed Allah before), the battle of Badr by committing disbelief in Him,

(So He gave (you) power over them), causing them to be captured in Badr,

(And Allah is All-Knower, All-Wise.)

He is Ever Aware of his actions and All-Wise in what He decides.

Surah: 8 Ayah: 72

﴿ إِنَّ ٱلَّذِينَ ءَامَنُواْ وَهَاجَرُواْ وَجَٰهَدُواْ بِأَمْوَٰلِهِمْ وَأَنفُسِهِمْ فِى سَبِيلِ ٱللَّهِ وَٱلَّذِينَ ءَاوَواْ وَّنَصَرُواْ أُوْلَٰٓئِكَ بَعْضُهُمْ أَوْلِيَآءُ بَعْضٍۚ وَٱلَّذِينَ ءَامَنُواْ وَلَمْ يُهَاجِرُواْ مَا لَكُم مِّن وَلَٰيَتِهِم مِّن شَىْءٍ حَتَّىٰ يُهَاجِرُواْۚ وَإِنِ ٱسْتَنصَرُوكُمْ فِى ٱلدِّينِ فَعَلَيْكُمُ ٱلنَّصْرُ إِلَّا عَلَىٰ قَوْمٍۭ بَيْنَكُمْ وَبَيْنَهُم مِّيثَٰقٌۗ وَٱللَّهُ بِمَا تَعْمَلُونَ بَصِيرٌ ۝ ﴾

72. Verily, those who believed, and emigrated and strove hard and fought with their property and their lives in the Cause of Allâh as well as those who gave (them) asylum and help, - these are (all) allies to one another. And as to those who believed but did not emigrate (to you O Muhammad (peace be upon him)) you owe no duty of protection to them until they emigrate; but if they seek your help in religion, it is your duty to help them except against a people with whom you have a treaty of mutual alliance; and Allâh is the All-Seer of what you do.

Transliteration

72. Inna allatheena amanoo wahajaroo wajahadoo bi-amwalihim waanfusihim fee sabeeli Allahi waallatheena awaw wanasaroo ola-ika baAAduhum awliyao baAAdin

waallatheena amanoo walam yuhajiroo ma lakum min walayatihim min shay-in hatta yuhajiroo wa-ini istansarookum fee alddeeni faAAalaykumu alnnasru illa AAala qawmin baynakum wabaynahum meethaqun waAllahu bima taAAmaloona baseerun

Tafsir Ibn Kathir

The Muhajirin and Al-Ansar are the Supporters of One Another

Here Allah mentions the types of believers, dividing them into the Muhajirin, who left their homes and estates, emigrating to give support to Allah and His Messenger to establish His religion. They gave up their wealth and themselves in this cause. There are also the Ansar, the Muslims of Al-Madinah, who gave asylum to their Muhajirin brethren in their own homes and comforted them with their wealth. They also gave aid to Allah and His Messenger by fighting alongside the Muhajirun. Certainly they are,

(allies to one another), for each one of them has more right to the other than anyone else. This is why Allah's Messenger forged ties of brotherhood between the Muhajirin and Ansar, as Al-Bukhari recorded from Ibn `Abbas. They used to inherit from each other, having more right to inheritance than the deceased man's relatives, until Allah abrogated that practice with the fixed share for near relatives. Imam Ahmad recorded that Jarir bin `Abdullah Al-Bajali said that the Messenger of Allah said,

«الْمُهَاجِرُونَ وَالْأَنْصَارُ أَوْلِيَاءُ بَعْضُهُمْ لِبَعْضٍ، وَالطُّلَقَاءُ مِنْ قُرَيْشٍ، وَالْعُتَقَاءُ مِنْ ثَقِيفٍ بَعْضُهُمْ أَوْلِيَاءُ بَعْضٍ إِلَى يَوْمِ الْقِيَامَةِ»

(The Muhajirun and Al-Ansar are the supporters of each other, while the Tulaqa' of Quraysh (whom the Prophet set free after conquering Makkah) and `Utaqa' from Thaqif (whom the Prophet set free from captivity after the battle of Hunayn) are supporters of each other until the Day of Resurrection.)

Only Ahmad collected this Hadith.

Allah praised the Muhajirin and the Ansar in several Ayat of His Book and His Messenger (also praised them too). Allah said,

(And the foremost to embrace Islam of the Muhajirun and the Ansar and also those who followed them exactly. Allah is well-pleased with them as they are well-pleased with Him. He has prepared for them gardens under which rivers flow (Paradise).)(9:100), k

(Allah has forgiven the Prophet, the Muhajirin and the Ansar who followed him in the time of distress.) (9:117), and,

((And there is also a share in this booty) for the poor Muhajirin, who were expelled from their homes and their property, seeking bounties from Allah and (His) good pleasure, and helping Allah and His Messenger. Such are indeed the truthful. And those who, before them, had homes (in Al-Madinah) and adopted the faith, love those who emigrate to them, and have no jealousy in their breasts for that which they have been given, and give them (emigrants) preference over themselves even though they were in need of that) (59:8-9).

The best comment on Allah's statement,

(...and have no jealousy in their breasts for that which they have been given) is that it means, they do not envy the Muhajirin for the rewards that Allah gave them for their emigration. These Ayat indicate that the Muhajirin are better in grade than the Ansar, and there is a consensus on this ruling among the scholars.

The Believers Who did not emigrate did not yet receive the Benefits of Wilayah

Allah said,

(And as to those who believed but did not emigrate, you owe no duty of protection to them until they emigrate,) (8:72).

This is the third category of believers, those who believed, but did not perform Hijrah and instead remained in their areas. They do not have any share in the war booty or in the fifth (designated for Allah and His Messenger, the relatives of the Prophet , the orphans, the poor and the wayfarer), unless they attend battle.

Imam Ahmad recorded that Buraydah bin Al-Hasib Al-Aslami said, "When the Messenger of Allah would send a commander with an expedition force or an army, he would advise him to have Taqwa of Allah and be kind to the Muslims under his command. He used to say,

«اغْزُوا بِاسْمِ اللهِ فِي سَبِيلِ اللهِ، قَاتِلُوا مَنْ كَفَرَ بِاللهِ، إِذَا لَقِيتَ عَدُوَّكَ مِنَ الْمُشْرِكِينَ فَادْعُهُمْ إِلَى إِحْدَى ثَلَاثِ خِصَالٍ أَوْ خِلَالٍ فَأَيَّتُهُنَّ مَا أَجَابُوكَ إِلَيْهَا فَاقْبَلْ مِنْهُمْ، وَكُفَّ عَنْهُمْ. ادْعُهُمْ إِلَى الْإِسْلَامِ، فَإِنْ أَجَابُوكَ فَاقْبَلْ مِنْهُمْ وَكُفَّ عَنْهُمْ. ثُمَّ ادْعُهُمْ إِلَى التَّحَوُّلِ مِنْ دَارِهِمْ إِلَى دَارِ الْمُهَاجِرِينَ، وَأَعْلِمْهُمْ إِنْ فَعَلُوا ذَلِكَ أَنَّ لَهُمْ مَا لِلْمُهَاجِرِينَ، وَأَنَّ عَلَيْهِمْ مَا عَلَى الْمُهَاجِرِينَ، فَإِنْ أَبَوْا وَاخْتَارُوا دَارَهُمْ، فَأَعْلِمْهُمْ أَنَّهُمْ يَكُونُونَ كَأَعْرَابِ الْمُسْلِمِينَ، يَجْرِي عَلَيْهِمْ حُكْمُ اللهِ الَّذِي يَجْرِي عَلَى الْمُؤْمِنِينَ، وَلَا يَكُونُ لَهُمْ فِي الْفَيْءِ وَالْغَنِيمَةِ نَصِيبٌ، إِلَّا أَنْ يُجَاهِدُوا مَعَ الْمُسْلِمِينَ، فَإِنْ هُمْ أَبَوْا،

$$\text{فَادْعُهُمْ إِلَى إِعْطَاءِ الْجِزْيَةِ. فَإِنْ أَجَابُوا فَاقْبَلْ مِنْهُمْ وَكُفَّ عَنْهُمْ، فَإِنْ أَبَوْا فَاسْتَعِنْ بِاللهِ ثُمَّ قَاتِلْهُم}$$

(Fight in the Name of Allah, in the cause of Allah. Fight those who disbelieve in Allah. When you meet your Mushrik enemy, then call them to one of three choices, and whichever they agree to, then accept it and turn away from them. Call them to embrace Islam, and if they agree, accept it from them and turn away from them. Then call them to leave their area and come to areas in which the Muhajirin reside. Make known to them that if they do this, they will have the rights, as well as, the duties of the Muhajirin. If they refuse and decide to remain in their area, make known to them that they will be just like Muslim bedouins, and that Allah's law applies to them just as it does to all believers. However, they will not have a share in the war booty or Fai' (booty without war), unless they perform Jihad along with Muslims. If they refuse all of this, then call them to pay the Jizyah, and if they accept, then take it from them and turn away from them. If they refuse all these (three) options, then trust in Allah and fight them.)

Muslim collected this Hadith.

Allah said next,

(But if they seek your help in religion, it is your duty to help them.)

Allah commands, if these bedouins, who did not perform Hijrah, ask you to aid them against their enemy, then aid them. It is incumbent on you to aid them in this case, because they are your brothers in Islam, unless they ask you to aid them against disbelievers with whom you have a fixed-term treaty of peace. In that case, do not betray your treaties or break your promises with those whom you have treaties of peace. This was reported from Ibn `Abbas.

Surah: 8 Ayah: 73

$$\text{﴿ وَالَّذِينَ كَفَرُوا بَعْضُهُمْ أَوْلِيَاءُ بَعْضٍ ۚ إِلَّا تَفْعَلُوهُ تَكُن فِتْنَةٌ فِى ٱلْأَرْضِ وَفَسَادٌ كَبِيرٌ ﴾}$$

73. And those who disbelieve are allies of one another, (and) if you (Muslims of the whole world collectively) do not do so (i.e. become allies, as one united block under one Khalifah (a chief Muslim ruler for the whole Muslim world) to make victorious Allâh's Religion of Islâmic Monotheism), there will be Fitnah (wars, battles, polytheism) and oppression on the earth, and a great mischief and corruption (appearance of polytheism).

Chapter 8: Al-Anfal (Spoils of War, Booty), Verses 041-075

Transliteration

73. Waallatheena kafaroo baAAduhum awliyao baAAdin illa tafAAaloohu takun fitnatun fee al-ardi wafasadun kabeerun

Tafsir Ibn Kathir

The Disbelievers are Allies of Each Other; the Muslims are not their Allies

After Allah mentioned that the believers are the supporters of one another, He severed all ties of support between them and the disbelievers. In his Mustadrak, Al-Hakim recorded that Usamah said that the Prophet said,

«لَا يَتَوَارَثُ أَهْلُ مِلَّتَيْنِ، وَلَا يَرِثُ مُسْلِمٌ كَافِرًا، وَلَا كَافِرٌ مُسْلِمًا»

(No followers of two religions inherit from each other. Therefore, neither a Muslim inherits from a disbeliever nor a disbeliever from a Muslim.)

The Prophet recited this Ayah,

(And those who disbelieve are supporters of one another, (and) if you (Muslims) do not do so (protect one another), there will be Fitnah on the earth, and great corruption.) Al-Hakim said, "Its chain is Sahih, and they did not record it." However, the following, from Usamah bin Zayd, is in the Two Sahihs; the Messenger of Allah said,

«لَا يَرِثُ الْمُسْلِمُ الْكَافِرَ وَلَا الْكَافِرُ الْمُسْلِمَ»

(Neither a Muslim inherits from a disbeliever nor a disbeliever inherits from a Muslim.)

Allah said next,

(If you do not do so, there will be Fitnah and oppression on the earth, and a great corruption), meaning, if you do not shun the idolators and offer your loyalty to the believers, Fitnah will overcome the people. Then confusion (polytheism and corruption) will be rampant, for the believers will be mixed with disbelievers, resulting in tremendous, widespread trials (corruption and mischief) between people.

Surah: 8 Ayah: 74 & Ayah: 75

﴿ وَالَّذِينَ ءَامَنُواْ وَهَاجَرُواْ وَجَـٰهَدُواْ فِى سَبِيلِ ٱللَّهِ وَٱلَّذِينَ ءَاوَواْ وَّنَصَرُواْ أُوْلَـٰٓئِكَ هُمُ ٱلْمُؤْمِنُونَ حَقًّا لَّهُم مَّغْفِرَةٌ وَرِزْقٌ كَرِيمٌ ﴾

74. And those who believed, and emigrated and strove hard in the Cause of Allâh (Al-Jihâd), as well as those who gave (them) asylum and aid - these are the believers in truth, for them is forgiveness and Rizqun Karîm (a generous provision i.e. Paradise).

$$\left\{\text{وَالَّذِينَ ءَامَنُواْ مِنۢ بَعْدُ وَهَاجَرُواْ وَجَٰهَدُواْ مَعَكُمْ فَأُوْلَٰٓئِكَ مِنكُمْ ۚ وَأُوْلُواْ الْأَرْحَامِ بَعْضُهُمْ أَوْلَىٰ بِبَعْضٍ فِى كِتَٰبِ اللَّهِ ۗ إِنَّ اللَّهَ بِكُلِّ شَىْءٍ عَلِيمٌ ۝}\right.$$

75. And those who believed afterwards, and emigrated and strove hard along with you, (in the Cause of Allâh) they are of you. But kindred by blood are nearer to one another (regarding inheritance) in the decree ordained by Allâh. Verily, Allâh is the All-Knower of everything.

Transliteration

74. Waallatheena amanoo wahajaroo wajahadoo fee sabeeli Allahi waallatheena awaw wanasaroo ola-ika humu almu/minoona haqqan lahum maghfiratun warizqun kareemun 75. Waallatheena amanoo min baAAdu wahajaroo wajahadoo maAAakum faola-ika minkum waoloo al-arhami baAAduhum awla bibaAAdin fee kitabi Allahi inna Allaha bikulli shay-in AAaleemun

Tafsir Ibn Kathir

Believers in Truth

After Allah affirmed the ruling of loyalty and protection between the believers in this life, He then mentioned their destination in the Hereafter. Allah also affirmed the faith of the believers, just as mentioned in the beginning of this Surah, and that He will reward them with forgiveness and by erasing their sins, if they have any. He also promised them honorable provisions that are abundant, pure, everlasting and eternal; provisions that never end or run out, nor will they ever cause boredom, for they are delightful and come in great varieties. Allah then mentioned that those who follow the path of the believers in faith and performing good deeds, will be with them in the Hereafter. Just as Allah said,

(And the foremost to embrace Islam...) (9:100), until the end of the Ayah. He also said,

(And those who came after them ...) (59:10).

A Hadith that is in the Two Sahihs, which is Mutawatir and has several authentic chains of narrations, mentions that the Messenger of Allah said,

《الْمَرْءُ مَعَ مَنْ أَحَبَّ》

(One will be in the company of those whom he loves.) Another Hadith states,

《مَنْ أَحَبَّ قَوْمًا فَهُوَ مِنْهُمْ》

(He who loves a people is one of them), and in another narration, he said,

《حُشِرَ مَعَهُم》

(...will be gathered with them (on the Day of Resurrection).)

Inheritance is for Designated Degrees of Relatives

Allah said,

(But kindred by blood are nearer to one another (regarding inheritance) in the decree ordained by Allah), meaning, in Allah's decision. This Ayah encompasses all relatives, not only the degrees of relative who do not have a fixed, designated share in the inheritance, as some people claim and use this Ayah to argue. According to Ibn `Abbas, Mujahid, `Ikrimah, Al-Hasan, Qatadah and several others, this Ayah abrogated inheriting from those with whom one had ties of treaties or brotherhood, as was the case in the beginning of Islam. So it applies to all relatives, and as for those who do not inherit, then this is supported by the Hadith,

《إِنَّ اللهَ قَدْ أَعْطَى كُلَّ ذِي حَقٍّ حَقَّهُ فَلَا وَصِيَّةَ لِوَارِثٍ》

(Indeed Allah had alloted every right to the one who deserves it, so there may be no will for an heir.)

Therefore, this Ayah also includes those who have a fixed share of inheritance. Allah knows best.

This is the end of the Tafsir of Surat Al-Anfal, all praise and thanks are for Allah, in Him we trust, and He is sufficient for us, what an excellent supporter He is.

CHAPTER (SURAH) 9: AL-BARA'AT (THE IMMUNITY) OR AT-TAWBA (REPENTANCE, DISPENSATION), VERSES 001-092

Surah: 9 Ayah: 1 & Ayah: 2

﴿ بَرَآءَةٌ مِّنَ ٱللَّهِ وَرَسُولِهِ إِلَى ٱلَّذِينَ عَـٰهَدتُّم مِّنَ ٱلْمُشْرِكِينَ ۝ ﴾

1. Freedom from (all) obligations (is declared) from Allâh and His Messenger (peace be upon him) to those of the Mushrikûn (polytheists, pagans, idolaters, disbelievers in the Oneness of Allâh), with whom you made a treaty.

﴿ فَسِيحُوا۟ فِى ٱلْأَرْضِ أَرْبَعَةَ أَشْهُرٍ وَٱعْلَمُوٓا۟ أَنَّكُمْ غَيْرُ مُعْجِزِى ٱللَّهِ ۙ وَأَنَّ ٱللَّهَ مُخْزِى ٱلْكَـٰفِرِينَ ۝ ﴾

2. So travel freely (O Mushrikûn - See V.2:105) for four months (as you will) throughout the land, but know that you cannot escape (from the Punishment of) Allâh; and Allâh will disgrace the disbelievers.

Transliteration

1. Baraatun mina Allahi warasoolihi ila allatheena AAahadtum mina almushrikeena 2. Faseehoo fee al-ardi arbaAAata ashhurin waiAAlamoo annakum ghayru muAAjizee Allahi waanna Allaha mukhzee alkafireena

Tafsir Ibn Kathir
Why there is no Basmalah in the Beginning of This Surah

This honorable Surah (chapter 9) was one of the last Surahs to be revealed to the Messenger of Allah . Al-Bukhari recorded that Al-Bara' said, "The last Ayah to be revealed was,

(They ask you for a legal verdict. Say: "Allah directs (thus) about Al-Kalalah.") (4:176), while the last Surah to be revealed was Bara'ah." The Basmalah was not mentioned in the beginning of this Surah because the Companions did not write it in the complete copy of the Qur'an (Mushaf) they collected, following the Commander of the faithful, `Uthman bin `Affan, may Allah be pleased with him. The first part of this honorable Surah was revealed to the Messenger of Allah when he returned from the battle of Tabuk, during the Hajj season, which the Prophet thought about attending. But he remembered that the idolators would still attend that Hajj, as was usual in past years, and that they perform Tawaf around the House while naked. He disliked to associate with them and sent Abu Bakr As-Siddiq, may Allah be pleased with him, to lead Hajj that year and show the people their rituals, commanding him to inform the idolators that they would not be allowed to participate in Hajj after that season. He commanded him to proclaim,

(Freedom from (all) obligations (is declared) from Allah and His Messenger ()...), to the people. When Abu Bakr had left, the Messenger sent `Ali bin Abu Talib to be the one to deliver this news to the idolators on behalf of the Messenger , for he was the Messenger's cousin. We will mention this story later.

Publicizing the Disavowal of the Idolators

Allah said,

(Freedom from obligations from Allah and His Messenger ()), is a declaration of freedom from all obligations from Allah and His Messenger ,

(to those of the Mushrikin, with whom you made a treaty. So travel freely (Mushrikin) for four months (as you will) throughout the land) (9:1-2). This Ayah refers to idolators who had indefinite treaties and those, whose treaties with Muslims ended in less than four months. The terms of these treaties were restricted to four months only. As for those whose term of peace ended at a specific date later (than the four months), then their treaties would end when their terms ended, no matter how long afterwards, for Allah said,

(So fulfill their treaty for them until the end of their term)(9:4). So whoever had a coventant with Allah's Messenger then it would last until its period expired, this was reported from Muhammad bin Ka`b Al-Qurazi and others. We will also mention a

Chapter 9: At-Tawba (Repentance), Verses 001-092

Hadith on this matter. Abu Ma`shar Al-Madani said that Muhammad bin Ka`b Al-Qurazi and several others said, "The Messenger of Allah sent Abu Bakr to lead the Hajj rituals on the ninth year (of Hijrah). He also sent `Ali bin Abi Talib with thirty or forty Ayat from Bara'ah (At-Tawbah), and he recited them to the people, giving the idolators four months during which they freely move about in the land. He recited these Ayat on the day of `Arafah (ninth of Dhul-Hijjah). The idolators were given twenty more days (till the end) of Dhul-Hijjah, Muharram, Safar, Rabi` Al-Awwal and ten days from Rabi` Ath-Thani. He proclaimed to them in their camping areas, `No Mushrik will be allowed to perform Hajj after this year, nor a naked person to perform Tawaf around the House.'" So Allah said,

Surah: 9 Ayah: 3

﴿ وَأَذَٰنٌ مِّنَ ٱللَّهِ وَرَسُولِهِۦٓ إِلَى ٱلنَّاسِ يَوْمَ ٱلْحَجِّ ٱلْأَكْبَرِ أَنَّ ٱللَّهَ بَرِىٓءٌ مِّنَ ٱلْمُشْرِكِينَ ۙ وَرَسُولُهُۥ ۚ فَإِن تُبْتُمْ فَهُوَ خَيْرٌ لَّكُمْ ۖ وَإِن تَوَلَّيْتُمْ فَٱعْلَمُوٓاْ أَنَّكُمْ غَيْرُ مُعْجِزِى ٱللَّهِ ۗ وَبَشِّرِ ٱلَّذِينَ كَفَرُواْ بِعَذَابٍ أَلِيمٍ ﴾

3. And a declaration from Allâh and His Messenger to mankind on the greatest day (the 10th of Dhul-Hijjah - the 12th month of Islâmic calendar) that Allâh is free from (all) obligations to the Mushrikûn (See V.2:105) and so is His Messenger. So if you (Mushrikûn) repent, it is better for you, but if you turn away, then know that you cannot escape (from the Punishment of) Allâh. And give tidings (O Muhammad (peace be upon him)) of a painful torment to those who disbelieve.

Transliteration

3. Waathanun mina Allahi warasoolihi ila alnnasi yawma alhajji al-akbari anna Allaha baree-on mina almushrikeena warasooluhu fa-in tubtum fahuwa khayrun lakum wa-in tawallaytum faiAAlamoo annakum ghayru muAAjizee Allahi wabashshiri allatheena kafaroo biAAathabin aleemin

Tafsir Ibn Kathir

Allah says, this is a declaration,

(from Allah and His Messenger), and a preface warning to the people,

(on the greatest day of Hajj), the day of Sacrifice, the best and most apparent day of the Hajj rituals, during which the largest gathering confers.

(that Allah is free from (all) obligations to the Mushrikin and so is His Messenger.) also free from all obligations to them. Allah next invites the idolators to repent,

(So if you repent), from the misguidance and Shirk you indulge in,

(it is better for you, but if you turn away), and persist on your ways, (then know that you cannot escape Allah) Rather, Allah is capable over you, and you are all in His grasp, under His power and will,

(And give tidings of a painful torment for those who disbelieve) earning them disgrace and affliction in this life and the torment of chains and barbed iron bars in the Hereafter. Al-Bukhari recorded that Abu Hurayrah said, "Abu Bakr sent me during that Hajj with those dispatched on the day of Sacrifice to declare in Mina that no Mushrik will be allowed to attend Hajj after that year, nor will a naked person be allowed to perform Tawaf." Humayd said, "The Prophet then sent `Ali bin Abi Talib and commanded him to announce Bara'ah." Abu Hurayrah said, "Ali publicized Bara'ah with us to the gathering in Mina on the day of Sacrifice, declaring that no Mushrik shall perform Hajj after that year, nor shall a naked person perform Tawaf around the House." Al-Bukhari also collected this Hadith the this narration of which, Abu Hurayrah said, "On the day of Nahr, Abu Bakr sent me along with other announcers to Mina to make a public announcement that `No pagan is allowed to perform Hajj after this year, and no naked person is allowed to perform the Tawaf around the Ka`bah.' Abu Bakr was leading the people in that Hajj season, and in the year of `The Farewell Hajj' when the Prophet performed Hajj, no Mushrik performed Hajj.'" This is the narration that Al-Bukhari recorded in the Book on Jihad. Muhammad bin Ishaq reported a narration from Abu Ja`far Muhammad bin `Ali bin Al-Husayn who said, "When Bara'ah was revealed to Allah's Messenger , and he had sent Abu Bakr to oversee the Hajj rites for the people, he was asked, `O Messenger of Allah! Why not send this (message) to Abu Bakr' So he said,

«لَا يُؤَدِّي عَنِّي إِلَّا رَجُلٌ مِنْ أَهْلِ بَيْتِي»

(It will not be accepted to have been from me if it is not from a man from my family.) Then he called for `Ali and said to him,

«اخْرُجْ بِهذِهِ الْقِصَّةِ مِنْ صَدْرِ بَرَاءَةَ وَأَذِّنْ فِي النَّاسِ يَوْمَ النَّحْرِ إِذَا اجْتَمَعُوا بِمِنًى، أَنَّهُ لَا يَدْخُلُ الْجَنَّةَ كَافِرٌ، وَلَا يَحُجُّ بَعْدَ الْعَامِ مُشْرِكٌ، وَلَا يَطُوفُ بِالْبَيْتِ عُرْيَانٌ، وَمَنْ كَانَ لَهُ عِنْدَ رَسُولِ اللهِ صلى الله عليه وسلّم عَهْدٌ فَهُوَ لَهُ إِلَى مُدَّتِه»

(Take this section from the beginning of Bara'ah and proclaim to the people on the day of the Sacrifice while they are gathered at Mina that no disbeliever will enter Paradise, no idolator will be permitted to perform Hajj after the year, there will be no Tawaf while naked, and whoever has a covenant with Allah's Messenger, then it shall be valid until the time of its expiration.) `Ali rode the camel of Allah's Messenger named Al-`Adba' until he caught up with Abu Bakr in route. When Abu Bakr saw him he said, `Are you here as a commander or a follower.' `Ali replied, `A follower.' They

Chapter 9: At-Tawba (Repentance), Verses 001-092

continued on. Abu Bakr lead the people in Hajj while the Arabs were camping in their normal locations from Jahiliyyah. On the day of Sacrifice, `Ali bin Abi Talib stood and proclaimed, `O people! No disbeliever will be admitted into Paradise, no idolator will be permitted to perform Hajj next year, there shall be no Tawaf while naked, and whoever has a covenant with Allah's Messenger , then it shall be valid until its time of expiration.' So no idolator performed Hajj after that year, Tawaf around the House while naked ceased. Then they returned to Allah's Messenger . So this was the declaration of innocence, whoever among the idolators had no treaty, then he had a treaty of peace for one year, if he had a particular treaty, then it was valid until its date of expiration."

Surah: 9 Ayah: 4

﴿ إِلَّا ٱلَّذِينَ عَٰهَدتُّم مِّنَ ٱلۡمُشۡرِكِينَ ثُمَّ لَمۡ يَنقُصُوكُمۡ شَيۡـًٔا وَلَمۡ يُظَٰهِرُواْ عَلَيۡكُمۡ أَحَدٗا فَأَتِمُّوٓاْ إِلَيۡهِمۡ عَهۡدَهُمۡ إِلَىٰ مُدَّتِهِمۡۚ إِنَّ ٱللَّهَ يُحِبُّ ٱلۡمُتَّقِينَ ﴾

4. Except those of the Mushrikûn (See V.2:105) with whom you have a treaty, and who have not subsequently failed you in aught, nor have supported anyone against you. So fulfill their treaty to them for the end of their term. Surely Allâh loves Al-Mattaqûn (the pious - See V.2:2).

Transliteration

4. Illa allatheena AAahadtum mina almushrikeena thumma lam yanqusookum shay-an walam yuthahiroo AAalaykum ahadan faatimmoo ilayhim AAahdahum ila muddatihim inna Allaha yuhibbu almuttaqeena

Tafsir Ibn Kathir

Existing Peace Treaties remained valid until the End of Their Term

This is an exception regulating the longest extent of time for those who have a general treaty - with out time mentioned - to four months. They would have four months to travel the lands in search of sanctuary for themselves wherever they wish. Those whose treaty mentioned a specifec limited term, then the longest it would extend was to the point of its agreed upon termination date. Hadiths in this regard preceeded. So anyone who had a treaty with Allah's Messenger , it lasted until its specific termination date. However, those in this category were required to refrain from breaking the terms of the agreement with Muslims and from helping non-Muslims against Muslims. This is the type whose peace agreement with Muslims was carried out to its end. Allah encouraged honoring such peace treaties, saying,

(Surely, Allah loves those who have Taqwa) (9:4), who keep their promises.

Surah: 9 Ayah: 5

﴿ فَإِذَا ٱنسَلَخَ ٱلْأَشْهُرُ ٱلْحُرُمُ فَٱقْتُلُواْ ٱلْمُشْرِكِينَ حَيْثُ وَجَدتُّمُوهُمْ وَخُذُوهُمْ وَٱحْصُرُوهُمْ وَٱقْعُدُواْ لَهُمْ كُلَّ مَرْصَدٍ ۚ فَإِن تَابُواْ وَأَقَامُواْ ٱلصَّلَوٰةَ وَءَاتَوُاْ ٱلزَّكَوٰةَ فَخَلُّواْ سَبِيلَهُمْ ۚ إِنَّ ٱللَّهَ غَفُورٌ رَّحِيمٌ ﴾

5. Then when the Sacred Months (the 1st, 7th, 11th, and 12th months of the Islâmic calendar) have passed, then kill the Mushrikûn (See V.2:105) wherever you find them, and capture them and besiege them, and lie in wait for them in each and every ambush. But if they repent and perform As-Salât (Iqâmat-as-Salât), and give Zakât, then leave their way free. Verily, Allâh is Oft-Forgiving, Most Merciful.

Transliteration

5. Fa-itha insalakha al-ashhuru alhurumu faoqtuloo almushrikeena haythu wajadtumoohum wakhuthoohum waohsuroohum waoqAAudoo lahum kulla marsadin fa-in taboo waaqamoo alssalata waatawoo alzzakata fakhalloo sabeelahum inna Allaha ghafoorun raheemun

Tafsir Ibn Kathir

This is the Ayah of the Sword

Mujahid, `Amr bin Shu`ayb, Muhammad bin Ishaq, Qatadah, As-Suddi and `Abdur-Rahman bin Zayd bin Aslam said that the four months mentioned in this Ayah are the four-month grace period mentioned in the earlier Ayah,

(So travel freely for four months throughout the land.) Allah said next,

(So when the Sacred Months have passed...), meaning, `Upon the end of the four months during which We prohibited you from fighting the idolators, and which is the grace period We gave them, then fight and kill the idolators wherever you may find them.' Allah's statement next,

(then fight the Mushrikin wherever you find them), means, on the earth in general, except for the Sacred Area, for Allah said,

(And fight not with them at Al-Masjid Al-Haram, unless they fight you there. But if they attack you, then fight them.)(2:191) Allah said here,

(and capture them), executing some and keeping some as prisoners,

(and besiege them, and lie in wait for them in each and every ambush), do not wait until you find them. Rather, seek and besiege them in their areas and forts, gather intelligence about them in the various roads and fairways so that what is made wide looks ever smaller to them. This way, they will have no choice, but to die or embrace Islam,

(But if they repent and perform the Salah, and give the Zakah, then leave their way free. Verily, Allah is Oft-Forgiving, Most Merciful.) Abu Bakr As-Siddiq used this and other honorable Ayat as proof for fighting those who refrained from paying the Zakah. These Ayat allowed fighting people unless, and until, they embrace Islam and implement its rulings and obligations. Allah mentioned the most important aspects of Islam here, including what is less important. Surely, the highest elements of Islam after the Two Testimonials, are the prayer, which is the right of Allah, the Exalted and Ever High, then the Zakah, which benefits the poor and needy. These are the most honorable acts that creatures perform, and this is why Allah often mentions the prayer and Zakah together. In the Two Sahihs, it is recorded that Ibn `Umar said that the Messenger of Allah said,

«أُمِرْتُ أَنْ أُقَاتِلَ النَّاسَ حَتَّى يَشْهَدُوا أَنْ لَا إِلَهَ إِلَّا اللهُ وَأَنَّ مُحَمَّدًا رَسُولُ اللهِ وَيُقِيمُوا الصَّلَاةَ وَيُؤْتُوا الزَّكَاةَ»

(I have been commanded to fight the people until they testify that there is no deity worthy of worship except Allah and that Muhammad is the Messenger of Allah, establish the prayer and pay the Zakah.) This honorable Ayah (9:5) was called the Ayah of the Sword, about which Ad-Dahhak bin Muzahim said, "It abrogated every agreement of peace between the Prophet and any idolator, every treaty, and every term." Al-`Awfi said that Ibn `Abbas commented: "No idolator had any more treaty or promise of safety ever since Surah Bara'ah was revealed. The four months, in addition to, all peace treaties conducted before Bara'ah was revealed and announced had ended by the tenth of the month of Rabi` Al-Akhir."

Surah: 9 Ayah: 6

﴿ وَإِنْ أَحَدٌ مِّنَ ٱلْمُشْرِكِينَ ٱسْتَجَارَكَ فَأَجِرْهُ حَتَّىٰ يَسْمَعَ كَلَٰمَ ٱللَّهِ ثُمَّ أَبْلِغْهُ مَأْمَنَهُۥ ذَٰلِكَ بِأَنَّهُمْ قَوْمٌ لَّا يَعْلَمُونَ ۝ ﴾

6. And if anyone of the Mushrikûn (polytheists, idolaters, pagans, disbelievers in the Oneness of Allâh) seeks your protection then grant him protection so that he may hear the Word of Allâh (the Qur'ân), and then escort him to where he can be secure, that is because they are men who know not.

Transliteration

6. Wa-in ahadun mina almushrikeena istajaraka faajirhu hatta yasmaAAa kalama Allahi thumma ablighhu ma/manahu thalika bi-annahum qawmun la yaAAlamoona

Tafsir Ibn Kathir

Idolators are granted Safe Passage if They seek It

Allah said to His Prophet, peace be upon him,

(And if anyone of the Mushrikin), whom you were commanded to fight and We allowed you their blood and property,'

(seeks your protection), asked you for safe passage, then accept his request until he hears the Words of Allah, the Qur'an. Recite the Qur'an to him and mention a good part of the religion with which you establish Allah's proof against him,

(and then escort him to where he can be secure) and safe, until he goes back to his land, his home, and area of safety,

(that is because they are men who know not.) The Ayah says, `We legislated giving such people safe passage so that they may learn about the religion of Allah, so that Allah's call will spread among His servants. Ibn Abi Najih narrated that Mujahid said that this Ayah, "Refers to someone who comes to you to hear what you say and what was revealed to you (O Muhammad). Therefore, he is safe until he comes to you, hears Allah's Words and then proceeds to the safe area where he came from." The Messenger of Allah used to thereafter grant safe passage to those who came to him for guidance or to deliver a message. On the day of Hudaybiyyah, several emissaries from Quraysh came to him, such as `Urwah bin Mas`ud, Mikraz bin Hafs, Suhayl bin `Amr and several others. They came mediating between him and the Quraysh pagans. They witnessed the great respect the Muslims had for the Prophet , which astonished them, for they never before saw such respect for anyone, kings nor czars. They went back to their people and conveyed this news to them; this, among other reasons, was one reason that most of them accepted the guidance. When Musaylimah the Liar sent an emissary to the Messenger of Allah, he asked him, "Do you testify that Musaylimah is a messenger from Allah" He said, "Yes." The Messenger of Allah said,

«لَوْلَا أَنَّ الرُّسُلَ لَا تُقْتَلُ لَضَرَبْتُ عُنُقَكَ»

(I would have cut off your head, if it was not that emissaries are not killed.) That man, Ibn An-Nawwahah, was later beheaded when `Abdullah bin Mas`ud was the governor of Al-Kufah. When it became known that he still testified that Musaylimah was a messenger from Allah, Ibn Mas`ud summoned him and said to him, "You are not delivering a message now!" He commanded that Ibn An-Nawwahah be decapitated, may Allah curse him and deprive him of His mercy. In summary, those who come from a land at war with Muslims to the area of Islam, delivering a message, for business transactions, to negotiate a peace treaty, to pay the Jizyah, to offer an end to hostilities, and so forth, and request safe passage from Muslim leaders or their deputies, should be granted safe passage, as long as they remain in Muslim areas, until they go back to their land and sanctuary.

Surah: 9 Ayah: 7

﴿ كَيْفَ يَكُونُ لِلْمُشْرِكِينَ عَهْدٌ عِندَ ٱللَّهِ وَعِندَ رَسُولِهِۦٓ إِلَّا ٱلَّذِينَ عَـٰهَدتُّمْ عِندَ ٱلْمَسْجِدِ ٱلْحَرَامِ ۖ فَمَا ٱسْتَقَـٰمُوا۟ لَكُمْ فَٱسْتَقِيمُوا۟ لَهُمْ ۚ إِنَّ ٱللَّهَ يُحِبُّ ٱلْمُتَّقِينَ ﴿٧﴾ ﴾

7. How can there be a covenant with Allâh and with His Messenger for the Mushrikûn (polytheists, idolaters, pagans, disbelievers in the Oneness of Allâh) except those with whom you made a covenant near Al-Masjid-al-Harâm (at Makkah)? So long as they are true to you, stand you true to them. Verily, Allâh loves Al-Muttaqûn (the pious - see V.2:2).

Transliteration

7. Kayfa yakoonu lilmushrikeena AAahdun AAinda Allahi waAAinda rasoolihi illa allatheena AAahadtum AAinda almasjidi alharami fama istaqamoo lakum faistaqeemoo lahum inna Allaha yuhibbu almuttaqeena

Tafsir Ibn Kathir

Affirming the Disavowel of the Idolators

Allah mentions the wisdom in dissolving all obligations to the idolators and giving them a four month period of safety, after which they will meet the sharp sword wherever they are found,

(How can there be a covenant for the Mushrikin), a safe resort and refuge, while they persist in Shirk with Allah, and disbelief in Him and His Messenger,

(except those with whom you made a covenant near Al-Masjid Al-Haram), on the day of Hudaybiyyah. Allah said in another Ayah (concerning the day of Hudaybiyyah),

(They are the ones who disbelieved and hindered you from Al-Masjid Al-Haram and detained the sacrificial animals, from reaching their place of sacrifice.) (48:25) Allah said next,

(So long as they are true to you, stand you true to them.), if they keep the terms of the treaties you conducted with them, including peace between you and them for ten years,

(then stand you true to them. Verily, Allah loves those who have Taqwa.) The Messenger of Allah and the Muslims preserved the terms of the treaty with the people of Makkah from the month of Dhul-Qa`dah in the sixth year (of Hijrah), until the Quraysh broke it and helped their allies, Banu Bakr, against Khuza`ah, the allies of Allah's Messenger . Aided by the Quraysh, Banu Bakr killed some of Bani Khuza`ah in the Sacred Area! The Messenger of Allah led an invasion army in the month of Ramadan, of the eighth year, and Allah opened the Sacred Area for him to rule over them, all thanks are due to Allah. The Messenger of Allah freed the Quraysh who embraced Islam after they were overpowered and defeated. These numbered around two thousands, and they were refered to by the name `Tulaqa' afterwards. Those among them who remained in disbelief and ran away from Allah's Messenger were sent promises of safe refuge for four months, during which they were allowed to move about freely. They included Safwan bin Umayyah, `Ikrimah bin Abi Jahl and many others. Allah later on guided them to Islam, and they became excellent believers. Surely, Allah is worthy of all praise for all His actions and decrees.

Surah: 9 Ayah: 8

﴿ كَيْفَ وَإِن يَظْهَرُواْ عَلَيْكُمْ لَا يَرْقُبُواْ فِيكُمْ إِلاًّ وَلَا ذِمَّةً يُرْضُونَكُم بِأَفْوَاهِهِمْ وَتَأْبَىٰ قُلُوبُهُمْ وَأَكْثَرُهُمْ فَاسِقُونَ ﴾

8. How (can there be such a covenant with them) that when you are overpowered by them, they regard not the ties, either of kinship or of covenant with you? With (good words from) their mouths they please you, but their hearts are averse to you, and most of them are Fâsiqûn (rebellious, disobedient to Allâh).

Transliteration

8. Kayfa wa-in yathharoo AAalaykum la yarquboo feekum illan wala thimmatan yurdoonakum bi-afwahihim wata/ba quloobuhum waaktharuhum fasiqoona

Tafsir Ibn Kathir

Allah encourages the believers to show enmity to the idolators and to dissociate from them, affirming that they do not deserve to enjoy a covenant of peace, because of their Shirk in Allah and disbelief in Allah's Messenger.

If these disbelievers have a chance to defeat Muslims, they will cause great mischief, leave nothing unharmed, disregard the ties of kinship and the sanctity of their vows. `Ali bin Abi Talhah, `Ikrimah and Al-`Awfi narrated that Ibn `Abbas said, "Ill means kinship, while, Dhimmah means covenant." Ad-Dahhak and As-Suddi said similarly.

Surah: 9 Ayah: 9, Ayah: 10 & Ayah: 11

﴿ اشْتَرَوْاْ بِـَٔايَٰتِ ٱللَّهِ ثَمَنًا قَلِيلًا فَصَدُّواْ عَن سَبِيلِهِۦٓ إِنَّهُمْ سَآءَ مَا كَانُواْ يَعْمَلُونَ ﴾

9. They have purchased with the Ayât (proofs, evidences, verses, lessons, signs, revelations, etc.) of Allâh a little gain, and they hindered men from His Way; evil indeed is that which they used to do.

﴿ لَا يَرْقُبُونَ فِى مُؤْمِنٍ إِلًّا وَلَا ذِمَّةً وَأُوْلَٰٓئِكَ هُمُ ٱلْمُعْتَدُونَ ﴾

10. With regard to a believer, they respect not the ties, either of kinship or of covenant! It is they who are the transgressors.

﴿ فَإِن تَابُوا۟ وَأَقَامُوا۟ ٱلصَّلَوٰةَ وَءَاتَوُا۟ ٱلزَّكَوٰةَ فَإِخْوَٰنُكُمْ فِى ٱلدِّينِ ۗ وَنُفَصِّلُ ٱلْءَايَٰتِ لِقَوْمٍ يَعْلَمُونَ ﴿١١﴾ ﴾

11. But if they repent, perform As-Salât (Iqâmat-as-Salât) and give Zakât, then they are your brethren in religion. (In this way) We explain the Ayât (proofs, evidences, verses, lessons, signs, revelations, etc.) in detail for a people who know.

Transliteration

9. Ishtaraw bi-ayati Allahi thamanan qaleelan fasaddoo AAan sabeelihi innahum saa ma kanoo yaAAmaloona 10. La yarquboona fee mu/minin illan wala thimmatan waola-ika humu almuAAtadoona 11. Fa-in taboo waaqamoo alssalata waatawoo alzzakata fa-ikhwanukum fee alddeeni wanufassilu al-ayati liqawmin yaAAlamoona

Tafsir Ibn Kathir

Allah admonishes the idolators and encourages the believers to fight against them because,

(They have purchased with the Ayat of Allah a little gain,) idolators exchanged following the Ayat of Allah with the lower affairs of life that they indulged in,

(and they hindered men from His way), trying to prevent the believers from following the truth,

(evil indeed is that which they used to do. With regard to a believer, they respect not the ties, either of kinship or of covenant!) (9:9-10). We explained these meanings before, as well as, the meaning of,

(But if they repent, perform the Salah...)

Surah: 9 Ayah: 12

﴿ وَإِن نَّكَثُوٓا۟ أَيْمَٰنَهُم مِّنۢ بَعْدِ عَهْدِهِمْ وَطَعَنُوا۟ فِى دِينِكُمْ فَقَٰتِلُوٓا۟ أَئِمَّةَ ٱلْكُفْرِ إِنَّهُمْ لَآ أَيْمَٰنَ لَهُمْ لَعَلَّهُمْ يَنتَهُونَ ﴿١٢﴾ ﴾

12. But if they violate their oaths after their covenant, and attack your religion with disapproval and criticism then fight (you) the leaders of disbelief (chiefs of Quraish pagans of Makkah) - for surely their oaths are nothing to them - so that they may stop (evil actions).

Transliteration

12. Wa-in nakathoo aymanahum min baAAdi AAahdihim wataAAanoo fee deenikum faqatiloo a-immata alkufri innahum la aymana lahum laAAallahum yantahoona

Tafsir Ibn Kathir

The Oaths of the Leaders of Disbelief mean nothing to Them

Allah says, if the idolators with whom you conducted peace treaties for an appointed term break

(their oaths) meaning, terms of their treaties, and covenants

(and attack your religion...) with disapproval and criticism, it is because of this that one who curses the Messenger, peace be upon him, or attacks the religion of Islam by way of criticism and disapproval, they are to be fought. This is why Allah said afterwards,

(then fight (you) against the leaders of disbelief -- for surely, their oaths are nothing to them -- so that they may stop.) so that they may refrain from the disbelief, rebellion and the transgression they indulge in. Qatadah and others said that the leaders of disbelief were Abu Jahl, `Utbah and Shaybah, Umayyah bin Khalaf, and he went on to mention several others. Al-A`mash narrated from Zayd bin Wahb from Hudhayfah; "The people of this Ayah were never fought again." A similar statement was reported from `Ali bin Abi Talib, may Allah be pleased with him. However, this Ayah is general, even though the specific reason behind revealing it was the idolators of Quraysh. So this Ayah generally applies to them and others as well, Allah knows best. Al-Walid bin Muslim said that Safwan bin `Amr narrated that `Abdur-Rahman bin Jubayr bin Nufayr said that when Abu Bakr sent an army to Ash-Sham, he advised them, "You will find some people with shaved heads. Therefore, strike the swords upon the parts that contain the devil, for by Allah, it is better to me to kill one of these people than to kill seventy other men. This is because Allah said,

(then fight (you) against the leaders of disbelief.)" Ibn Abi Hatim collected it.

Surah: 9 Ayah: 13, Ayah: 14 & Ayah: 15

﴿ أَلَا تُقَاتِلُونَ قَوْمًا نَّكَثُوٓاْ أَيْمَـٰنَهُمْ وَهَمُّواْ بِإِخْرَاجِ ٱلرَّسُولِ وَهُم بَدَءُوكُمْ أَوَّلَ مَرَّةٍ أَتَخْشَوْنَهُمْ فَٱللَّهُ أَحَقُّ أَن تَخْشَوْهُ إِن كُنتُم مُّؤْمِنِينَ ﴾

13. Will you not fight a people who have violated their oaths (pagans of Makkah) and intended to expel the Messenger while they did attack you first? Do you fear them? Allâh has more right that you should fear Him if you are believers.

﴿ قَـٰتِلُوهُمْ يُعَذِّبْهُمُ ٱللَّهُ بِأَيْدِيكُمْ وَيُخْزِهِمْ وَيَنصُرْكُمْ عَلَيْهِمْ وَيَشْفِ صُدُورَ قَوْمٍ مُّؤْمِنِينَ ﴾

14. Fight against them so that Allâh will punish them by your hands and disgrace them and give you victory over them and heal the breasts of a believing people,

Chapter 9: At-Tawba (Repentance), Verses 001-092

﴿ وَيُذْهِبْ غَيْظَ قُلُوبِهِمْ ۗ وَيَتُوبُ ٱللَّهُ عَلَىٰ مَن يَشَآءُ ۗ وَٱللَّهُ عَلِيمٌ حَكِيمٌ ۝ ﴾

15. And remove the anger of their (believers') hearts. Allâh accepts the repentance of whom He wills. Allâh is All-Knowing, All-Wise.

Transliteration

13. Ala tuqatiloona qawman nakathoo aymanahum wahammoo bi-ikhraji alrrasooli wahum badaookum awwala marratin atakhshawnahum faAllahu ahaqqu an takhshawhu in kuntum mu/mineena 14. Qatiloohum yuAAaththibhumu Allahu bi-aydeekum wayukhzihim wayansurkum AAalayhim wayashfi sudoora qawmin mu/mineena 15. Wayuthhib ghaytha quloobihim wayatoobu Allahu AAala man yashao waAllahu AAaleemun hakeemun

Tafsir Ibn Kathir

Encouragement to fight the Disbelievers, and some Benefits of fighting Them

These Ayat encourage, direct and recommend fighting against the idolators who break the terms of their covenants, those who tried to expel the Messenger from Makkah. Allah said in other Ayat,

(And (remember) when the disbelievers plotted against you to imprison you, or to kill you, or to expell you; they were plotting and Allah too was plotting; and Allah is the best of those who plot.) (8:30),

(...and have driven out the Messenger and yourselves (from your homeland) because you believe in Allah your Lord!) (60:1), and,

(And verily, they were about to frighten you so much as to drive you out from the land.) (17:76) Allah's statement,

(while they did attack you first), refers to the battle of Badr when the idolators marched to protect their caravan. When they knew that their caravan escaped safely, they still went ahead with their intent to fight Muslims out of arrogance, as we mentioned before. It was also said that these Ayat refer to the idolators breaking the peace agreement with Muslims and aiding Bani Bakr, their allies, against Khuza`ah, the ally of the Messenger of Allah . This is why the Messenger of Allah marched to Makkah in the year of the victory, thus conquering it, all thanks and praise is due to Allah. Allah said,

(Do you fear them Allah has more right that you should fear Him if you are believers.) Allah says here, `Do not fear idolators, but fear Me instead, for I am worthy of being feared by the servants due to My might and punishment. In My Hand lies the matter; whatever I will occurs, and whatever I do not will does not occur.' Allah next said, while ordering the believers and explaining the wisdom of ordaining Jihad against them, all the while able to destroy their enemies with a command from Him,

(Fight against them so that Allah will punish them by your hands, and disgrace them and give you victory over them, and heal the breasts of a believing people.) This Ayah includes all believers, even though Mujahid, `Ikrimah and As-Suddi said that it refers to Khuza`ah. Concerning the believers, Allah said;

(and remove the anger of their hearts), then

(Allah accepts the repentance of whom He wills), from His servants,

(Allah is All-Knowing), in what benefits His servants,

(All-Wise), in His actions and statements, whether narrative or legislative. Allah does what He wills, decides what He wills, and He is the Just Who never wrongs any. Not even the weight of an atom of good or evil is ever neglected with Him, but rather, He compensates for it in this life and the Hereafter.

Surah: 9 Ayah: 16

﴿ أَمْ حَسِبْتُمْ أَن تُتْرَكُواْ وَلَمَّا يَعْلَمِ ٱللَّهُ ٱلَّذِينَ جَـٰهَدُواْ مِنكُمْ وَلَمْ يَتَّخِذُواْ مِن دُونِ ٱللَّهِ وَلَا رَسُولِهِۦ وَلَا ٱلْمُؤْمِنِينَ وَلِيجَةً وَٱللَّهُ خَبِيرٌۢ بِمَا تَعْمَلُونَ ﴾

16. Do you think that you shall be left alone while Allâh has not yet tested those among you who have striven hard and fought and have not taken Walîjah ((Bitânah - helpers, advisors and consultants from disbelievers, pagans.) giving openly to them their secrets) besides Allâh and His Messenger, and the believers. Allâh is Well-Acquainted with what you do.

Transliteration

16. Am hasibtum an tutrakoo walamma yaAAlami Allahu allatheena jahadoo minkum walam yattakhithoo min dooni Allahi wala rasoolihi wala almu/mineena waleejatan waAllahu khabeerun bima taAAmaloona

Tafsir Ibn Kathir

Among the Wisdom of Jihad is to test the Muslims

Allah said,

(Do you think), O believers that We will leave you untested with matters that make apparent those who have pure, good intent from those who have false intent This is why Allah said next,

(while Allah has not yet tested those among you who have striven hard and fought and have not taken Walijah besides Allah and His Messenger, and the believers...), meaning, supporters and confidants. Rather, they are sincere for Allah and His Messenger inwardly and outwardly. Allah also said;

(Alif-Lam-Mim. Do people think that they will be left alone because they say: "We believe," and will not be tested. And We indeed tested those who were before them.

Chapter 9: At-Tawba (Repentance), Verses 001-092

And Allah will certainly make known those who are true, and will certainly make known those who are liars...) (29:1-3),

(Do you think that you will enter Paradise before Allah tests those of you who fought (in His cause) and (also) tests those who are patient)(3: 142), and,

(Allah will not leave the believers in the state in which you are now, until He distinguishes the wicked from the good)(3:179). In summary, since Allah legislated Jihad for His servants, He explained that the wisdom behind doing so includes testing His servants, distinguishing between those who obey Him and those who disobey Him. Allah, the Exalted, is the All-Knower of what occurred, what will occur, and the true essence of what might occur had He decided it. Therefore, Allah knows everything before it occurs and how it will occur, there is no deity worthy of worship except Him, nor a Lord except Him. Truly, there is none who can avert Allah's judgment and decision.

Surah: 9 Ayah: 17 & Ayah: 18

﴿ مَا كَانَ لِلْمُشْرِكِينَ أَن يَعْمُرُوا مَسَاجِدَ ٱللَّهِ شَاهِدِينَ عَلَىٰ أَنفُسِهِم بِٱلْكُفْرِ أُوْلَٰٓئِكَ حَبِطَتْ أَعْمَالُهُمْ وَفِى ٱلنَّارِ هُمْ خَالِدُونَ ۝ ﴾

17. It is not for the Mushrikûn (polytheists, idolaters, pagans, disbelievers in the Oneness of Allâh), to maintain the Mosques of Allâh (i.e. to pray and worship Allâh therein, to look after their cleanliness and their building,), while they witness against their own selves of disbelief. The works of such are in vain and in Fire shall they abide.

﴿ إِنَّمَا يَعْمُرُ مَسَاجِدَ ٱللَّهِ مَنْ ءَامَنَ بِٱللَّهِ وَٱلْيَوْمِ ٱلْءَاخِرِ وَأَقَامَ ٱلصَّلَوٰةَ وَءَاتَى ٱلزَّكَوٰةَ وَلَمْ يَخْشَ إِلَّا ٱللَّهَ فَعَسَىٰ أُوْلَٰٓئِكَ أَن يَكُونُوا مِنَ ٱلْمُهْتَدِينَ ۝ ﴾

18. The Mosques of Allâh shall be maintained only by those who believe in Allâh and the Last Day, perform As-Salât (Iqâmat-as-Salât), and give Zakât and fear none but Allâh. It is they who are expected to be on true guidance.

Transliteration

17. Ma kana lilmushrikeena an yaAAmuroo masajida Allahi shahideena AAala anfusihim bialkufri ola-ika habitat aAAmaluhum wafee alnnari hum khalidoona 18. Innama yaAAmuru masajida Allahi man amana biAllahi waalyawmi al-akhiri waaqama alssalata waata alzzakata walam yakhsha illa Allaha faAAasa ola-ika an yakoonoo mina almuhtadeena

Tafsir Ibn Kathir

It is not for Idolators to maintain the Masjids of Allah

Allah says that it is not fitting that those who associate others with Allah in worship should maintain the Masjids of Allah that were built in His Name alone without partners. Those who read the Ayah, "Masjid Allah", said that it refers to Al-Masjid Al-Haram, the most honored Masjid on the earth, which was built, from the first day, for the purpose of worshipping Allah alone without partners. It was built by Khalil Ar-Rahman (the Prophet Ibrahim) peace be upon him. The idolators do this while they themselves testify to their disbelief with their statements and actions. As-Suddi said, "If you ask a Christian, `What is your religion', He will tell you he is a Christian. If you ask a Jew about his religion, he will say he is a Jew, and the same for a Sabi' and a Mushrik!'"

(The works of such are in vain), because of their Shirk,

(and in Fire shall they abide.) Allah said in another Ayah,

(And why should not Allah punish them while they hinder (men) from Al-Masjid Al-Haram, and they are not its guardians None can be its guardians except those with Taqwa, but most of them know not.)(8:34).

Believers are the True Maintainers of the Masjids

Allah said,

(The Masjids of Allah shall be maintained only by those who believe in Allah and the Last Day.) Therefore, Allah testifies to the faith of those who maintain the Masjids. `Abdur-Razzaq narrated that `Amr bin Maymun Al-Awdi said, "I met the Companions of the Prophet and they were saying, `The Masjids are the Houses of Allah on the earth. It is a promise from Allah that He is generous to those who visit Him in the Masjids.," Allah said next,

(perform the Salah), one of the major acts of worship practiced by the body,

(and give the Zakah), which is the best act that benefits other people,

(and fear none but Allah), they fear only Allah, the Exalted, and none else,

(It is they who are on true guidance.) `Ali bin Abi Talhah said that Ibn `Abbas said about Allah's statement,

(The Masjids of Allah shall be maintained only by those who believe in Allah and the Last Day;) "He who singles out Allah (in worship), has faith in the Last Day." (And he said); "He who believes in what Allah has revealed,

(perform the Salah), establishes the five daily prayers,

(and fear none but Allah.), worships Allah alone,

(it may be they who are on true guidance.) Allah says, `It is they who are the successful ones in truth.' Similarly, Allah said to His Prophet ,

(It may be that your Lord will raise you to Maqam Mahmud)(17:79). Allah says here, `Your Lord (O Muhammad) shall grant you a station of praise, that is, the intercession (on the Day of Resurrection).' Every `might' in the Qur'an means `shall'."

Surah: 9 Ayah: 19, Ayah: 20, Ayah: 21 & Ayah: 22

﴿ ۞ أَجَعَلْتُمْ سِقَايَةَ ٱلْحَاجِّ وَعِمَارَةَ ٱلْمَسْجِدِ ٱلْحَرَامِ كَمَنْ ءَامَنَ بِٱللَّهِ وَٱلْيَوْمِ ٱلْءَاخِرِ وَجَـٰهَدَ فِى سَبِيلِ ٱللَّهِ ۚ لَا يَسْتَوُۥنَ عِندَ ٱللَّهِ ۗ وَٱللَّهُ لَا يَهْدِى ٱلْقَوْمَ ٱلظَّـٰلِمِينَ ﴾

19. Do you consider the providing of drinking water to the pilgrims and the maintenance of Al-Masjid-al-Harâm (at Makkah) as equal to the worth of those who believe in Allâh and the Last Day, and strive hard and fight in the Cause of Allâh? They are not equal before Allâh. And Allâh guides not those people who are the Zâlimûn (polytheists and wrong-doers).

﴿ ٱلَّذِينَ ءَامَنُوا۟ وَهَاجَرُوا۟ وَجَـٰهَدُوا۟ فِى سَبِيلِ ٱللَّهِ بِأَمْوَٰلِهِمْ وَأَنفُسِهِمْ أَعْظَمُ دَرَجَةً عِندَ ٱللَّهِ ۚ وَأُو۟لَـٰٓئِكَ هُمُ ٱلْفَآئِزُونَ ﴾

20. Those who believed (in the Oneness of Allâh - Islâmic Monotheism) and emigrated and strove hard and fought in Allâh's Cause with their wealth and their lives are far higher in degree with Allâh. They are the successful.

﴿ يُبَشِّرُهُمْ رَبُّهُم بِرَحْمَةٍ مِّنْهُ وَرِضْوَٰنٍ وَجَنَّـٰتٍ لَّهُمْ فِيهَا نَعِيمٌ مُّقِيمٌ ﴾

21. Their Lord gives them glad tidings of a Mercy from Him, and His being pleased (with them), and of Gardens (Paradise) for them wherein are everlasting delights.

﴿ خَـٰلِدِينَ فِيهَآ أَبَدًا ۚ إِنَّ ٱللَّهَ عِندَهُۥٓ أَجْرٌ عَظِيمٌ ﴾

22. They will dwell therein forever. Verily, with Allâh is a great reward.

Transliteration

19. AjaAAaltum siqayata alhajji waAAimarata almasjidi alharami kaman amana biAllahi waalyawmi al-akhiri wajahada fee sabeeli Allahi la yastawoona AAinda Allahi waAllahu la yahdee alqawma aiththalimeena 20. Allatheena amanoo wahajaroo wajahadoo fee sabeeli Allahi bi-amwalihim waanfusihim aAAthamu darajatan AAinda Allahi waola-ika humu alfa-izoona 21. Yubashshiruhum rabbuhum birahmatin minhu waridwanin wajannatin lahum feeha naAAeemun muqeemun 22. Khalideena feeha abadan inna Allaha AAindahu ajrun AAatheemun

Tafsir Ibn Kathir

Providing Pilgrims with Water and maintaining the Sacred Masjid are not equal to Faith and Jihad

In his Tafsir, Al-`Awfi reported that Ibn `Abbas explained this Ayah: "The idolators said, `Maintaining Al-Masjid Al-Haram and providing water for pilgrims are better than embracing the faith and performing Jihad.' They used to boast and show off among the people because they claimed, they were the people and maintainers of Al-Masjid Al-Haram. Allah mentioned their arrogance and rejection (of the faith), saying to 'the people of Al-Haram', who were idolators,

(Indeed My Ayat used to be recited to you, but you used to turn back on your heels (denying them, and refusing to listen to them with hatred). In pride, talking evil about it (the Qur'an) by night.) (23:66-67). They used to boast about being those who maintained the Sacred Sanctuary,

(talking about it by night). They used to talk about this by night while shunning the Qur'an and the Prophet . Allah declared that faith and Jihad with the Prophet are better than the idolators' maintaining Al-Masjid Al-Haram and providing water for pilgrims. These actions -- maintaining and serving Allah's House -- will not benefit them with Allah because they associate others with Him. Allah the Exalted said,

(They are not equal before Allah. And Allah guides not those people who are the wrongdoers.) those who claimed they are the maintainers of the House. Allah described them with injustice, on account of their Shirk, and thus, their maintaining the Masjid will not avail them." `Ali bin Abi Talhah reported that Ibn `Abbas said, "This Ayah was revealed about Al-`Abbas bin `Abdul-Muttalib, for when he was captured in the battle of Badr, he said, `If you rushed before us to embrace Islam, perform Hijrah and Jihad, we were maintaining Al-Masjid Al-Haram, providing water for the pilgrims and setting the indebted free.' Allah, the Exalted and Ever High, said,

(Do you consider the providing of drinking water to the pilgrims), until,

(and Allah guides not those people who are the wrongdoers). Allah says, `All these actions were performed while committing Shirk, and I do not accept the (good deeds) that are performed while in a state of Shirk.'" Ad-Dahhak bin Muzahim said, "Muslims came to Al-`Abbas and his friends who were captured during the battle of Badr and admonished them for their Shirk. Al-`Abbas said, `By Allah! We used to maintain Al-Masjid Al-Haram, release the indebted, serve the House (or cover it, or maintain it) and provide water for pilgrims.' Allah revealed this verse,

(Do you consider the providing of drinking water to the pilgrims...)'" There is a Hadith (from the Prophet) about the Tafsir of this Ayah that we should mention. `Abdur-Razzaq recorded that An-Nu`man bin Bashir said that a man said, "I do not care if I do not perform an action after embracing Islam other than providing drinking water for pilgrims (who visit the Ka`bah at Makkah)." Another man said, "I do not care if I do not perform an action after embracing Islam other than maintaining Al-Masjid Al-Haram." A third man said, "Jihad in the cause of Allah is more righteous than what you have said." `Umar admonished them, "Do not raise your voices next to the Minbar of the Messenger of Allah," and as it was a Friday, he said, "but after we pray the Friday prayer, we will go to the Prophet and ask him." This verse was revealed,

(Do you consider the providing of drinking water to the pilgrims and the maintenance of Al-Masjid Al-Haram), until,

(They are not equal before Allah.)

Chapter 9: At-Tawba (Repentance), Verses 001-092

Surah: 9 Ayah: 23 & Ayah: 24

﴿ يَٰٓأَيُّهَا ٱلَّذِينَ ءَامَنُوا۟ لَا تَتَّخِذُوٓا۟ ءَابَآءَكُمْ وَإِخْوَٰنَكُمْ أَوْلِيَآءَ إِنِ ٱسْتَحَبُّوا۟ ٱلْكُفْرَ عَلَى ٱلْإِيمَٰنِ ۚ وَمَن يَتَوَلَّهُم مِّنكُمْ فَأُو۟لَٰٓئِكَ هُمُ ٱلظَّٰلِمُونَ ﴾ ﴿٢٣﴾

23. O you who believe! Take not for Auliyâ' (supporters and helpers) your fathers and your brothers if they prefer disbelief to Belief. And whoever of you does so, then he is one of the Zâlimûn (wrong-doers).

﴿ قُلْ إِن كَانَ ءَابَآؤُكُمْ وَأَبْنَآؤُكُمْ وَإِخْوَٰنُكُمْ وَأَزْوَٰجُكُمْ وَعَشِيرَتُكُمْ وَأَمْوَٰلٌ ٱقْتَرَفْتُمُوهَا وَتِجَٰرَةٌ تَخْشَوْنَ كَسَادَهَا وَمَسَٰكِنُ تَرْضَوْنَهَآ أَحَبَّ إِلَيْكُم مِّنَ ٱللَّهِ وَرَسُولِهِۦ وَجِهَادٍ فِى سَبِيلِهِۦ فَتَرَبَّصُوا۟ حَتَّىٰ يَأْتِىَ ٱللَّهُ بِأَمْرِهِۦ ۗ وَٱللَّهُ لَا يَهْدِى ٱلْقَوْمَ ٱلْفَٰسِقِينَ ﴾ ﴿٢٤﴾

24. Say: If your fathers, your sons, your brothers, your wives, your kindred, the wealth that you have gained, the commerce in which you fear a decline, and the dwellings in which you delight are dearer to you than Allâh and His Messenger, and striving hard and fighting in His Cause, then wait until Allâh brings about His Decision (torment). And Allâh guides not the people who are Al-Fâsiqûn (the rebellious, disobedient to Allâh).

Transliteration

23. Ya ayyuha allatheena amanoo la tattakhithoo abaakum wa-ikhwanakum awliyaa ini istahabboo alkufra AAala al-eemani waman yatawallahum minkum faola-ika humu alththalimoona   24. Qul in kana abaokum waabnaokum wa-ikhwanukum waazwajukum waAAasheeratukum waamwalun iqtaraftumooha watijaratun takhshawna kasadaha wamasakinu tardawnaha ahabba ilaykum mina Allahi warasoolihi wajihadin fee sabeelihi fatarabbasoo hatta ya/tiya Allahu bi-amrihi waAllahu la yahdee alqawma alfasiqeena

Tafsir Ibn Kathir

The Prohibition of taking the Idolators as Supporters, even with Relatives

Allah commands shunning the disbelievers, even if they are one's parents or children, and prohibits taking them as supporters if they choose disbelief instead of faith. Allah warns,

i(You will not find any people who believe in Allah and the Last Day, making friendship with those who oppose Allah and His Messenger, even though they were their fathers or their sons or their brothers or their kindred (people). For such He has written (predetermined) faith in their hearts, and strengthened them with a Ruh (proof, light and true guidance) from Himself. And He will admit them to Gardens (Paradise) under which rivers flow.) (58:22) Al-Hafiz Al-Bayhaqi recorded that `Abdullah bin Shawdhab said, "The father of Abu `Ubaydah bin Al-Jarrah was repeatedly praising the idols to his son on the day of Badr, and Abu `Ubaydah kept avoiding him. When Al-Jarrah persisted, his son Abu `Ubaydah headed towards him and killed him. Allah revealed this Ayah in his case,

(You will not find any people who believe in Allah and the Last Day, making friendship with those who oppose Allah and His Messenger.")(58:22) Allah commanded His Messenger to warn those who prefer their family, relatives or tribe to Allah, His Messenger and Jihad in His cause,

(Say: If your fathers, your sons, your brothers, your wives, your kindred, the wealth that you have gained), amassed and collected,

(the commerce in which you fear a decline, and the dwellings in which you delight), and prefer and love because they are comfortable and good. If all these things,

(are dearer to you than Allah and His Messenger, and striving hard and fighting in His cause, then wait...) for what will befall you of Allah's punishment and torment,

(until Allah brings about His decision. And Allah guides not the people who are rebellious.) Imam Ahmad recorded that Zuhrah bin Ma`bad said that his grandfather said, "We were with the Messenger of Allah , while he was holding the hand of `Umar bin Al-Khattab. `Umar said, `By Allah! You, O Messenger of Allah, are dearer to me than everything, except for myself.' The Messenger of Allah said,

«لَا يُؤْمِنُ أَحَدُكُمْ حَتَّى أَكُونَ أَحَبَّ إِلَيْهِ مِنْ نَفْسِه»

(None among you will attain faith until I become dearer to him than even himself.) `Umar said, `Verily, now, you are dearer to me than myself, by Allah!' The Messenger of Allah said,

«الْآنَ يَا عُمَر»

(Now, O `Umar!)" Al-Bukhari also collected this Hadith. Imam Ahmad and Abu Dawud (this is the version of Abu Dawud) recorded that Ibn `Umar said, "I heard the Messenger of Allah saying,

«إِذَا تَبَايَعْتُمْ بِالْعِينَةِ وَأَخَذْتُمْ بِأَذْنَابِ الْبَقَرِ وَرَضِيتُمْ بِالزَّرْعِ، وَتَرَكْتُمُ الْجِهَادَ سَلَّطَ اللهُ عَلَيْكُمْ ذُلًّا لَا يَنْزِعُهُ حَتَّى تَرْجِعُوا إِلَى دِينِكُم»

(If you transact in `Iynah (a type of Riba), follow the tails of cows (tilling the land), become content with agriculture and abandoned Jihad, Allah will send on you disgrace that He will not remove until, you return to your religion.)"

Surah: 9 Ayah: 25, Ayah: 26 & Ayah: 27

﴿ لَقَدْ نَصَرَكُمُ ٱللَّهُ فِى مَوَاطِنَ كَثِيرَةٍ وَيَوْمَ حُنَيْنٍ إِذْ أَعْجَبَتْكُمْ كَثْرَتُكُمْ فَلَمْ تُغْنِ عَنكُمْ شَيْئًا وَضَاقَتْ عَلَيْكُمُ ٱلْأَرْضُ بِمَا رَحُبَتْ ثُمَّ وَلَّيْتُم مُّدْبِرِينَ ۝ ﴾

25. Truly Allâh has given you victory on many battle fields, and on the Day of Hunain (battle) when you rejoiced at your great number, but it availed you naught and the earth, vast as it is, was straitened for you, then you turned back in flight.

﴿ ثُمَّ أَنزَلَ ٱللَّهُ سَكِينَتَهُ عَلَىٰ رَسُولِهِ وَعَلَى ٱلْمُؤْمِنِينَ وَأَنزَلَ جُنُودًا لَّمْ تَرَوْهَا وَعَذَّبَ ٱلَّذِينَ كَفَرُوا۟ وَذَٰلِكَ جَزَآءُ ٱلْكَافِرِينَ ۝ ﴾

26. Then Allâh did send down His Sakînah (calmness, tranquillity and reassurance) on the Messenger (Muhammad (peace be upon him)) and on the believers, and sent down forces (angels) which you saw not, and punished the disbelievers. Such is the recompense of disbelievers.

﴿ ثُمَّ يَتُوبُ ٱللَّهُ مِنۢ بَعْدِ ذَٰلِكَ عَلَىٰ مَن يَشَآءُ وَٱللَّهُ غَفُورٌ رَّحِيمٌ ۝ ﴾

27. Then after that Allâh will accept the repentance of whom He wills. And Allâh is Oft-Forgiving, Most Merciful.

Transliteration

25. Laqad nasarakumu Allahu fee mawatina katheeratin wayawma hunaynin ith aAAjabatkum kathratukum falam tughni AAankum shay-an wadaqat AAalaykumu al-ardu bima rahubat thumma wallaytum mudbireena   26. Thumma anzala Allahu sakeenatahu AAala rasoolihi waAAala almu/mineena waanzala junoodan lam tarawha waAAaththaba allatheena kafaroo wathalika jazao alkafireena   27. Thumma yatoobu Allahu min baAAdi thalika AAala man yashao waAllahu ghafoorun raheemun

Tafsir Ibn Kathir

The Outcome of Victory by Way of the Unseen Aid

Ibn Jurayj reported from Mujahid that this was the first Ayah of Bara'ah in which Allah, the Exalted, reminds the believers how He favored and blessed them by giving them victory in many battles with His Messenger . Allah mentioned that victory comes from Him, by His aid and decree, not because of their numbers or adequate supplies, whether the triumphs are few or many. On the day of Hunayn, the Muslims were proud because of their large number, which did not avail them in the least; they retreated and fled from battle. Only a few of them remained with the Messenger of Allah Allah then sent down His aid and support to His Messenger and the believers who remained with him, so that they were aware that victory is from Allah alone and through His aid, even if the victorious were few. Many a small group overcame a larger opposition by Allah's leave, and Allah is ever with those who are patient. We will explain this subject in detail below, Allah willing.

The Battle of Hunayn

The battle of Hunayn occurred after the victory of Makkah, in the month of Shawwal of the eighth year of Hijrah. After the Prophet conquered Makkah and things settled, most of its people embraced Islam and he set them free. News came to the Messenger of Allah that the tribe of Hawazin were gathering their forces to fight him, under the command of Malik bin `Awf An-Nadri, as well as, the entire tribe of Thaqif, the tribes of Banu Jusham, Banu Sa`d bin Bakr, a few people of Awza` from Banu Hilal and some people from Bani `Amr bin `Amir and `Awf bin `Amir. They brought their women, children, sheep and camels along, in addition to their armed forces and adequate supplies. The Messenger of Allah marched to meet them with the army that he brought to conquer Makkah, ten thousand from the Muhajirin, the Ansar and various Arab tribes. Along with them came the Tulaqa' numbering two thousand men. The Messenger took them along to meet the enemy. The two armies met in Humayn, a valley between Makkah and At-Ta'if. The battle started in the early part of the morning, when the Huwazin forces, who were lying in ambush, descended on the valley when the Muslims entered. Muslims were suddenly struck by the ambush, the arrows descended on them and the swords struck them. The Huwazin commander ordered them to descend and attack the Muslims as one block, and when they did that, the Muslims retreated in haste, just as Allah described them. The Messenger of Allah remained firm in his position while riding his mule, Ash-Shahba'. He was leading his mule towards the enemy, while his uncle Al-`Abbas was holding its right-hand rope and (his cousin) Abu Sufyan bin Al-Harith bin `Abdul-Muttalib was holding the left rope. They tried to hold the mule back so it would not run faster toward the enemy. Meanwhile, the Messenger of Allah was declaring his name aloud and saying,

«إِلَيَّ عِبَادَ اللهِ إِلَيَّ أَنَا رَسُولُ اللهِ»

(O servants of Allah! Come back to me! I am the Messenger of Allah! He repeated these words,

«أَنَا النَّبِيُّ لَا كَذِبْ. أَنَا ابْنُ عَبْدِ الْمُطَّلِب»

(I am the Prophet, not lying! I am the son of Abdul-Muttalib!) There remained between a hundred and eighty Companions with the Prophet. These included Abu Bakr, `Umar, Al-`Abbas, `Ali, Al-Fadl bin `Abbas, Abu Sufyan bin Al-Harith, Ayman the son of Umm Ayman and Usamah bin Zayd. There were many other Companions, may Allah be pleased with them. The Prophet commanded his uncle Al-`Abbas, whose voice was rather loud, to call at the top of his voice, "O Companions of the Samurah (tree)" referring to the Muhajirin and Ansar who gave their pledge under the tree during the pledge of Ridwan, not to run away and retreat. He also called, "O Companions of Surat Al-Baqarah." Upon hearing that, those heralded started saying, "Here we are! Here we are!" Muslims started returning in the direction of the

Chapter 9: At-Tawba (Repentance), Verses 001-092

Messenger of Allah. If the camel of one of them did not obey him (as the people were rushing to the other direction in flight) he would wear his shield and descend from his camel and rush to the side of the Messenger of Allah on foot. When a large crowd gathered around the Messenger of Allah, he commanded them to fight in sincerity and took a handful of sand and threw it in the faces of the disbelievers, after supplicating to Allah,

»اَللّٰهُمَّ أَنْجِزْ لِي مَا وَعَدْتَنِي«

(O Allah! Fulfill Your promise to me!) Then he threw that handful of sand which entered the eyes and mouth of all the disbelievers, thus distracting them from fighting, and they retreated in defeat. The Muslims pursued the enemy, killing and capturing them. The rest of the Muslim army (returning to battle gradually) rejoined their positions and found many captured disbelieving soldiers kept tied before the Messenger of Allah. In the Two Sahihs, it is recorded that Shu`bah said that Abu Ishaq said that Al-Bara' bin `Azib said to a man who asked him, "O Abu `Amarah! Did you run away during Hunayn and leave the Messenger of Allah " Al-Bara' said, "But the Messenger of Allah did not run away. Hawazin was a tribe proficient with their arrows. When we met them we attacked their forces and they ran away in defeat. The Muslims started to worry about collecting the spoils of war and the Hawazin started shooting arrows at us, then the Muslims fled. I saw the Messenger of Allah proclaiming, -- while Abu Sufyan was holding the bridle of his white mule,

»أَنَا النَّبِيُّ لَا كَذِبْ أَنَا ابْنُ عَبْدِ الْمُطَّلِب«

(I am the Prophet, not lying, I am the son of `Abdul-Muttalib!) This shows the great courage on behalf of the Prophet in the midst of confusion, when his army ran away and left him behind. Yet, the Messenger remained on his mule, which is a slow animal, not suitable for fast battle moves or even escape. Yet, the Messenger of Allah was encouraging his mule to move forward towards the enemy announcing who he was, so that those among them who did not know who he was came to know him. May Allah's peace and blessings be on the Messenger until the Day of Resurrection. This indicates the tremendous trust in Allah and reliance upon Him, as well as, sure knowledge that He will give him victory, complete what He has sent him for and give prominence to his religion above all other religions. Allah said,

(Then Allah did send down His Sakinah on His Messenger), He sent down tranquillity and reassurance to His Messenger,

(and on the believers), who remained with him,

(and sent down forces which you saw not,) this refers to angels. Imam Abu Ja`far bin Jarir (At-Tabari) said that Al-Qasim narrated to them, that Al-Hasan bin `Arafah said that Al-Mu`tamir bin Sulayman said from `Awf bin Abi Jamilah Al-`Arabi who said that he heard `Abdur-Rahman, the freed slave of Ibn Barthan saying, "A man who participated in Hunayn with the idolators narrated to me, `When we met the

Messenger of Allah and his Companions on the day of Hunayn, they did not remain in battle more than the time it takes to milk a sheep! When we defeated them, we pursued them until we ended at the rider of the white mule, the Messenger of Allah. At that time, men with white handsome faces intercepted us and said: `Disgraced be the faces! Go back. So we ran away, but they followed us. That was the end for us.'" Allah said,

(Then after that Allah will accept the repentance of whom He wills. And Allah is Oft-Forgiving, Most Merciful.) Allah forgave the rest of Huwazin when they embraced Islam and went to the Prophet, before he arrived at Makkah in the Ji`ranah area. This occurred twenty days after the battle of Hunayn. The Messenger gave them the choice between taking those who were prisoner or the war spoils they lost, and they chose the former. The Prophet released six thousand prisoners to them, but divided the war spoils between the victors, such as some of the Tulaqa', so that their hearts would be inclined towards Islam. He gave each of them a hundred camels, and the same to Malik bin `Awf An-Nasri whom he appointed chief of his people (Huwazin) as he was before. Malik bin `Awf said a poem in which he praised the Messenger of Allah for his generosity and extraordinary courage.

Surah: 9 Ayah: 28 & Ayah: 29

﴿ يَـٰٓأَيُّهَا ٱلَّذِينَ ءَامَنُوٓاْ إِنَّمَا ٱلْمُشْرِكُونَ نَجَسٌ فَلَا يَقْرَبُواْ ٱلْمَسْجِدَ ٱلْحَرَامَ بَعْدَ عَامِهِمْ هَـٰذَا ۚ وَإِنْ خِفْتُمْ عَيْلَةً فَسَوْفَ يُغْنِيكُمُ ٱللَّهُ مِن فَضْلِهِۦٓ إِن شَآءَ ۚ إِنَّ ٱللَّهَ عَلِيمٌ حَكِيمٌ ﴿٢٨﴾

28. O you who believe (in Allâh's Oneness and in His Messenger Muhammad (peace be upon him))! Verily, the Mushrikûn (polytheists, pagans, idolaters, disbelievers in the Oneness of Allâh, and in the Message of Muhammad (peace be upon him)) are Najasun (impure). So let them not come near Al-Masjid-al-Harâm (at Makkah) after this year; and if you fear poverty, Allâh will enrich you if He wills, out of His Bounty. Surely, Allâh is All-Knowing, All-Wise.

﴿ قَـٰتِلُواْ ٱلَّذِينَ لَا يُؤْمِنُونَ بِٱللَّهِ وَلَا بِٱلْيَوْمِ ٱلْأَخِرِ وَلَا يُحَرِّمُونَ مَا حَرَّمَ ٱللَّهُ وَرَسُولُهُۥ وَلَا يَدِينُونَ دِينَ ٱلْحَقِّ مِنَ ٱلَّذِينَ أُوتُواْ ٱلْكِتَـٰبَ حَتَّىٰ يُعْطُواْ ٱلْجِزْيَةَ عَن يَدٍ وَهُمْ صَـٰغِرُونَ ﴿٢٩﴾

29. Fight against those who believe not in Allâh, nor in the Last Day, nor forbid that which has been forbidden by Allâh and His Messenger (Muhammad (peace be upon him)) and those who acknowledge not the religion of truth (i.e. Islâm) among the people of the Scripture (Jews and Christians), until they pay the Jizyah with willing submission, and feel themselves subdued.

Chapter 9: At-Tawba (Repentance), Verses 001-092

Transliteration

28. Ya ayyuha allatheena amanoo innama almushrikoona najasun fala yaqraboo almasjida alharama baAAda AAamihim hatha wa-in khiftum AAaylatan fasawfa yughneekumu Allahu min fadlihi in shaa inna Allaha AAaleemun hakeemun 29. Qatiloo allatheena la yu/minoona biAllahi wala bialyawmi al-akhiri wala yuharrimoona ma harrama Allahu warasooluhu wala yadeenoona deena alhaqqi mina allatheena ootoo alkitaba hatta yuAAtoo aljizyata AAan yadin wahum saghiroona

Tafsir Ibn Kathir

Idolators are no longer allowed into Al-Masjid Al-Haram

Allah commands His believing servants, who are pure in religion and person, to expel the idolators who are filthy in the religious sense, from Al-Masjid Al-Haram. After the revelation of this Ayah, idolators were no longer allowed to go near the Masjid. This Ayah was revealed in the ninth year of Hijrah. The Messenger of Allah sent `Ali in the company of Abu Bakr that year to publicize to the idolators that no Mushrik will be allowed to perform Hajj after that year, nor a naked person allowed to perform Tawaf around the House. Allah completed this decree, made it a legislative ruling, as well as, a fact of reality. `Abdur-Razzaq recorded that Jabir bin `Abdullah commented on the Ayah,

(O you who believe! Verily, the Mushrikin are impure. So let them not come near Al-Masjid Al-Haram after this year) "Unless it was a servant or one of the people of Dhimmah." Imam Abu `Amr Al-Awza'i said, "Umar bin `Abdul-`Aziz wrote (to his governors) to prevent Jews and Christians from entering the Masjids of Muslims, and he followed his order with Allah's statement,

(Verily, the Mushrikin are impure.) `Ata' said, "All of the Sacred Area (the Haram) is considered a Masjid, for Allah said,

(So let them not come near Al-Masjid Al-Haram (at Makkah) after this year.)" This Ayah indicates that idolators are impure and that the believers are pure. In the Sahih is the following,

«الْمُؤْمِنُ لَا يَنْجُسُ»

(The believer does not become impure.) Allah said,

(and if you fear poverty, Allah will enrich you, out of His bounty.) Muhammad bin Ishaq commented, "The people said, `Our markets will be closed, our commerce disrupted, and what we earned will vanish.' So Allah revealed this verse,

(and if you fear poverty, Allah will enrich you, out of His bounty), from other resources,

(if He wills), until,

(...and feel themselves subdued.) This Ayah means, `this will be your compensation for the closed markets that you feared would result.' Therefore, Allah compensated them for the losses they incurred because they severed ties with idolators, by the Jizyah they earned from the People of the Book.'' Similar statements were reported from Ibn `Abbas, Mujahid, `Ikrimah, Sa`id bin Jubayr, Qatadah and Ad-Dahhak and others. Allah said,

(Surely, Allah is All-Knowing), in what benefits you,

(All-Wise), in His orders and prohibitions, for He is All-Perfect in His actions and statements, All-Just in His creations and decisions, Blessed and Hallowed be He. This is why Allah compensated Muslims for their losses by the amount of Jizyah that they took from the people of Dhimmah.

The Order to fight People of the Scriptures until They give the Jizyah

Allah said,

(Fight against those who believe not in Allah, nor in the Last Day, nor forbid that which has been forbidden by Allah and His Messenger, and those who acknowledge not the religion of truth among the People of the Scripture, until they pay the Jizyah with willing submission, and feel themselves subdued.) Therefore, when People of the Scriptures disbelieved in Muhammad , they had no beneficial faith in any Messenger or what the Messengers brought. Rather, they followed their religions because this conformed with their ideas, lusts and the ways of their forefathers, not because they are Allah's Law and religion. Had they been true believers in their religions, that faith would have directed them to believe in Muhammad , because all Prophets gave the good news of Muhammad's advent and commanded them to obey and follow him. Yet when he was sent, they disbelieved in him, even though he is the mightiest of all Messengers. Therefore, they do not follow the religion of earlier Prophets because these religions came from Allah, but because these suit their desires and lusts. Therefore, their claimed faith in an earlier Prophet will not benefit them because they disbelieved in the master, the mightiest, the last and most perfect of all Prophets . Hence Allah's statement,

(Fight against those who believe not in Allah, nor in the Last Day, nor forbid that which has been forbidden by Allah and His Messenger, and those who acknowledge not the religion of truth among the People of the Scripture,) This honorable Ayah was revealed with the order to fight the People of the Book, after the pagans were defeated, the people entered Allah's religion in large numbers, and the Arabian Peninsula was secured under the Muslims' control. Allah commanded His Messenger to fight the People of the Scriptures, Jews and Christians, on the ninth year of Hijrah, and he prepared his army to fight the Romans and called the people to Jihad announcing his intent and destination. The Messenger sent his intent to various Arab areas around Al-Madinah to gather forces, and he collected an army of thirty thousand. Some people from Al-Madinah and some hypocrites, in and around it, lagged behind, for that year was a year of drought and intense heat. The Messenger of Allah marched, heading towards Ash-Sham to fight the Romans until he reached Tabuk, where he set camp for about twenty days next to its water resources. He then prayed to Allah for a decision and went back to Al-Madinah because it was a hard year and the people were weak, as we will mention, Allah willing.

Paying Jizyah is a Sign of Kufr and Disgrace

Allah said,

(until they pay the Jizyah), if they do not choose to embrace Islam,

(with willing submission), in defeat and subservience,

(and feel themselves subdued.), disgraced, humiliated and belittled. Therefore, Muslims are not allowed to honor the people of Dhimmah or elevate them above Muslims, for they are miserable, disgraced and humiliated. Muslim recorded from Abu Hurayrah that the Prophet said,

«لَا تَبْدَءُوا الْيَهُودَ وَالنَّصَارَى بِالسَّلَامِ، وَإِذَا لَقِيتُمْ أَحَدَهُمْ فِي طَرِيقٍ فَاضْطَرُّوهُ إِلَى أَضْيَقِهِ»

(Do not initiate the Salam to the Jews and Christians, and if you meet any of them in a road, force them to its narrowest alley.) This is why the Leader of the faithful `Umar bin Al-Khattab, may Allah be pleased with him, demanded his well-known conditions be met by the Christians, these conditions that ensured their continued humiliation, degradation and disgrace. The scholars of Hadith narrated from `Abdur-Rahman bin Ghanm Al-Ash`ari that he said, "I recorded for `Umar bin Al-Khattab, may Allah be pleased with him, the terms of the treaty of peace he conducted with the Christians of Ash-Sham: `In the Name of Allah, Most Gracious, Most Merciful. This is a document to the servant of Allah `Umar, the Leader of the faithful, from the Christians of such and such city. When you (Muslims) came to us we requested safety for ourselves, children, property and followers of our religion. We made a condition on ourselves that we will neither erect in our areas a monastery, church, or a sanctuary for a monk, nor restore any place of worship that needs restoration nor use any of them for the purpose of enmity against Muslims. We will not prevent any Muslim from resting in our churches whether they come by day or night, and we will open the doors (of our houses of worship) for the wayfarer and passerby. Those Muslims who come as guests, will enjoy boarding and food for three days. We will not allow a spy against Muslims into our churches and homes or hide deceit (or betrayal) against Muslims. We will not teach our children the Qur'an, publicize practices of Shirk, invite anyone to Shirk or prevent any of our fellows from embracing Islam, if they choose to do so. We will respect Muslims, move from the places we sit in if they choose to sit in them. We will not imitate their clothing, caps, turbans, sandals, hairstyles, speech, nicknames and title names, or ride on saddles, hang swords on the shoulders, collect weapons of any kind or carry these weapons. We will not encrypt our stamps in Arabic, or sell liquor. We will have the front of our hair cut, wear our customary clothes wherever we are, wear belts around our waist, refrain from erecting crosses on the outside of our churches and demonstrating them and our books in public in Muslim fairways and markets. We will not sound the bells in our churches, except discretely, or raise our voices while reciting our holy books inside our churches in the presence of Muslims, nor raise our voices (with prayer) at our funerals, or light torches in funeral processions in the fairways of Muslims, or their markets. We will not bury our dead next to Muslim dead, or buy servants who were captured by Muslims. We will be guides for Muslims and refrain from breaching their privacy in their homes.' When I gave this document to `Umar, he added to it, `We will not beat any Muslim. These are the conditions that we set against ourselves and followers of our religion in return for safety and protection. If we break any of these promises that we set for your benefit against ourselves, then our Dhimmah (promise of protection) is broken and you are allowed to do with us what you are allowed of people of defiance and rebellion.'"

Surah: 9 Ayah: 30 & Ayah: 31

﴿ وَقَالَتِ ٱلْيَهُودُ عُزَيْرٌ ٱبْنُ ٱللَّهِ وَقَالَتِ ٱلنَّصَـٰرَى ٱلْمَسِيحُ ٱبْنُ ٱللَّهِ ۖ ذَٰلِكَ قَوْلُهُم بِأَفْوَٰهِهِمْ ۖ يُضَـٰهِـُٔونَ قَوْلَ ٱلَّذِينَ كَفَرُوا۟ مِن قَبْلُ ۚ قَـٰتَلَهُمُ ٱللَّهُ ۚ أَنَّىٰ يُؤْفَكُونَ ﴾

30. And the Jews say: 'Uzair (Ezra) is the son of Allâh, and the Christians say: Messiah is the son of Allâh. That is their saying with their mouths, resembling the saying of those who disbelieved aforetime. Allâh's Curse be on them, how they are deluded away from the truth!

﴿ ٱتَّخَذُوٓا۟ أَحْبَارَهُمْ وَرُهْبَـٰنَهُمْ أَرْبَابًا مِّن دُونِ ٱللَّهِ وَٱلْمَسِيحَ ٱبْنَ مَرْيَمَ وَمَآ أُمِرُوٓا۟ إِلَّا لِيَعْبُدُوٓا۟ إِلَـٰهًا وَٰحِدًا ۖ لَّآ إِلَـٰهَ إِلَّا هُوَ ۚ سُبْحَـٰنَهُۥ عَمَّا يُشْرِكُونَ ﴾

31. They (Jews and Christians) took their rabbis and their monks to be their lords besides Allâh (by obeying them in things which they made lawful or unlawful according to their own desires without being ordered by Allâh), and (they also took as their Lord) Messiah, son of Maryam (Mary), while they (Jews and Christians) were commanded (in the Taurât (Torah) and the Injeel (Gospel)) to worship none but One Ilâh (God - Allâh) Lâ ilâha illa Huwa (none has the right to be worshipped but He). Praise and glory is to Him, (far above is He) from having the partners they associate (with Him)."

Transliteration

30. Waqalati alyahoodu AAuzayrun ibnu Allahi waqalati alnnasara almaseehu ibnu Allahi thalika qawluhum bi-afwahihim yudahi-oona qawla allatheena kafaroo min qablu qatalahumu Allahu anna yu/fakoona 31. Ittakhathoo ahbarahum waruhbanahum arbaban min dooni Allahi waalmaseeha ibna maryama wama omiroo illa liyaAAbudoo ilahan wahidan la ilaha illa huwa subhanahu AAamma yushrikoona

Chapter 9: At-Tawba (Repentance), Verses 001-092 79

Tafsir Ibn Kathir

Fighting the Jews and Christians is legislated because They are Idolators and Disbelievers

Allah the Exalted encourages the believers to fight the polytheists, disbelieving Jews and Christians, who uttered this terrible statement and utter lies against Allah, the Exalted. As for the Jews, they claimed that `Uzayr was the son of God, Allah is free of what they attribute to Him. As for the misguidance of Christians over `Isa, it is obvious. This is why Allah declared both groups to be liars,

(That is their saying with their mouths), but they have no proof that supports their claim, other than lies and fabrications,

(resembling), imitating,

(the saying of those who disbelieved aforetime.) They imitate the previous nations who fell into misguidance just as Jews and Christians did,

(may Allah fight them), Ibn `Abbas said, "May Allah curse them."

(how they are deluded away from the truth!) how they deviate from truth, when it is apparent, exchanging it for misguidance. Allah said next,

(They took their rabbis and their monks to be their lords besides Allah, and the Messiah, son of Maryam) (9:31). Imam Ahmad, At-Tirmidhi and Ibn Jarir At-Tabari recorded a Hadith via several chains of narration, from `Adi bin Hatim, may Allah be pleased with him, who became Christian during the time of Jahiliyyah. When the call of the Messenger of Allah reached his area, `Adi ran away to Ash-Sham, and his sister and several of his people were captured. The Messenger of Allah freed his sister and gave her gifts. So she went to her brother and encouraged him to become Muslim and to go to the Messenger of Allah . `Adi, who was one of the chiefs of his people (the tribe of Tai') and whose father, Hatim At-Ta'i, was known for his generosity, went to Al-Madinah. When the people announced his arrival, `Adi went to the Messenger of Allah wearing a silver cross around his neck. The Messenger of Allah recited this Ayah;

(They took their rabbis and their monks to be their lords besides Allah). `Adi commented, "I said, `They did not worship them.'" The Prophet said,

«بَلَى إِنَّهُمْ حَرَّمُوا عَلَيْهِمُ الْحَلَالَ وَأَحَلُّوا لَهُمُ الْحَرَامَ فَاتَّبَعُوهُمْ فَذَلِكَ عِبَادَتُهُمْ إِيَّاهُم»

(Yes they did. They (rabbis and monks) prohibited the allowed for them (Christians and Jews) and allowed the prohibited, and they obeyed them. This is how they worshipped them.) The Messenger of Allah said to `Adi,

«يَا عَدِيُّ مَا تَقُولُ؟ أَيُفِرُّكَ أَنْ يُقَالَ: اللهُ أَكْبَرُ؟ فَهَلْ تَعْلَمُ شَيْئًا أَكْبَرَ مِنَ اللهِ؟ مَا يُفِرُّكَ؟ أَيُفِرُّكَ أَنْ يُقَالَ: لَا إِلَهَ إِلَّا اللهُ؟ فَهَلْ تَعْلَمُ مَنْ إِلَهٌ إِلَّا اللهُ؟»

(O `Adi what do you say Did you run away (to Ash-Sham) so that 'Allahu Akbar' (Allah is the Great) is not pronounced Do you know of anything greater than Allah What made you run away Did you run away so that `La ilaha illallah' is not pronounced Do you know of any deity worthy of worship except Allah)

The Messenger invited `Adi to embrace Islam, and he embraced Islam and pronounced the Testimony of Truth. The face of the Messenger of Allah beamed with pleasure and he said to `Adi,

«إِنَّ الْيَهُودَ مَغْضُوبٌ عَلَيْهِمْ وَالنَّصَارَى ضَالُّونَ»

(Verily, the Jews have earned the anger (of Allah) and the Christians are misguided.) Hudhayfah bin Al-Yaman, `Abdullah bin `Abbas and several others said about the explanation of,

(They took their rabbis and their monks to be their lords besides Allah...) that the Christians and Jews obeyed their monks and rabbis in whatever they allowed or prohibited for them. This is why Allah said,

(while they were commanded to worship none but One God), Who, whatever He renders prohibited is the prohibited, whatever He allowed is the allowed, whatever He legislates, is to be the law followed, and whatever He decides is to be adhered to;

(None has the right to be worshipped but He. Hallowed be He above what they associate (with Him).) Meaning, exalted, sanctified, hallowed above partners, equals, aids, rivals or children, there is no deity or Lord worthy of worship except Him.

Surah: 9 Ayah: 32 & Ayah: 33

﴿يُرِيدُونَ أَن يُطْفِئُواْ نُورَ ٱللَّهِ بِأَفْوَٰهِهِمْ وَيَأْبَى ٱللَّهُ إِلَّآ أَن يُتِمَّ نُورَهُۥ وَلَوْ كَرِهَ ٱلْكَٰفِرُونَ ۝﴾

32. They (the disbelievers, the Jews and the Christians) want to extinguish Allâh's Light (with which Muhammad (peace be upon him) has been sent - Islâmic Monotheism) with their mouths, but Allâh will not allow except that His Light should be perfected even though the Kâfirûn (disbelievers) hate (it).

﴿هُوَ ٱلَّذِىٓ أَرْسَلَ رَسُولَهُۥ بِٱلْهُدَىٰ وَدِينِ ٱلْحَقِّ لِيُظْهِرَهُۥ عَلَى ٱلدِّينِ كُلِّهِۦ وَلَوْ كَرِهَ ٱلْمُشْرِكُونَ ۝﴾

33. It is He Who has sent His Messenger (Muhammad (peace be upon him)) with guidance and the religion of truth (Islâm), to make it superior over all religions even though the Mushrikûn (polytheists, pagans, idolaters, disbelievers in the Oneness of Allâh) hate (it).

Transliteration

32. Yureedoona an yutfi-oo noora Allahi bi-afwahihim waya/ba Allahu illa an yutimma noorahu walaw kariha alkafiroona   33. Huwa allathee arsala rasoolahu bialhuda wadeeni alhaqqi liyuthhirahu AAala alddeeni kullihi walaw kariha almushrikoona

Tafsir Ibn Kathir

People of the Scriptures try to extinguish the Light of Islam

Allah says, the disbelieving idolators and People of the Scriptures want to,

(extinguish the Light of Allah). They try through argument and lies to extinguish the guidance and religion of truth that the Messenger of Allah was sent with. Their example is the example of he who wants to extinguish the light of the sun or the moon by blowing at them! Indeed, such a person will never accomplish what he sought. Likewise, the light of what the Messenger was sent with will certainly shine and spread. Allah replied to the idolators' desire and hope,

(but Allah will not allow except that His Light should be perfected even though the disbelievers (Kafirun) hate (it)) (9:32). (Linguistincally) a Kafir is the person who covers something. For instance, night is called Kafiran (covering) because it covers things (with darkness). The farmer is called Kafiran, because he covers seeds in the ground. Allah said in an Ayah,

(thereof the growth is pleasing to the (Kuffar) tillers)(57:20).

Islam is the Religion That will dominate over all Other Religions

Allah said next,

(It is He Who has sent His Messenger with guidance and the religion of truth.) `Guidance' refers to the true narrations, beneficial faith and true religion that the Messenger came with. `religion of truth' refers to the righteous, legal deeds that bring about benefit in this life and the Hereafter.

(to make it (Islam) superior over all religions) It is recorded in the Sahih that the Messenger of Allah said,

»إِنَّ اللهَ زَوَى لِي الْأَرْضَ مَشَارِقَهَا وَمَغَارِبَهَا، وَسَيَبْلُغُ مُلْكُ أُمَّتِي مَا زُوِيَ لِيبِيمِنْهَا«

(Allah made the eastern and western parts of the earth draw near for me (to see), and the rule of my Ummah will extend as far as I saw.) Imam Ahmad recorded from Tamim Ad-Dari that he said, "I heard the Messenger of Allah saying,

«لَيَبْلُغَنَّ هَذَا الْأَمْرُ مَا بَلَغَ اللَّيْلُ وَالنَّهَارُ، وَلَا يَتْرُكُ اللهُ بَيْتَ مَدَرٍ وَلَا وَبَرٍ إِلَّا أَدْخَلَهُ هَذَا الدِّينَ، يُعِزُّ عَزِيزًا وَيُذِلُّ ذَلِيلًا، عِزًّا يُعِزُّ اللهُ بِهِ الْإِسْلَامَ وَذُلًّا يُذِلُّ اللهُ بِهِ الْكُفْرَ»

(This matter (Islam) will keep spreading as far as the night and day reach, until Allah will not leave a house made of mud or hair, but will make this religion enter it, while bringing might to a mighty person (a Muslim) and humiliation to a disgraced person (who rejects Islam). Might with which Allah elevates Islam (and its people) and disgrace with which Allah humiliates disbelief (and its people).) Tamim Ad-Dari (who was a Christian before Islam) used to say, "I have come to know the meaning of this Hadith in my own people. Those who became Muslims among them acquired goodness, honor and might. Disgrace, humiliation and Jizyah befell those who remained disbelievers."

Surah: 9 Ayah: 34 & Ayah: 35

﴿ ۞ يَٰٓأَيُّهَا ٱلَّذِينَ ءَامَنُوٓا۟ إِنَّ كَثِيرًا مِّنَ ٱلْأَحْبَارِ وَٱلرُّهْبَانِ لَيَأْكُلُونَ أَمْوَٰلَ ٱلنَّاسِ بِٱلْبَٰطِلِ وَيَصُدُّونَ عَن سَبِيلِ ٱللَّهِ ۗ وَٱلَّذِينَ يَكْنِزُونَ ٱلذَّهَبَ وَٱلْفِضَّةَ وَلَا يُنفِقُونَهَا فِى سَبِيلِ ٱللَّهِ فَبَشِّرْهُم بِعَذَابٍ أَلِيمٍ ۝ ﴾

34. O you who believe! Verily, there are many of the (Jewish) rabbis and the (Christian) monks who devour the wealth of mankind in falsehood, and hinder (them) from the Way of Allâh (i.e. Allâh's Religion of Islâmic Monotheism). And those who hoard up gold and silver (al-Kanz: the money, the Zakât of which has not been paid), and spend them not in the Way of Allâh, announce unto them a painful torment.

﴿ يَوْمَ يُحْمَىٰ عَلَيْهَا فِى نَارِ جَهَنَّمَ فَتُكْوَىٰ بِهَا جِبَاهُهُمْ وَجُنُوبُهُمْ وَظُهُورُهُمْ ۖ هَٰذَا مَا كَنَزْتُمْ لِأَنفُسِكُمْ فَذُوقُوا۟ مَا كُنتُمْ تَكْنِزُونَ ۝ ﴾

35. On the Day when that (Al-Kanz: money, gold and silver the Zakât of which has not been paid) will be heated in the Fire of Hell and with it will be branded their foreheads, their flanks, and their backs, (and it will be said unto them): "This is the treasure which you hoarded for yourselves. Now taste of what you used to hoard."

Transliteration

34. Ya ayyuha allatheena amanoo inna katheeran mina al-ahbari waalrruhbani laya/kuloona amwala alnnasi bialbatili wayasuddoona AAan sabeeli Allahi waallatheena yaknizoona aththahaba waalfiddata wala yunfiqoonaha fee sabeeli Allahi fabashshirhum biAAathabin aleemin 35. Yawma yuhma AAalayha fee nari jahannama fatukwa biha jibahuhum wajunoobuhum wathuhooruhum hatha ma kanaztum li-anfusikum fathooqoo ma kuntum taknizoona

Tafsir Ibn Kathir

Warning against Corrupt Scholars and Misguided Worshippers

As-Suddi said that the Ahbar are Jewish rabbis, while the Ruhban are Christian monks. This statement is true, for Ahbar are Jewish rabbis, just as Allah said,

(Why do not the Ahbar (rabbis) and the religious learned men forbid them from uttering sinful words and eating unlawful things.) (5:63) The Ruhban are Christian monks or worshippers, while the `Qissisun' are their scholars. Allah said in another Ayah,

(This is because among them, there are Qissisin and Ruhban...)(5:82). This Ayah warns against corrupt scholars and misguided worshippers. Sufyan bin `Uyaynah said, "Those among our scholars who become corrupt are similar to the Jews, while those among our worshippers who become misguided are like Christians." An authentic Hadith declares,

《لَتَرْكَبُنَّ سُنَنَ مَنْ كَانَ قَبْلَكُمْ حَذْوَ الْقُذَّةِ بِالْقُذَّة》

(You will follow the ways of those who were before you, step by step.) They asked, "Jews and Christians" He said,

《فَمَن》

? (Who else) In another narration, they asked, "Persia and Rome" He said,

《فَمَنِ النَّاسِ إِلَّا هَؤُلَاءِ؟》

(And who else if it was not them) These texts warn against imitating them in action and statement, for they, as Allah stated,

(devour the wealth of mankind in falsehood, and hinder (them) from the way of Allah.) They sell the religion in return for worldly gains, using their positions and status among people to illegally devour their property. For instance, the Jews were respected by the people of Jahiliyyah and collected gifts, taxes and presents from them. When Allah sent His Messenger , the Jews persisted in their misguidance, disbelief and rebellion, hoping to keep their status and position. However, Allah extinguished all this and took it away from them with the light of Prophethood and instead gave them disgrace and degradation, and they incurred the anger of Allah, the Exalted. Allah said next,

(and hinder (them) from the way of Allah.) Therefore, they illegally devour people's property and hinder them from following the truth. They also confuse truth with falsehood and pretend before their ignorant followers that they call to righteousness. The true reality is that they call to the Fire and will not find any helpers on the Day of Resurrection.

Torment of Those Who hoard Gold and Silver

Allah said,

(And those who hoard (Kanz) gold and silver and spend them not in the way of Allah, announce unto them a painful torment.) (9:34). This is the third category of leaders, for people rely on their scholars, worshippers and the wealthy among them. When these categories of people become corrupt, the society in general becomes corrupt. Ibn Al-Mubarak once said, "What corrupted the religion, except kings and wicked Ahbar and Ruhban." As for Kanz, it refers to the wealth on which Zakah has not been paid, according to Malik, who narrated this from `Abdullah bin Dinar from Ibn `Umar. Al-Bukhari recorded that Az-Zuhri said that Khalid bin Aslam said that `Abdullah bin `Umar said, "This was before Zakah was ordained. When Zakah was ordained, Allah made it a cleanser for wealth." `Umar bin `Abdul-`Aziz and `Irak bin Malik said that this Ayah was abrogated by Allah's statement,

(Take Sadaqah (alms) from their wealth) There are many Hadiths that admonish hoarding gold and silver. We will mention here some of these Hadiths. `Abdur-Razzaq recorded a Hadith from `Ali about Allah's statement,

(And those who hoard up gold and silver...) `Ali said that the Prophet said,

«تَبًّا لِلذَّهَبِ تَبًّا لِلْفِضَّةِ»

(Woe to gold! Woe to silver.) He repeated this statement thrice, and this Hadith was hard on the Companions of the Messenger of Allah , who said, "What type of wealth should we use" `Umar said, "I will find out for you," and he asked, "O Allah's Messenger! Your statement was hard for your Companions. They asked, `What wealth should we use'" The Prophet answered,

«لِسَانًا ذَاكِرًا وَقَلْبًا شَاكِرًا وَزَوْجَةً تُعِينُ أَحَدَكُمْ عَلَى دِينِهِ»

(A remembering tongue, an appreciative heart and a wife that helps one of you implement his religion.) Allah's statement,

Chapter 9: At-Tawba (Repentance), Verses 001-092

(On the Day when that will be heated in the fire of Hell and with it will be branded their foreheads, their flanks, and their backs, (and it will be said unto them) "This is the treasure which you hoarded for yourselves. Now taste of what you used to hoard.") These words will be said to them as a way of admonishing, criticizing and mocking them. Allah also said;

(Then pour over his head the torment of boiling water. "Taste you (this)! Verily, you were (pretending to be) the mighty, the generous!") (44:48-49). There is a saying that goes, "He who covets a thing and prefers it to Allah's obedience, will be punished with it." Because hoarding money was better to these people than Allah's pleasure, they were punished with it. For instance, Abu Lahab, may Allah curse him, was especially active in defying the Messenger of Allah , and his wife was helping him in this regard. Therefore, on the Day of Resurrection, she will help in punishing him, for there will be a twisted rope of palm fiber on her neck. She will be gathering wood from the Fire and throwing it on him so that his torment is made harder by the hand of someone whom he used to care for in this life. Likewise, money was precious to those who hoarded it in this life. Therefore, money will produce the worst harm for them in the Hereafter, when it will be heated in the Fire of Jahannam, whose heat is quiet sufficient, and their forehead, sides and back will be branded with it. Imam Abu Ja`far Ibn Jarir recorded that Thawban said that the Messenger of Allah used to declare,

«مَنْ تَرَكَ بَعْدَهُ كَنْزًا مُثِّلَ لَهُ يَوْمَ الْقِيَامَةِ شُجَاعًا أَقْرَعَ لَهُ زَبِيبَتَانِ يَتْبَعُهُ وَيَقُولُ: وَيْلَكَ مَا أَنْتَ؟ فَيَقُولُ: أَنَا كَنْزُكَ الَّذِي تَرَكْتَهُ بَعْدَكَ وَلَا يَزَالُ يَتْبَعُهُ حَتَّى يُلْقِمَهُ يَدَهُ فَيَقْضِمَهَا ثُمَّ يَتْبَعُهَا سَائِرَ جَسَدِه»

(Whoever leaves a treasure behind (on which he did not pay the Zakah), then on the Day of Resurrection his wealth will be made like a bald-headed poisonous male snake with two black spots over the eyes. The snake will follow him, and he will say, `Woe to you! Who are you' The snake will say, `I am your treasure that you left behind,' and will keep following him until the man gives it his hand; the snake will devour it and then devour his whole body.) Ibn Hibban also collected this Hadith in his Sahih. Part of this Hadith was also collected in the Two Sahihs from Abu Hurayrah. In his Sahih, Muslim recorded from Abu Hurayrah that the Messenger of Allah said,

«مَا مِنْ رَجُلٍ لَا يُؤَدِّي زَكَاةَ مَالِهِ إِلَّا جُعِلَ لَهُ يَوْمَ الْقِيَامَةِ صَفَائِحُ مِنْ نَارٍ، فَيُكْوَى بِهَا جَنْبُهُ وَجَبْهَتُهُ وَظَهْرُهُ فِي يَوْمٍ كَانَ مِقْدَارُهُ خَمْسِينَ أَلْفَ سَنَةٍ، حَتَّى يُقْضَى بَيْنَ الْعِبَادِ ثُمَّ يُرَى سَبِيلُهُ إِمَّا إِلَى الْجَنَّةِ وَإِمَّا إِلَى النَّار»

(Every man who does not pay the Zakah due on his money, then on the Day of Resurrection, his side, forehead and back will be branded with rods made of fire on a Day the length of which is fifty thousand years, until when the servants will be judged; that man will be shown his destination, either to Paradise or the Fire.) and in the Tafsir of this Ayah, Al-Bukhari recorded that Zayd bin Wahb said, "I passed by Abu Dharr in the area of Rabadhah and asked him, `What made you reside in this area' He said, `We were in Ash-Sham when I recited this Ayah,

(And those who hoard up gold and silver and spend them not in the way of Allah, announce unto them a painful torment.) Mu`awiyah said, `This Ayah is not about us, it is only about the People of the Book.' So I (Abu Dharr) said, `Rather, it is about us and them."

Surah: 9 Ayah: 36

﴿ إِنَّ عِدَّةَ ٱلشُّهُورِ عِندَ ٱللَّهِ ٱثْنَا عَشَرَ شَهْرًا فِى كِتَبِ ٱللَّهِ يَوْمَ خَلَقَ ٱلسَّمَوَتِ وَٱلْأَرْضَ مِنْهَا أَرْبَعَةٌ حُرُمٌ ذَلِكَ ٱلدِّينُ ٱلْقَيِّمُ فَلَا تَظْلِمُوا فِيهِنَّ أَنفُسَكُمْ وَقَتِلُوا ٱلْمُشْرِكِينَ كَافَّةً كَمَا يُقَتِلُونَكُمْ كَافَّةً وَٱعْلَمُوا أَنَّ ٱللَّهَ مَعَ ٱلْمُتَّقِينَ ﴾ ۝

36. Verily, the number of months with Allâh is twelve months (in a year), so was it ordained by Allâh on the Day when He created the heavens and the earth; of them four are Sacred, (i.e. the 1st, the 7th, the 11th and the 12th months of the Islâmic calendar). That is the right religion, so wrong not yourselves therein, and fight against the Mushrikûn (polytheists, pagans, idolaters, disbelievers in the Oneness of Allâh) collectively, as they fight against you collectively. But know that Allâh is with those who are Al-Muttaqûn (the pious - see V.2:2).

Transliteration

36. Inna AAiddata alshshuhoori AAinda Allahi ithna AAashara shahran fee kitabi Allahi yawmakhalaqa alssamawati waal-arda minha arbaAAatun hurumun thalika alddeenu alqayyimu fala tathlimoo feehinna anfusakum waqatiloo almushrikeena kaffatan kama yuqatiloonakum kaffatan waiAAlamoo anna Allaha maAAa almuttaqeena

Tafsir Ibn Kathir

The Year consists of Twelve Months

Imam Ahmad recorded that Abu Bakrah said that the Prophet said in a speech during his Hajj,

Chapter 9: At-Tawba (Repentance), Verses 001-092

(The division of time has turned to its original form which was current when Allah created the heavens and the earth. The year is of twelve months, out of which four months are sacred: Three are in succession Dhul-Qa`dah, Dhul-Hijjah and Muharram, and (the fourth is) Rajab of (the tribe of) Mudar which comes between Jumada (Ath-Thaniyah) and Sha`ban." The Prophet then asked,

«أَيُّ يَوْمٍ هَذَا؟»

(What is the day today') We said, "Allah and His Messenger know better. He kept quiet until we thought that he might give that day another name. He said

«أَلَيْسَ يَوْمَ النَّحْرِ؟»

(Isn't it the day of Nahr) We replied, "Yes." He further asked,

«أَيُّ شَهْرٍ هَذَا؟»

(Which month is this) We again said, "Allah and His Messenger know better," and he kept quiet and made us think that he might give it another name. Then he said,

«أَلَيْسَ ذَا الحِجَّةِ؟»

(Isn't it the month of Dhul-Hijjah) We replied, "Yes." He asked,

«أَيُّ بَلَدٍ هَذَا؟»

(What town is this) We said, "Allah and His Messenger know better," and he kept quiet until we thought that he might change its name. He asked,

«أَلَيْسَتِ الْبَلْدَةَ؟»

(Isn't this the (Sacred) Town) We said, "Yes." He said,

«فَإِنَّ دِمَاءَكُمْ وَأَمْوَالَكُمْ وَأَعْرَاضَكُمْ عَلَيْكُمْ حَرَامٌ كَحُرْمَةِ يَوْمِكُمْ هَذَا فِي شَهْرِكُمْ هَذَا، فِي بَلَدِكُمْ هَذَا. وَسَتَلْقَوْنَ رَبَّكُمْ فَيَسْأَلُكُمْ عَنْ أَعْمَالِكُمْ، أَلَا لَا تَرْجِعُوا بَعْدِي ضُلَّالًا يَضْرِبُ بَعْضُكُمْ رِقَابَ بَعْضٍ أَلَا هَلْ

$$\text{بَلَّغْتُ؟ أَلَا لِيُبَلِّغِ الشَّاهِدُ مِنْكُمُ الْغَائِبَ فَلَعَلَّ مَنْ يُبَلِّغُهُ يَكُونُ أَوْعَى لَهُ مِنْ بَعْضِ مَنْ سَمِعَه}$$

(Verily! Your blood, property and honor are sacred to one another like the sanctity of this day of yours, in this month of yours and in this city of yours. Verily, you will meet your Lord and He will question you about your actions. Behold! Do not revert to misguidance after me by striking the necks of one another. Have I conveyed It is incumbent upon those who are present to inform those who are absent, because those who are absent might comprehend (what I have said) better than some who are present.) Al-Bukhari and Muslim collected this Hadith. In a small book collected by Shaykh `Alam ad-Din As-Sakhawi, entitled, Al-Mashhur fi Asma' Al-Ayam wash-Shuhur, he mentioned that Muharram is so named because it is a sacred month. To me, it was so named to emphasize its sacredness. This is because the Arabs would switch it around. One year they would say it was a sacred month, the following year they would say that it was not. The author said, "...and Safar is so named because they used to leave their homes during that month for fighting and traveling. When saying `Safir' a place, it means to leave it... Rabi` Al-Awwal is called that because they used to do Irtiba` in it, that is to maintain one's property... and Rabi` Al-Akhir, was so named for the same reasons. Jumada is called that because the water would dry up (Jamud) then....They say Jumada Al-Uwla and Al-Awwal, or Jumada Al-Akhar or Al-Akhirah. Rajab comes from Tarjib, meaning to honor. Sha`ban because the tribes would separate and return to their homes. Ramadan was so named because of the severity of the Ramda' - that is - the heat, and they say that the branch Ramadat when it is thirsty...And the saying that it is a Name of Allah is a mistake, for there is no proof or support for that..."

The Sacred Months

Allah said,

(of them four are sacred). The Arabs used to consider these months sacred during the time of Jahiliyyah, except for a group of them called Al-Basl, who held eight months of the year to be sacred as way of exaggeration in religion. The Prophet said,

$$\text{«ثَلَاثَةٌ مُتَوَالِيَاتٌ: ذُو الْقَعْدَةِ وَذُو الْحِجَّةِ وَالْمُحَرَّمُ وَرَجَبُ مُضَرَ الَّذِي بَيْنَ جُمَادَى وَشَعْبَان»}$$

(Three are in succession; Dhul-Qa`dah, Dhul-Hijjah and Muharram, and (the fourth is) Rajab (of (the tribe of) Mudar which comes between Jumada (Ath-Thani)) and Sha`ban). The Prophet said "Rajab of Mudar" to attest to the custom of Mudar, in saying that Rajab is the month that is between Jumada and Sha`ban, not as the tribe of Rabi`ah thought, that it is between Sha`ban and Shawwal, which is Ramadan in the present calendar. The four Sacred Months were made four, three in succession and one alone, so that the Hajj and `Umrah are performed with ease. Dhul-Qa`dah, the month before the Hajj month, was made sacred because they refrained from fighting during that month. Dhul-Hijjah, the next month, was made sacred because it is the month of Hajj, during which they performed Hajj rituals. Muharram, which comes next, was made sacred so that they are able to go back to their areas in safety (after performing Hajj). Rajab, in the middle of the lunar year, was made sacred so that those coming from the farthest areas of Arabia are able to perform `Umrah and visit the House and then go back to their areas safely. Allah said next,

(That is the right religion), that is the Straight Law, requiring implementing Allah's order concerning the months that He made sacred and their true count as it was originally written by Allah. Allah said,

(so wrong not yourselves therein) during these Sacred Months, for sin in them is worse than sin in other months. Likewise, sins in the Sacred City are written multiplied,

(...and whoever inclines to evil actions therein (in Makkah) or to do wrong, him We shall cause to taste from a painful torment) (22:25). Similarly, sin in general is worse during the Sacred Months `Ali bin Abi Talhah narrated that Ibn `Abbas said, Allah's statement,

(Verily, the number of months with Allah...), is connected to

(so wrong not yourselves therein), "In all (twelve) months. Allah then chose four out of these months and made them sacred, emphasizing their sanctity, making sinning in them greater, in addition to, multiplying rewards of righteous deeds during them." Qatadah said about Allah's statement,

(so wrong not yourselves therein), "Injustice during the Sacred Months is worse and graver than injustice in other months. Verily, injustice is always wrong, but Allah makes things graver than others as He will." He also said, "Allah has chosen some of His creation above others. He chose Messengers from angels and from men. He also chose His Speech above all speech, the Masajid above other areas of the earth, Ramadan and the Sacred Months above all months, Friday above the other days and Laylatul-Qadr (The Night of Decree) above all nights. Therefore, sanctify what Allah has sanctified, for doing so is the practice of people of understanding and comprehension."

Fighting in the Sacred Months

Allah said,

(and fight against the idolators collectively), all of you,

(as they fight against you collectively.), all of them,

(But know that Allah is with those who have Taqwa), and know that initiating battle during the Sacred Months is forbidden. Allah said in other Ayat,

(O you who believe! Violate not the sanctity of the symbols of Allah, nor of the sacred month.) (5:2),

(The Sacred Month is for the Sacred Month, and for the prohibited things, there is the law of equality (Qisas). Then whoever transgresses the prohibition against you, you transgress likewise against him) (2:194), and,

(Then when the Sacred Months have passed, kill the idolators...) (9:5). As for Allah's statement,

(And fight against the idolators collectively as they fight against you collectively), it includes permission for the believers to fight the idolators in the Sacred Month, if the idolators initiate hostilities therein. Allah said in other Ayat,

(The Sacred Month is for the Sacred Month, and for the prohibited things, there is the law of equality (Qisas)) (2:194), and,

(And fight not with them at Al-Masjid Al-Haram, unless they (first) fight you there. But if they attack you, then kill them.) (2:191). As for the Messenger of Allah laying siege to At-Ta'if until the Sacred Month started, it was a continuation of the battle against Hawazin and their allies from Thaqif. They started the fighting and gathered their men for the purpose of conducting war. The Messenger of Allah marched to meet them and when they took refuge in At-Ta'if, the Prophet laid siege to them so that they descend from their forts, but they inflicted casualties on Muslims. The siege continued for about forty days, during which a Sacred Month began, and the siege continued for several days in that month. The Messenger broke the siege and went back (to Makkah). So fighting that carries over into it (the Sacred Month) is not the same as initiating warfare during it, Allah knows best.

Surah: 9 Ayah: 37

﴿ إِنَّمَا ٱلنَّسِىٓءُ زِيَادَةٌ فِى ٱلْكُفْرِ يُضَلُّ بِهِ ٱلَّذِينَ كَفَرُواْ يُحِلُّونَهُۥ عَامًا وَيُحَرِّمُونَهُۥ عَامًا لِّيُوَاطِـُٔواْ عِدَّةَ مَا حَرَّمَ ٱللَّهُ فَيُحِلُّواْ مَا حَرَّمَ ٱللَّهُ زُيِّنَ لَهُمْ سُوٓءُ أَعْمَـٰلِهِمْ وَٱللَّهُ لَا يَهْدِى ٱلْقَوْمَ ٱلْكَـٰفِرِينَ ﴾

37. The postponing (of a Sacred Month) is indeed an addition to disbelief: thereby the disbelievers are led astray, for they make it lawful one year and forbid it another year in order to adjust the number of months forbidden by Allâh, and make such forbidden ones lawful. The evil of their deeds is made fair-seeming to them. And Allâh guides not the people who disbelieve.

Transliteration

37. Innama alnnasee-o ziyadatun fee alkufri yudallu bihi allatheena kafaroo yuhilloonahu AAaman wayuharrimoonahu AAaman liyuwati-oo AAiddata ma harrama Allahu fayuhilloo ma harrama Allahu zuyyina lahum soo-o aAAmalihim waAllahu la yahdee alqawma alkafireena

Chapter 9: At-Tawba (Repentance), Verses 001-092

Tafsir Ibn Kathir

Admonishing the Preference of Opinion in a Religious Matter

Allah admonishes the idolators for choosing their wicked opinions over Allah's Law. They changed Allah's legislation based upon their vain desires, allowing what Allah prohibited and prohibiting what Allah allowed. They thought that three consecutive sacred months were rather long for them to remain without fighting, for they were full of anger and rage. This is why before Islam they innovated a change in the Sacred Month of Muharram, delaying it to the month of Safar! Therefore, they allowed fighting in the Sacred Month and made the non-sacred month sacred, to make the Sacred Months in a year four, as Allah decided! `Ali bin Abi Talhah said that Ibn `Abbas commented on Allah's statement,

(The postponing (of a Sacred Month) is indeed an addition to disbelief), "Junadah bin `Awf bin Umayyah Al-Kinani, known as Abu Thumamah, used to attend the Hajj season every year and declare, `Abu Thumamah is never rejected nor refuted!,' and he used to treat Safar as sacred for people one year (and un-sanctify Muharram) and treat Muharram as sacred another year (and un-sanctify Safar in that year). This is why Allah said,

(The postponing (of a Sacred Month) is indeed an addition to disbelief.) nAllah says, `They allow Muharram one year and make it sacred another year.'" Al-`Awfi narrated a similar statement from Ibn `Abbas. Layth bin Abi Sulaym narrated that Mujahid said, "There was a man from Bani Kinanah who would attend the Hajj season every year riding his donkey. He would proclaim, `O people! I am never rejected, denied or refuted in what I say. We made this coming Muharram sacred, and Safar not!' The following year he would come again and declare the same words then say, `We made this coming Safar sacred and delayed Muharram (revoked its sanctity).' This is the meaning of Allah's statement,

(in order to adjust the number of months forbidden by Allah), to four months. Allah says, `They allow what Allah disallowed by delaying the Sacred Month.'" The idolators used to allow Muharram one year and sanctify Safar in its place. They would continue the months of the year according to their normal count and names. The next year they would sanctify Muharram and continue the year, Safar, Rabi`, until the end of the year.

(They make it lawful one year and forbid it another year in order to adjust the number of months forbidden by Allah, and make such forbidden ones lawful.) Therefore, they would still sanctify four months every year, but would one year sanctify the third from the three consecutive Sacred Months, Muharram, and postpone and delay it another year to Safar. In his book of Sirah, Imam Muhammad bin Ishaq presented a very useful beneficial discussion on this matter. He said; "The first to start the practice of overlooking the sanctity of months for the Arabs, thus allowing what Allah sanctified of them and sanctifying what Allah allowed of them, was "Al-Qalammas". He was Hudhayfah bin `Abd Fuqaym bin `Adi bin `Amr bin Tha`labah bin Al-Harith bin Malik bin Kinanah bin Khuzaymah bin Mudrikah bin Ilyas bin Mudar bin Nizar bin Ma`dd bin `Adnan. His son `Abbad maintained this practice, then after him his son Qala` bin

`Abbad did the same, Then his son Umayyah bin Qala`, then his son `Awf bin Umayyah, then his son Abu Thumamah Junadah bin `Awf. He was the last one of his sons (to continue this practice) before Islam. The Arabs used to gather around him when Hajj finished, and he would stand and give them a speech in which he sanctifies Rajab, Dhul-Qa`dah and Dhul-Hijjah. He would defer the sanctity of Muharram to Safar one year and uphold its sanctity another year, so as to appear upholding the number (of Sacred Months) Allah made sacred. Therefore, he would allow what Allah prohibited and prohibit what Allah allowed." Allah knows best.

Surah: 9 Ayah: 38 & Ayah: 39

﴿ يَـٰٓأَيُّهَا ٱلَّذِينَ ءَامَنُوا۟ مَا لَكُمْ إِذَا قِيلَ لَكُمُ ٱنفِرُوا۟ فِى سَبِيلِ ٱللَّهِ ٱثَّاقَلْتُمْ إِلَى ٱلْأَرْضِ أَرَضِيتُم بِٱلْحَيَوٰةِ ٱلدُّنْيَا مِنَ ٱلْـَٔاخِرَةِ فَمَا مَتَـٰعُ ٱلْحَيَوٰةِ ٱلدُّنْيَا فِى ٱلْـَٔاخِرَةِ إِلَّا قَلِيلٌ ۝ ﴾

38. O you who believe! What is the matter with you, that when you are asked to march forth in the Cause of Allâh (i.e. Jihâd) you cling heavily to the earth? Are you pleased with the life of this world rather than the Hereafter? But little is the enjoyment of the life of this world as compared to the Hereafter.

﴿ إِلَّا تَنفِرُوا۟ يُعَذِّبْكُمْ عَذَابًا أَلِيمًا وَيَسْتَبْدِلْ قَوْمًا غَيْرَكُمْ وَلَا تَضُرُّوهُ شَيْـًٔا ۗ وَٱللَّهُ عَلَىٰ كُلِّ شَىْءٍ قَدِيرٌ ۝ ﴾

39. If you march not forth, He will punish you with a painful torment and will replace you by another people; and you cannot harm Him at all, and Allâh is Able to do all things.

Transliteration

38. Ya ayyuha allatheena amanoo ma lakum itha qeela lakumu infiroo fee sabeeli Allahi iththaqaltum ila al-ardi aradeetum bialhayati alddunya mina al-akhirati fama mataAAu alhayati alddunya fee al-akhirati illa qaleelun   39. Illa tanfiroo yuAAaththibkum AAathaban aleeman wayastabdil qawman ghayrakum wala tadurroohu shay-an waAllahu AAala kulli shay-in qadeerun

Tafsir Ibn Kathir

Admonishing clinging to Life rather than rushing to perform Jihad

Allah admonishes those who lagged behind the Messenger of Allah in the battle of Tabuk, at a time when fruits were ripe and shades tempting in the intense and terrible heat,

(O you who believe! What is the matter with you, that when you are asked to march forth in the cause of Allah), if you are called to perform Jihad in the cause of Allah,

Chapter 9: At-Tawba (Repentance), Verses 001-092

(you cling heavily to the earth), reclining to remain in peace, shade and ripe fruits.

(Are you pleased with the life of this world rather than the Hereafter), why do you do this, is it because you prefer this life instead of the Hereafter Allah next diminishes the eagerness for this worldly life and increases it for the Hereafter,

(But little is the enjoyment of the life of this world compared to the Hereafter.) Imam Ahmad recorded that Al-Mustawrid, a member of Bani Fihr, said that the Messenger of Allah said,

«مَا الدُّنْيَا فِي الْآخِرَةِ إِلَّا كَمَا يَجْعَلُ أَحَدُكُمْ إِصْبَعَهُ هَذِهِ فِي الْيَمِّ، فَلْيَنْظُرْ بِمَ تَرْجِعُ؟»

(The life of this world, compared to the Hereafter, is just like when one of you dips his finger in the sea, let him contemplate how much of it his finger would carry.) The Prophet pointed with his index finger. Muslim collected this Hadith. Ath-Thawri narrated that Al-A`mash said about the Ayah,

(But little is the enjoyment of the life of this world compared to the Hereafter.) "What compares to the provision a traveler takes." `Abdul-`Aziz bin Abi Hazim narrated that his father said, "When `Abdul-`Aziz bin Marwan was dying he said, `Bring the shroud I will be covered with so that I inspect it.' When it was placed before him, he looked at it and said, `Is this what I will end up with from this life' He then turned his back and cried, while saying, `Woe to you, O life! Your abundance is truly little, your little is short lived, we were deceived by you.'" Allah warns those who do not join Jihad,

(If you march not forth, He will punish you with a painful torment) Ibn `Abbas said, "Allah's Messenger called some Arabs to mobilize, but they lagged behind and Allah witheld rain from coming down on them, and this was their torment." Allah said,

(and will replace you by another people), who will give aid to His Prophet and establish his religion. Allah said in another Ayah,

(And if you turn away (from the obedience to Allah), He will exchange you for some other people and they will not be your likes.) (47:38)

(and you cannot harm Him at all), you can never harm Allah when you lag behind and stay away from joining Jihad,

(and Allah is able to do all things.) He is able to destroy the enemies without your help.

Surah: 9 Ayah: 40

﴿إِلَّا تَنصُرُوهُ فَقَدْ نَصَرَهُ ٱللَّهُ إِذْ أَخْرَجَهُ ٱلَّذِينَ كَفَرُوا۟ ثَانِىَ ٱثْنَيْنِ إِذْ هُمَا فِى ٱلْغَارِ إِذْ يَقُولُ لِصَـٰحِبِهِۦ لَا تَحْزَنْ إِنَّ ٱللَّهَ مَعَنَا ۖ فَأَنزَلَ ٱللَّهُ سَكِينَتَهُۥ عَلَيْهِ وَأَيَّدَهُۥ بِجُنُودٍ لَّمْ تَرَوْهَا وَجَعَلَ كَلِمَةَ ٱلَّذِينَ كَفَرُوا۟ ٱلسُّفْلَىٰ ۗ وَكَلِمَةُ ٱللَّهِ هِىَ ٱلْعُلْيَا ۗ وَٱللَّهُ عَزِيزٌ حَكِيمٌ﴾

40. If you help him (Muhammad (peace be upon him)) not (it does not matter), for Allâh did indeed help him when the disbelievers drove him out, the second of two; when they (Muhammad (peace be upon him) and Abu Bakr (may Allah be pleased with him))were in the cave, and he (peace be upon him) said to his companion (Abu Bakr (may Allah be pleased with him)) "Be not sad (or afraid), surely Allâh is with us." Then Allâh sent down His Sakînah (calmness, tranquillity, peace) upon him, and strengthened him with forces (angels) which you saw not, and made the word of those who disbelieved the lowermost, while the Word of Allâh that became the uppermost, and Allâh is All-Mighty, All-Wise.

Transliteration

40. Illa tansuroohu faqad nasarahu Allahu ith akhrajahu allatheena kafaroo thaniya ithnayni ith huma fee alghari ith yaqoolu lisahibihi la tahzan inna Allaha maAAana faanzala Allahu sakeenatahu AAalayhi waayyadahu bijunoodin lam tarawha wajaAAala kalimata allatheena kafaroo alssufla wakalimatu Allahi hiya alAAulya waAllahu AAazeezun hakeemun

Tafsir Ibn Kathir

Allah supports His Prophet

Allah said,

(If you help him not), if you do not support His Prophet, then it does not matter, for Allah will help, support, suffice and protect him, just as He did,

(when the disbelievers drove him out, the second of the two;) During the year of the Hijrah, the idolators tried to kill, imprison or expel the Prophet, who escaped with his friend and Companion, Abu Bakr bin Abi Quhafah, to the cave of Thawr. They remained in the cave for three days so that the pagans who were sent in their pursuit, returned (to Makkah), and they proceed to Al-Madinah. While in the cave, Abu Bakr was afraid the pagans might discover them for fear that some harm might touch the Messenger. The Prophet kept reassuring him and strengthening his resolve, saying,

«يَا أَبَا بَكْرٍ، مَا ظَنُّكَ بِاثْنَيْنِ اللهُ ثَالِثُهُمَا»

(O Abu Bakr! What do you think about two, with Allah as their third) Imam Ahmad recorded from Anas that Abu Bakr said to him, "I said to the Prophet when we were in the cave, `If any of them looks down at his feet, he will see us.' He said,

«يَا أَبَا بَكْرٍ، مَا ظَنُّكَ بِاثْنَيْنِ اللهُ ثَالِثُهُمَا»

(O Abu Bakr! What do you think about two with Allah as their third)" This is recorded in the Two Sahihs. This is why Allah said,

(Then Allah sent down His Sakinah upon him) sent His aid and triumph to His Messenger , or they say it refers to Abu Bakr,

(and strengthened him with forces which you saw not), the angels,

(and made the word of those who disbelieved the lowermost, while the Word of Allah that became the uppermost;) Ibn `Abbas commented, "'The word of those who disbelieved', is Shirk, while, `The Word of Allah' is `La ilaha illallah." It is recorded in the Two Sahihs that Abu Musa Al-Ash`ari said, "The Messenger of Allah was asked about a man who fights because of courage, or out of rage for his honor, or to show off. Whom among them is in the cause of Allah' The Prophet said,

«مَنْ قَاتَلَ لِتَكُونَ كَلِمَةُ اللهِ هِيَ الْعُلْيَا فَهُوَ فِي سَبِيلِ اللهِ»

(He who fights so that Allah's Word is superior, then he fights in Allah's cause.)" Allah said next,

(and Allah is All-Mighty), in His revenge and taking retribution, He is the Most Formidable and those who seek refuge with Him and take shelter by adhering to what He instructs are never made to suffer injustice,

(All-Wise), in His statements and actions.

Surah: 9 Ayah: 41

﴿ انْفِرُواْ خِفَافًا وَثِقَالاً وَجَاهِدُواْ بِأَمْوَالِكُمْ وَأَنفُسِكُمْ فِي سَبِيلِ اللَّهِ ذَلِكُمْ خَيْرٌ لَّكُمْ إِن كُنتُمْ تَعْلَمُونَ ﴿٤١﴾

41. March forth, whether you are light (being healthy, young and wealthy) or heavy (being ill, old and poor), strive hard with your wealth and your lives in the Cause of Allâh. This is better for you, if you but knew.

Transliteration

41. Infiroo khifafan wathiqalan wajahidoo bi-amwalikum waanfusikum fee sabeeli Allahi thalikum khayrun lakum in kuntum taAAlamoona

Tafsir Ibn Kathir

Jihad is required in all Conditions

Sufyan Ath-Thawri narrated from his father from Abu Ad-Duha, Muslim bin Subayh, who said, "This Ayah,

(March forth, whether you are light or heavy) was the first part to be revealed from Surah Bara'ah." Mu`tamir bin Sulayman narrated that his father said, "Hadrami claimed that he was told that some people used to declare that they will not gain sin (if they lag behind the forces of Jihad) because they are ill or old. This Ayah was revealed,

(March forth, whether you are light or heavy.)" Allah commanded mass mobilization together with the Messenger of Allah for the battle of Tabuk, to fight the disbelieving People of the Book, the Romans, Allah's enemies. Allah ordained that the believers all march forth with the Messenger regardless whether they felt active, lazy, at ease or had difficult circumstances,

(March forth, whether you are light or heavy) `Ali bin Zayd narrated that Anas said that Abu Talhah commented (on this Ayah), "Whether you are old or young, Allah did not leave an excuse for anyone." Abu Talhah marched to Ash-Sham and fought until he was killed. In another narration, Abu Talhah recited Surah Bara'ah until he reached this Ayah,

(March forth, whether you are light or heavy, and strive hard with your wealth and your lives in the cause of Allah.) He then said, "I see that Allah had called us to mobilize whether we are old or young. O my children! Prepare my supplies." His children said, `May Allah grant you His mercy! You conducted Jihad along with the Messenger of Allah until he died, then with Abu Bakr until he died, then with `Umar until he died. Let us perform Jihad in your place." Abu Talhah refused and he went to the sea (under the command of Mu`awiyah) where he died. They could not find an island to bury him on until nine days later, during which his body did not deteriorate or change and they buried him on the island. As-Suddi said,

(March forth, whether you are light or heavy), whether you are rich, poor, strong, or weak. A man came forward, and he was fat, complained, and asked for permission to stay behind (from Jihad), but the Prophet refused. Then this Ayah,

(March forth, whether you are light or heavy) was revealed, and it became hard on the people. So Allah abrogated it with this Ayah,

(There is no blame on those who are weak or ill or who find no resources to spend, if they are sincere and true (in duty) to Allah and His Messenger) (9:91)." Ibn Jarir said that Hibban bin Zayd Ash-Shar`abi narrated to him, "We mobilized our forces with Safwan bin `Amr, who was the governor of Hims towards the city of Ephsos appointed to the Jerajima Christian expatriates (in Syria). I saw among the army an old, yet active man, whose eyebrows had sunk over his eyes (from old age), from the residents of Damascus, riding on his animal. I said to him, `O uncle! Allah has given you an excuse (to lag behind).' He said, `O my nephew! Allah has mobilized us

Chapter 9: At-Tawba (Repentance), Verses 001-092

whether we are light or heavy. Verily, those whom Allah loves, He tests them. Then to Allah is their return and eternal dwelling. Allah tests from His servants whoever thanks (Him) and observes patience and remembrance of Him, all the while worshipping Allah, the Exalted and Most Honored, and worshipping none else."' Next, Allah encourages spending in His cause and striving with one's life in His pleasure and the pleasure of His Messenger ,

(and strive hard with your wealth and your lives in the cause of Allah. This is better for you, if you but knew.) Allah says, this is better for you in this life and the Hereafter. You might spend small amounts, but Allah will reward you the property of your enemy in this life, as well as, the honor that He will keep for you in the Hereafter. The Prophet said,

«تَكَفَّلَ اللهُ لِلْمُجَاهِدِ فِي سَبِيلِهِ إِنْ تَوَفَّاهُ أَنْ يُدْخِلَهُ الْجَنَّةَ، أَوْ يَرُدَّهُ إِلَى مَنْزِلِهِ بِمَا نَالَ مِنْ أَجْرٍ أَوْ غَنِيمَة»

(Allah promised the Mujahid in His cause that if He brings death to him, He will enter him into Paradise. Or, He will return him to his house with whatever reward and war spoils he earns.) So Allah said;

(Jihad is ordained for you (Muslims) though you dislike it, and it may be that you dislike a thing which is good for you and that you like a thing which is bad for you. Allah knows but you do not know.)(2:216) Imam Ahmad recorded that Anas said that the Messenger of Allah said to a man,

«أَسْلِم»

(Embrace Islam,) but the man said, "I dislike doing so." The Messenger said,

«أَسْلِمْ وَإِنْ كُنْتَ كَارِهًا»

(Embrace Islam even if you dislike it)."

Surah: 9 Ayah: 42

﴿ لَوْ كَانَ عَرَضًا قَرِيبًا وَسَفَرًا قَاصِدًا لَّاتَّبَعُوكَ وَلَـٰكِن بَعُدَتْ عَلَيْهِمُ ٱلشُّقَّةُ ۚ وَسَيَحْلِفُونَ بِٱللَّهِ لَوِ ٱسْتَطَعْنَا لَخَرَجْنَا مَعَكُمْ يُهْلِكُونَ أَنفُسَهُمْ وَٱللَّهُ يَعْلَمُ إِنَّهُمْ لَكَـٰذِبُونَ ﴿٤٢﴾ ﴾

42. Had it been a near gain (booty in front of them) and an easy journey, they would have followed you, but the distance (Tabuk expedition) was long for them; and

they would swear by Allâh, "If we only could, we would certainly have come forth with you." They destroy their own selves, and Allâh knows that they are liars.

Transliteration

42. Law kana AAaradan qareeban wasafaran qasidan laittabaAAooka walakin baAAudat AAalayhimu alshshuqqatu wasayahlifoona biAllahi lawi istataAAna lakharajna maAAakum yuhlikoona anfusahum waAllahu yaAAlamu innahum lakathiboona

Tafsir Ibn Kathir

Why Hypocrites would not join in Jihad

Allah admonishes those who lagged behind and did not join the Prophet for the battle of Tabuk, those who asked the Prophet for permission to remain behind, falsely pretending to have legitimate reasons to do so,

(Had it been a near gain), booty right in front of them, according to Ibn `Abbas,

(and an easy journey), travel for only a short distance,

(they would have followed you.) But,

(the distance was long for them), to Ash-Sham,

(and they would swear by Allah), when you return to them,

(If we only could, we would certainly have come forth with you), had not there been a valid excuse, we would have gone out with you,

(They destroy themselves, and Allah knows that they are liars.)

Surah: 9 Ayah: 43, Ayah: 44 & Ayah: 45

﴿ عَفَا ٱللَّهُ عَنكَ لِمَ أَذِنتَ لَهُمْ حَتَّىٰ يَتَبَيَّنَ لَكَ ٱلَّذِينَ صَدَقُوا۟ وَتَعْلَمَ ٱلْكَـٰذِبِينَ ۝ ﴾

43. May Allâh forgive you (O Muhammad (peace be upon him)) Why did you grant them leave (for remaining behind; you should have persisted as regards your order to them to proceed on Jihâd), until those who told the truth were seen by you in a clear light, and you had known the liars?

﴿ لَا يَسْتَـْٔذِنُكَ ٱلَّذِينَ يُؤْمِنُونَ بِٱللَّهِ وَٱلْيَوْمِ ٱلْـَٔاخِرِ أَن يُجَـٰهِدُوا۟ بِأَمْوَٰلِهِمْ وَأَنفُسِهِمْ ۗ وَٱللَّهُ عَلِيمٌۢ بِٱلْمُتَّقِينَ ۝ ﴾

44. Those who believe in Allâh and the Last Day would not ask your leave to be exempted from fighting with their properties and their lives; and Allâh is the All-Knower of Al-Muttaqûn (the pious - see V.2:2).

﴿ إِنَّمَا يَسْتَـْٔذِنُكَ ٱلَّذِينَ لَا يُؤْمِنُونَ بِٱللَّهِ وَٱلْيَوْمِ ٱلْـَٔاخِرِ وَٱرْتَابَتْ قُلُوبُهُمْ فَهُمْ فِى رَيْبِهِمْ يَتَرَدَّدُونَ ﴾

45. It is only those who believe not in Allâh and the Last Day and whose hearts are in doubt that ask your leave (to be exempted from Jihâd). So in their doubts they waver.

Transliteration

43. AAafa Allahu AAanka lima athinta lahum hatta yatabayyana laka allatheena sadaqoo wataAAlama alkathibeena 44. La yasta/thinuka allatheena yu/minoona biAllahi waalyawmi al-akhiri an yujahidoo bi-amwalihim waanfusihim waAllahu AAaleemun bialmuttaqeena 45. Innama yasta/thinuka allatheena la yu/minoona biAllahi waalyawmi al-akhiri wairtabat quloobuhum fahum fee raybihim yataraddadoona

Tafsir Ibn Kathir

Moderately criticizing the Prophet for allowing the Hypocrites to stay behind

Ibn Abi Hatim recorded that `Awn said, "Have you heard criticism softer than this, starting with forgiveness before criticism,

(May Allah forgive you. Why did you grant them leave...)" Muwarriq Al-`Ijli and others said similarly. Qatadah said, "Allah criticized him as you read here, then later revealed to him the permission to allow them to lag behind if he wants, in Surat An-Nur,

(So if they ask your permission for some affairs of theirs, give permission to whom you will of them) (24:62)." `Ata' Al-Khurasani said similarly. Mujahid said, "This Ayah was revealed about some people who said, `Ask permission from the Messenger of Allah (to stay behind), and whether he agrees, or disagrees, remain behind!'" Allah said,

(...until those who told the truth were manifest to you), in reference to valid excuses,

(and you had known the liars) Allah says, `Why did you not refuse to give them permission to remain behind when they asked you, so that you know those who truly obey you and the liars, who were intent on remaining behind even if you do not give them permission to do so, Allah asserts that none who believe in Allah and His Messenger seek his permission to remain behind from fighting,

(would not ask your leave), to stay behind from Jihad,

(Those who believe in Allah and the Last Day, to be exempted from fighting with their properties and their lives.) because they consider Jihad an act of worship. This is why when Allah called them to perform Jihad, they obeyed and hasten to act in His obedience,

(and Allah is the All-Knower of those who have Taqwa. Those who ask your leave), to remain behind, without a valid excuse,

(those who believe not in Allah and the Last Day), they do not hope for Allah's reward in the Hereafter for their good actions,

(and whose hearts are in doubt), about the validity of what you brought them,

(so in their doubts they waver.) They waver in doubt, taking one step forward and one step back. They do not have a firm stance in anything, for they are unsure and destroyed, neither belonging to these nor to those. Verily, those whom Allah misguides, will never find a way for themselves to guidance.

Surah: 9 Ayah: 46 & Ayah: 47

﴿ ۞ وَلَوْ أَرَادُواْ ٱلْخُرُوجَ لَأَعَدُّواْ لَهُۥ عُدَّةً وَلَـٰكِن كَرِهَ ٱللَّهُ ٱنۢبِعَاثَهُمْ فَثَبَّطَهُمْ وَقِيلَ ٱقْعُدُواْ مَعَ ٱلْقَـٰعِدِينَ ﴾ ﴿٤٦﴾

46. And if they had intended to march out, certainly, they would have made some preparation for it; but Allâh was averse to their being sent forth, so He made them lag behind, and it was said (to them), "Sit you among those who sit (at home)."

﴿ لَوْ خَرَجُواْ فِيكُم مَّا زَادُوكُمْ إِلَّا خَبَالًا وَلَأَوْضَعُواْ خِلَـٰلَكُمْ يَبْغُونَكُمُ ٱلْفِتْنَةَ وَفِيكُمْ سَمَّـٰعُونَ لَهُمْ ۗ وَٱللَّهُ عَلِيمٌۢ بِٱلظَّـٰلِمِينَ ﴾ ﴿٤٧﴾

47. Had they marched out with you, they would have added to you nothing except disorder, and they would have hurried about in your midst (spreading corruption) and sowing sedition among you - and there are some among you who would have listened to them. And Allâh is the All-Knower of the Zâlimûn (polytheists and wrong-doers).

Transliteration

46. Walaw aradoo alkhurooja laaAAaddoo lahu AAuddatan walakin kariha Allahu inbiAAathahum fathabbatahum waqeela oqAAudoo maAAa alqaAAideena   47. Law kharajoo feekum ma zadookum illa khabalan walaawdaAAoo khilalakum yabghoonakumu alfitnata wafeekum sammaAAoona lahum waAllahu AAaleemun bialththalimeena

Tafsir Ibn Kathir

Exposing Hypocrites

Allah said,

(And if they had intended to march out,), with you to participate in Jihad

(certainly, they would have made some preparation for it) they would have prepared for such task,

(but Allah was averse to their being sent forth) Allah hated that they should go with you,

(so He made them lag behind, and stay away (from Jihad),

(and it was said (to them): "Sit you among those who sit (at home)") as a part of what was decreed for them (not that He legislated that they stay behind). Allah then explained why He disliked that they march with the believers, saying,

(Had they marched out with you, they would have added to you nothing except disorder), because they are cowards and failures,

(and they would have hurried about in your midst sowing sedition among you) They would have rushed to spread false stories, hatred and discord among you,

(and there are some among you who would have listened to them.) who would have obeyed them, given preference to their speech and words and asked them for advice, unaware of the true reality of these hypocrites. This might have caused corruption and great evil between the believers. Muhammad bin Ishaq said, "Those who sought permission (from the Messenger to lag behind) included some of the chiefs, such as `Abdullah bin Ubayy bin Salul and Al-Jadd bin Qays, who were masters of their people. Allah also made them lag behind because He knew that if they went along with the Messenger they would sow sedition in his army." There were some in the Prophet's army who liked these chiefs and were ready to obey them, because they considered them honorable,

(and there are some among you who would have listened to them) (9:47). Allah next reminds of His perfect knowledge, saying,

(And Allah is the All-Knower of the wrongdoers.) Allah says that He knows what occurred, what will occur and if anything would have occurred, how it would occur, such as,

(Had they marched out with you, they would have added to you nothing except disorder,) indicating what they would have done had they marched, even though they did not. Allah said in similar Ayat,

(But if they were returned (to the world), they would certainly revert to that which they were forbidden. And indeed they are liars.) (6:28),

(Had Allah known of any good in them, He would indeed have made them listen; and even if He had made them listen, they would but have turned away with aversion (to the truth)) (8:23), and,

(And if We had ordered them (saying), "Kill yourselves (the innocent ones kill the guilty ones) or leave your homes," very few of them would have done it; but if they had done what they were told, it would have been better for them, and would have strengthened their conviction. And indeed We would then have bestowed upon them a great reward from Ourselves. And indeed We would have guided them to the straight way) (4:66-68).

Surah: 9 Ayah: 48

﴿ لَقَدِ ٱبْتَغَوُاْ ٱلْفِتْنَةَ مِن قَبْلُ وَقَلَّبُواْ لَكَ ٱلْأُمُورَ حَتَّىٰ جَآءَ ٱلْحَقُّ وَظَهَرَ أَمْرُ ٱللَّهِ وَهُمْ كَـٰرِهُونَ ﴾

48. Verily, they had plotted sedition before, and had upset matters for you, until the truth (victory) came and the Decree of Allâh (His Religion, Islâm) became manifest though they hated it.

Transliteration

48. Laqadi ibtaghawoo alfitnata min qablu waqallaboo laka al-omoora hatta jaa alhaqqu wathahara amru Allahi wahum karihoona

Tafsir Ibn Kathir

Allah encourages His Prophet against hypocrites,

(Verily, they had plotted sedition before, and had upset matters for you,) `For a long time,' Allah says, hypocrites thought and plotted against you and your Companions, as well as, failing and attempting to extinguish your religion.' This occurred soon after the Prophet migrated to Al-Madinah, when pagan Arabs joined force and the Jews and hypocrites of Al-Madinah waged war against the Messenger . When Allah gave victory to the Prophet in Badr and raised high his word, `Abdullah bin Ubayy and his fellows said, "This (Islam) is a matter that has prevailed." They embraced Islam outwardly, and whenever Allah elevated Islam and its people in might, hypocrites increased in rage and disappointment,

(until the truth (victory) came and the decree of Allah became manifest though they hated it.)

Surah: 9 Ayah: 49

﴿ وَمِنْهُم مَّن يَقُولُ ٱئْذَن لِّى وَلَا تَفْتِنِّىٓ أَلَا فِى ٱلْفِتْنَةِ سَقَطُواْ وَإِنَّ جَهَنَّمَ لَمُحِيطَةٌ بِٱلْكَـٰفِرِينَ ﴾

Chapter 9: At-Tawba (Repentance), Verses 001-092

49. And among them is he who says: "Grant me leave (to be exempted from Jihâd) and put me not into trial." Surely, they have fallen into trial. And verily, Hell is surrounding the disbelievers.

Transliteration

49. Waminhum man yaqoolu i/than lee wala taftinnee ala fee alfitnati saqatoo wa-inna jahannama lamuheetatun bialkafireena

Tafsir Ibn Kathir

Allah says, some hypocrites say to you, O Muhammad ,

(Grant me leave), to stay behind,

(and put me not into trial.), if I go with you and see the women of the Romans. Allah, the Exalted, replied,

5(Surely, they have fallen into trial) because of the statement they uttered. Muhammad bin Ishaq reported from Az-Zuhri, Yazid bin Ruwman, `Abdullah bin Abi Bakr, `Asim bin Qatadah and several others that they said, "The Messenger of Allah said to Al-Jadd bin Qays from Bani Salimah,

«هَلْ لَكَ يَا جَدُّ الْعَامَ فِي جَلَادِ بَنِي الْأَصْفَرِ؟»

(`Would you like to fight the yellow ones (Romans) this year) He said, `O Allah's Messenger! Give me permission (to remain behind) and do not cause Fitnah for me. By Allah! My people know that there is not a man who is more fond of women than I. I fear that if I see the women of the yellow ones, I would not be patient.' The Messenger of Allah turned away from him and said,

«قَدْ أَذِنْتُ لَكَ»

(I give you permission.) In Al-Jadd's case, this Ayah was revealed,

(And among them is he who says: "Grant me leave and put me not into trial.") Therefore, Allah says that the Fitnah that he fell into because of not joining the Messenger of Allah (in Jihad) and preferring his safety to the safety of the Messenger is worse than the Fitnah that he falsely claimed to fear." It was reported from Ibn `Abbas, Mujahid and several others that this Ayah was revealed in the case of Al-Jadd bin Qays, who was among the chiefs of Bani Salimah. It is also recorded in the Sahih that the Messenger of Allah asked,

«مَنْ سَيِّدُكُمْ يَا بَنِي سَلَمَةَ؟»

(Who is your chief, O Bani Salamah) They said, "Al-Jadd bin Qays, although we consider him a miser." The Messenger of Allah said,

«وَأَيُّ دَاءٍ أَدْوَأُ مِنَ الْبُخْلِ وَلَكِنْ سَيِّدُكُمْ الْفَتَى الْجَعْدُ الْأَبْيَضُ بِشْرُ بْنُ الْبَرَاءِ بْنِ مَعْرُورٍ»

(There is not a disease worse than stinginess! Therefore, your chief is the white young man with curly hair, Bishr bin Al-Bara' bin Ma'rur.) Allah said next,

(And verily, Hell is surrounding the disbelievers.) and they will never be able to avoid, avert, or escape from it.

Surah: 9 Ayah: 50 & Ayah: 51

﴿ إِن تُصِبْكَ حَسَنَةٌ تَسُؤْهُمْ ۖ وَإِن تُصِبْكَ مُصِيبَةٌ يَقُولُوا۟ قَدْ أَخَذْنَآ أَمْرَنَا مِن قَبْلُ وَيَتَوَلَّوا۟ وَّهُمْ فَرِحُونَ ۝ ﴾

50. If good befalls you (O Muhammad (peace be upon him)) it grieves them, but if a calamity overtakes you, they say: "We took our precaution beforehand," and they turn away rejoicing.

﴿ قُل لَّن يُصِيبَنَآ إِلَّا مَا كَتَبَ ٱللَّهُ لَنَا هُوَ مَوْلَىٰنَا ۚ وَعَلَى ٱللَّهِ فَلْيَتَوَكَّلِ ٱلْمُؤْمِنُونَ ۝ ﴾

51. Say: "Nothing shall ever happen to us except what Allâh has ordained for us. He is our Maulâ (Lord, Helper and Protector)." And in Allâh let the believers put their trust.

Transliteration

50. In tusibka hasanatun tasu/hum wa-in tusibka museebatun yaqooloo qad akhathna amrana min qablu wayatawallaw wahum farihoona 51. Qul lan yuseebana illa ma kataba Allahu lana huwa mawlana waAAala Allahi falyatawakkali almu/minoona

Tafsir Ibn Kathir

Allah emphasizes the enmity that the hypocrites have for the Prophet.

If a blessing, such as victory and triumph over the enemies, is given to the Prophet, thus pleasing him and his Companions, it grieves the hypocrites,

(but if a calamity overtakes you, they say: "We took our precaution beforehand,"), they say, we took precautions when we did not join him,

Chapter 9: At-Tawba (Repentance), Verses 001-092

(and they turn away rejoicing.) Allah directed His Prophet to reply to the perfect enmity they have towards him,

(Say), to them,

(Nothing shall ever happen to us except what Allah has ordained for us.) for we are under His control and decree,

(He is our Mawla.), Master and protector,

(And in Allah let the believers put their trust) (9:51), and we trust in Him. Verily, He is sufficient for us and what an excellent guardian.

Surah: 9 Ayah: 52, Ayah: 53 & Ayah: 54

﴿ قُلْ هَلْ تَرَبَّصُونَ بِنَا إِلَّا إِحْدَى ٱلْحُسْنَيَيْنِ ۖ وَنَحْنُ نَتَرَبَّصُ بِكُمْ أَن يُصِيبَكُمُ ٱللَّهُ بِعَذَابٍ مِّنْ عِندِهِۦٓ أَوْ بِأَيْدِينَا ۖ فَتَرَبَّصُوٓا۟ إِنَّا مَعَكُم مُّتَرَبِّصُونَ ۝ ﴾

52. Say: "Do you wait for us (anything) except one of the two best things (martyrdom or victory); while we await for you either that Allâh will afflict you with a punishment from Himself or at our hands. So wait, we too are waiting with you."

﴿ قُلْ أَنفِقُوا۟ طَوْعًا أَوْ كَرْهًا لَّن يُتَقَبَّلَ مِنكُمْ ۖ إِنَّكُمْ كُنتُمْ قَوْمًا فَٰسِقِينَ ۝ ﴾

53. Say: "Spend (in Allâh's Cause) willingly or unwillingly, it will not be accepted from you. Verily, you are ever a people who are Fâsiqûn (rebellious, disobedient to Allâh)."

﴿ وَمَا مَنَعَهُمْ أَن تُقْبَلَ مِنْهُمْ نَفَقَٰتُهُمْ إِلَّآ أَنَّهُمْ كَفَرُوا۟ بِٱللَّهِ وَبِرَسُولِهِۦ وَلَا يَأْتُونَ ٱلصَّلَوٰةَ إِلَّا وَهُمْ كُسَالَىٰ وَلَا يُنفِقُونَ إِلَّا وَهُمْ كَٰرِهُونَ ۝ ﴾

54. And nothing prevents their contributions from being accepted from them except that they disbelieved in Allâh and in His Messenger (Muhammad (peace be upon him)) and that they came not to As-Salât (the prayer) except in a lazy state, and that they offer not contributions but unwillingly.

Transliteration

52. Qul hal tarabbasoona bina illa ihda alhusnayayni wanahnu natarabbasu bikum an yuseebakumu Allahu biAAathabin min AAindihi aw bi-aydeena fatarabbasoo inna maAAakum mutarabbisoona   53. Qul anfiqoo tawAAan aw karhan lan yutaqabbala minkum innakum kuntum qawman fasiqeena   54. Wama manaAAahum an tuqbala minhum nafaqatuhum illa annahum kafaroo biAllahi wabirasoolihi wala ya/toona alssalata illa wahum kusala wala yunfiqoona illa wahum karihoona

Tafsir Ibn Kathir

Allah said,

(Say), O Muhammad to them,

(Do you wait for us), anything,

(except one of the two best things), martyrdom or victory over you, according to the meaning given by Ibn `Abbas, Mujahid, Qatadah, and others.

(while we await for you), that this will touch you,

(either that Allah will afflict you with a punishment from Himself or at our hands), either capture or killing,

(So wait, we too are waiting with you.) Allah said next,

(Say: Spend willingly or unwillingly), for whatever you spend either way,

(it will not be accepted from you. Verily, you are ever a people who are rebellious.) Allah mentions the reason behind not accepting their charity from them,

(except that they disbelieved in Allah and in His Messenger.) and the deeds are accepted if they are preceded with faith,

(and that they came not to the Salah except in a lazy state.) Therefore, they neither have good intention nor eagerness to perform the acts (of faith),

(And nothing prevents their contributions from being accepted from them except that they disbelieved in Allah and in His Messenger, and that they came not to the Salah (the prayer) except in a lazy state, and that they offer not contributions but unwillingly.) The Truthful, to whom the Truth was revealed, Muhammad, peace be upon him, said that Allah does not stop giving rewards until you (believers) stop performing good deeds, and that Allah is Tayyib (Good and Pure) and only accepts what is Tayyib. This is why Allah does not accept charity or good deeds from the people described in these Ayat, because He only accepts it from those who have Taqwa.

Surah: 9 Ayah: 55

﴿ فَلَا تُعْجِبْكَ أَمْوَالُهُمْ وَلَا أَوْلَادُهُمْ إِنَّمَا يُرِيدُ اللَّهُ لِيُعَذِّبَهُم بِهَا فِي الْحَيَوٰةِ الدُّنْيَا وَتَزْهَقَ أَنفُسُهُمْ وَهُمْ كَافِرُونَ ﴾

55. So let not their wealth or their children amaze you (O Muhammad (peace be upon him)) in reality Allâh's Plan is to punish them with these things in the life of the this world, and that their souls shall depart (die) while they are disbelievers.

Transliteration

55. Fala tuAAjibka amwaluhum wala awladuhum innama yureedu Allahu liyuAAaththibahum biha fee alhayati alddunya watazhaqa anfusuhum wahum kafiroona

Tafsir Ibn Kathir

Allah says to His Messenger ,

(So let not their wealth nor their children amaze you...) In similar Ayat, Allah said,

(And strain not your eyes in longing for the things We have given for enjoyment to various groups of them, the splendor of the life of this world, that We may test them thereby. But the provision (good reward in the Hereafter) of your Lord is better and more lasting) (20:131), and,

(Do they think that in wealth and children with which We enlarge them. We hasten unto them with good things. Nay, but they perceive not.) (23:55-56). Allah said next,

(in reality Allah's plan is to punish them with these things in the life of this world,) by taking the Zakah due on their money from them and spending it in Allah's cause, according to the meaning given by Al-Hasan Al-Basri. Allah's statement,

(and that their souls shall depart while they are disbelievers) means, so that when Allah brings death to them, they will still be disbelievers, to make matters worse for them and the torment more severe. We seek refuge from such an end, which includes being led astray gradually by these things which they have.

Surah: 9 Ayah: 56 & Ayah: 57

﴿ وَيَحْلِفُونَ بِاللَّهِ إِنَّهُمْ لَمِنكُمْ وَمَا هُم مِّنكُمْ وَلَـٰكِنَّهُمْ قَوْمٌ يَفْرَقُونَ ۝ ﴾

56. They swear by Allâh that they are truly of you while they are not of you, but they are a people (hypocrites) who are afraid (that you may kill them).

﴿ لَوْ يَجِدُونَ مَلْجَأً أَوْ مَغَـٰرَٰتٍ أَوْ مُدَّخَلاً لَّوَلَّوْاْ إِلَيْهِ وَهُمْ يَجْمَحُونَ ۝ ﴾

57. Should they find a refuge, or caves, or a place of concealment, they would turn straightway thereto with a swift rush.

Transliteration

56. Wayahlifoona biAllahi innahum laminkum wama hum minkum walakinnahum qawmun yafraqoona 57. Law yajidoona maljaan aw magharatin aw muddakhalan lawallaw ilayhi wahum yajmahoona

Tafsir Ibn Kathir

Exposing Hypocrites' Fright and Fear

Allah describes to His Prophet the fright, fear, anxiety and nervousness of the hypocrites,

(They swear by Allah that they are truly of you), swearing a sure oath,

(while they are not of you), in reality,

(but they are a people who are afraid), and this is what made them swear.

(Should they find a refuge), such as a fort in which they hide and fortify themselves,

(or caves), in some mountains,

(or a place of concealment), a tunnel or a hole in the ground, according to the explanation given by Ibn `Abbas, Mujahid and Qatadah,

(they would turn straightway thereto with a swift rush) away from you because they associate with you unwillingly, not because they are fond of you. They prefer that they do not have to mix with you, but necessity has its rules! It is because of this that they feel grief, sadness and sorrow, seeing Islam and its people enjoying ever more might, triumph and glory. Therefore, whatever pleases Muslims brings them grief, and this is why they prefer to disassociate themselves from the believers. Hence Allah's statement,

(Should they find a refuge, or caves, or a place of concealment, they would turn straightway thereto with a swift rush.)

Surah: 9 Ayah: 58 & Ayah: 59

﴿ وَمِنْهُم مَّن يَلْمِزُكَ فِى ٱلصَّدَقَٰتِ فَإِنْ أُعْطُوا۟ مِنْهَا رَضُوا۟ وَإِن لَّمْ يُعْطَوْا۟ مِنْهَآ إِذَا هُمْ يَسْخَطُونَ ۝ ﴾

58. And of them are some who accuse you (O Muhammad (peace be upon him)) in the matter of (the distribution of) the alms. If they are given part thereof, they are pleased, but if they are not given thereof, behold! They are enraged!

﴿ وَلَوْ أَنَّهُمْ رَضُوا۟ مَآ ءَاتَىٰهُمُ ٱللَّهُ وَرَسُولُهُۥ وَقَالُوا۟ حَسْبُنَا ٱللَّهُ سَيُؤْتِينَا ٱللَّهُ مِن فَضْلِهِۦ وَرَسُولُهُۥٓ إِنَّآ إِلَى ٱللَّهِ رَٰغِبُونَ ۝ ﴾

59. Would that they were contented with what Allâh and His Messenger (peace be upon him) gave them and had said: "Allâh is Sufficient for us. Allâh will give us of His Bounty, and so will His Messenger (from alms). We implore Allâh (to enrich us)."

Chapter 9: At-Tawba (Repentance), Verses 001-092

Transliteration

58. Waminhum man yalmizuka fee alssadaqati fa-in oAAtoo minha radoo wa-in lam yuAAtaw minha itha hum yaskhatoona   59. Walaw annahum radoo ma atahumu Allahu warasooluhu waqaloo hasbuna Allahu sayu/teena Allahu min fadlihi warasooluhu inna ila Allahi raghiboona

Tafsir Ibn Kathir

Hypocrites question the Integrity of the Messenger when distributing Alms

Allah said next,

(And of them), among the hypocrites,

(who accuse you) or question your integrity,

(concerning), division of,

(the alms), when you divide them. They question your fairness, even though it is they who deserve that their integrity be questioned. The hypocrites do not do this in defense of the religion, but to gain more for themselves. This is why,

(If they are given) meaning, from the Zakah,

(They are pleased, but if they are not given thereof, behold! They are enraged!) (9:58), angry for themselves. Qatadah commented on Allah's statement,

(And of them are some who accuse you concerning the alms.) "Allah says, `Some of them question your integrity in the matter of distribution of the alms.' We were told that a bedouin man, who had recently embraced Islam, came to the Prophet , when he was dividing some gold and silver, and said to him, `O Muhammad! Even though Allah commanded you to divide in fairness, you have not done so.' The Prophet of Allah said,

«وَيْلَكَ فَمَنْ ذَا الَّذِي يَعْدِلُ عَلَيْكَ بَعْدِي؟»

(Woe to you! Who would be fair to you after me then) The Prophet of Allah said next,

«احْذَرُوا هَذَا وَأَشْبَاهَهُ فَإِنَّ فِي أُمَّتِي أَشْبَاهُ هَذَا يَقْرَءُونَ الْقُرْآنَ لَا يُجَاوِزُ تَرَاقِيهِمْ فَإِذَا خَرَجُوا فَاقْتُلُوهُمْ، ثُمَّ إِذَا خَرَجُوا فَاقْتُلُوهُمْ، ثُمَّ إِذَا خَرَجُوا فَاقْتُلُوهُمْ»

(Beware of this man and his likes! There are similar persons in my Ummah who recite the Qur'an, but the Qur'an will not go beyond their throat. If they rise (against Muslims rulers) then kill them, if they rise, kill them, then if they rise kill them.) We were also told that the Prophet of Allah used to say,

$$\text{«وَالَّذِي نَفْسِي بِيَدِهِ مَا أُعْطِيكُمْ شَيْئًا وَلَا أَمْنَعُكُمُوهُ إِنَّمَا أَنَا خَازِنٌ»}$$

(By He in Whose Hand is my life! I do not give or withhold anything; I am only a keeper.)" This statement from Qatadah is similar to the Hadith that the Two Shaykhs narrated from Abu Sa`id about the story of Dhul-Khuwaysirah, whose name was Hurqus. Hurqus protested against the Prophet's division of the war spoils of Hunayn, saying, "Be fair, for you have not been fair!" The Prophet said,

$$\text{«لَقَدْ خِبْتُ وَخَسِرْتُ إِنْ لَمْ أَكُنْ أَعْدِلُ»}$$

(I would have become a loser and a failure if I was not fair!) The Messenger said after that man left,

$$\text{«إِنَّهُ يَخْرُجُ مِنْ ضِئْضِىءِ هَذَا قَوْمٌ يَحْقِرُ أَحَدُكُمْ صَلَاتَهُ مَعَ صَلَاتِهِمْ وَصِيَامَهُ مَعَ صِيَامِهِمْ، يَمْرُقُونَ مِنَ الدِّينِ مُرُوقَ السَّهْمِ مِنَ الرَّمِيَّةِ، فَأَيْنَمَا لَقِيتُمُوهُمْ فَاقْتُلُوهُمْ؛ فَإِنَّهُمْ شَرُّ قَتْلَى تَحْتَ أَدِيمِ السَّمَاءِ»}$$

(Among the offspring of this man will be some with whose prayer, when one of you sees it, would belittle his prayer, and his fast as compared to their fast. They will be renegades from the religion, just like an arrow goes through the game's body. Wherever you find them, kill them, for verily, they are the worst dead people under the cover of the sky.) Allah said next, while directing such people to what is more beneficial for them than their behavior,

(Would that they were content with what Allah and His Messenger gave them and had said: "Allah is sufficient for us. Allah will give us of His bounty, and so will His Messenger (from alms). We implore Allah (to enrich us).") This honorable Ayah contains a gracious type of conduct and an honorable secret. Allah listed; contentment with what He and His Messenger give, trusting in Allah alone -- by saying;

(and they had said: Allah is sufficient for us), and hoping in Allah alone, and He made these the indications of obedience to the Messenger , adhering to his commands, avoiding his prohibitions, believing his narrations and following his footsteps.

Surah: 9 Ayah: 60

﴿ ۞ إِنَّمَا ٱلصَّدَقَٰتُ لِلْفُقَرَآءِ وَٱلْمَسَٰكِينِ وَٱلْعَٰمِلِينَ عَلَيْهَا وَٱلْمُؤَلَّفَةِ قُلُوبُهُمْ وَفِى ٱلرِّقَابِ وَٱلْغَٰرِمِينَ وَفِى سَبِيلِ ٱللَّهِ وَٱبْنِ ٱلسَّبِيلِ ۖ فَرِيضَةً مِّنَ ٱللَّهِ ۗ وَٱللَّهُ عَلِيمٌ حَكِيمٌ ﴾ ۝

60. As-Sadaqât (here it means Zakât) are only for the Fuqarâ' (poor), and Al-Masâkin (the poor) and those employed to collect (the funds), and to attract the hearts of those who have been inclined (towards Islâm); and to free the captives, and for those in debt, and for Allâh's Cause (i.e. for Mujâhidûn - those fighting in a holy battle), and for the wayfarer (a traveler who is cut off from everything); a duty imposed by Allâh. And Allâh is All-Knower, All-Wise.

Transliteration

60. Innama alssadaqatu lilfuqara-i waalmasakeeni waalAAamileena AAalayha waalmu-allafati quloobuhum wafee alrriqabi waalgharimeena wafee sabeeli Allahi waibni alssabeeli fareedatan mina Allahi waAllahu AAaleemun hakeemun

Tafsir Ibn Kathir

Expenditures of Zakah (Alms)

After Allah mentioned the protest that the ignorant hypocrites mentioned to the Prophet about the distribution of alms. He stated that it is He who divided the alms, explained its rulings and decided in its division; He did not delegate this decision to anyone else. Allah mentioned the expenditures of Zakah in this Ayah, starting with the Fuqara' (the poor) because they have more need than the other categories, since their need is pressing and precarious. It was reported that Ibn `Abbas, Mujahid, Al-Hasan Al-Basri, Ibn Zayd and several others said that the Faqir is a graceful person who does not ask anyone for anything, while the Miskin is the one who follows after people, begging. Qatadah said, "The Faqir is the ill person, while the Miskin is physically fit." We will now mention the Hadiths about each of these eight categories

The Fuqara' (Poor)

Ibn `Umar said that the Messenger of Allah said,

«لَا تَحِلُّ الصَّدَقَةُ لِغَنِيٍّ وَلَا لِذِي مِرَّةٍ سَوِيٍّ»

(The alms should not be given to the wealthy and the physically fit.) Ahmad, Abu Dawud and At-Tirmidhi collected this Hadith.

The Masakin (Needy)

Abu Hurayrah narrated that the Messenger of Allah said,

«لَيْسَ الْمِسْكِينُ بِهَذَا الطَّوَّافِ الَّذِي يَطُوفُ عَلَى النَّاسِ فَتَرُدُّهُ اللُّقْمَةُ وَاللُّقْمَتَانِ، وَالتَّمْرَةُ وَالتَّمْرَتَانِ»

(The needy person is not the one who goes round the people and asks them for a mouthful or two (of meals) or a date or two). They asked, "Then who is the needy person, O Allah's Messenger!" He said,

«الَّذِي لَا يَجِدُ غِنًى يُغْنِيهِ، وَلَا يُفْطَنُ لَهُ فَيُتَصَدَّقَ عَلَيْهِ، وَلَا يَسْأَلُ النَّاسَ شَيْئًا»

(The one who does not have enough to satisfy his needs and whose condition is not known to others, that others may give him something in charity, and who does not beg of people.) The Two Shaykhs collected this Hadith

Those employed to collect Alms

Those employed to collect alms deserve a part of the alms, unless they are relatives of the Messenger of Allah , who are not allowed to accept any Sadaqah. Muslim recorded that `Abdul-Muttalib bin Rabi`ah bin Al-Harith and Al-Fadl bin Al-`Abbas went to the Messenger of Allah asking him to employ them to collect the alms. The Messenger replied,

«إِنَّ الصَّدَقَةَ لَا تَحِلُّ لِمُحَمَّدٍ وَلَا لِآلِ مُحَمَّدٍ، إِنَّمَا هِيَ أَوْسَاخُ النَّاسِ»

(Verily, the alms are not allowed for Muhammad nor the relatives of Muhammad, for it is only the dirt that the people discard.) Al-Mu'allafatu Qulubuhum There are several types of Al-Mu'allafatu Qulubuhum. There are those who are given alms to embrace Islam. For instance, the Prophet of Allah gave something to Safwan bin Umayyah from the war spoils of Hunayn, even though he attended it while a Mushrik. Safwan said, "He kept giving me until he became the dearest person to me after he had been the most hated person to me." Imam Ahmad recorded that Safwan bin Umayyah said, "The Messenger of Allah gave me (from the spoils of) Hunayn while he was the most hateful person to me. He kept giving me until he became the most beloved person to me." Muslim and At-Tirmidhi collected this Hadith, as well. Some of Al-Mu'allafatu Qulubuhum are given from alms so that they become better in Islam and their heart firmer in faith. For instance, the Prophet gave some of the chiefs of the Tulaqa' a hundred camels each after the battle of Hunayn, saying,

Chapter 9: At-Tawba (Repentance), Verses 001-092

»إِنِّي لَأُعْطِي الرَّجُلَ وَغَيْرُهُ أَحَبُّ إِلَيَّ مِنْهُ خَشْيَةَ أَنْ يُكِبَّهُ اللهُ عَلَى وَجْهِهِ فِي نَارِ جَهَنَّمَ«

(I give a man (from the alms) while another man is dearer to me than him, for fear that Allah might throw him on his face in the fire of Jahannam.) It is recorded in the Two Sahihs that Abu Sa`id said that `Ali sent the Messenger of Allah a gold nugget still in its dirt from Yemen. The Prophet divided it between four men: Al-Aqra` bin Habis, `Uyaynah bin Badr, `Alqamah bin `Ulathah and Zayd Al-Khayr, saying,

»أَتَأَلَّفُهُم«

(To draw their hearts closer.) Some people are given because some of his peers might embrace Islam, while others are given to collect alms from surrounding areas, or to defend Muslim outposts. Allah knows best.

The Riqab

Al-Hasan Al-Basri, Muqatil bin Hayyan, `Umar bin `Abdul-`Aziz, Sa`id bin Jubayr, An-Nakha`i, Az-Zuhri and Ibn Zayd said Riqab means those slaves who make an agreement with the master to pay a certain ransom for their freedom." Similar was reported from Abu Musa Al-Ash`ari. Ibn `Abbas and Al-Hasan said, "It is allowed to use Zakah funds to buy the freedom of slaves," indicating that `Riqab' has more general meanings than merely giving money to slaves to buy their freedom or one's buying a slave and freeing him on an individual basis. A Hadith states that for every limb (of the servant) freed, Allah frees a limb of the one who freed him from slavery, even a sexual organ for a sexual organ, for the reward is equitable to the deed,

(And you will be requited nothing except for what you used to do.) (37:39)

Virtue of freeing Slaves

In the Musnad, there is a Hadith from Al-Bara' bin `Azib that a man asked, "O Allah's Messenger! Direct me to an action that draws me closer to Paradise and away from the Fire." The Messenger of Allah said,

»أَعْتِقِ النَّسَمَةَ وَفُكَّ الرَّقَبَةَ«

(Emancipate the person and free the neck (slave).) The man asked, "O Allah's Messenger! Are they not one and the same" He said,

»لَا، عِتْقُ النَّسَمَةِ أَنْ تُفْرِدَ بِعِتْقِهَا، وَفَكُّ الرَّقَبَةِ أَنْ تُعِينَ فِي ثَمَنِهَا«

(No, you emancipate a person by freeing him on your own, but you untie a neck (slave) by helping in its price.)

Al-Gharimun (the Indebted)

There are several types of indebted persons. They include those who incur expenses in solving disputes between people, those who guarantee a loan that became due, causing financial strain to them, and those whose funds do not sufficiently cover their debts. It also includes those who indulged in a sin and repented from it. These types have a right to a part of alms (designated for Al-Gharimun). Qabisah bin Mukhariq Al-Hilali said, "I carried a debt (resolving a dispute between people) and went to the Messenger of Allah asking him to help pay it. The Messenger said,

«أَقِمْ حَتَّى تَأْتِيَنَا الصَّدَقَةُ فَنَأْمُرَ لَكَ بِهَا»

(Be patient until some alms are brought to us so that we give it to you.) He then said,

«يَا قَبِيصَةُ إِنَّ الْمَسْأَلَةَ لَا تَحِلُّ إِلَّا لِأَحَدِ ثَلَاثَةٍ: رَجُلٍ تَحَمَّلَ حَمَالَةً فَحَلَّتْ لَهُ الْمَسْأَلَةُ حَتَّى يُصِيبَهَا ثُمَّ يُمْسِكَ، وَرَجُلٍ أَصَابَتْهُ جَائِحَةٌ اجْتَاحَتْ مَالَهُ فَحَلَّتْ لَهُ الْمَسْأَلَةُ حَتَّى يُصِيبَ قِوَامًا مِنْ عَيْشٍ أَوْ قَالَ: سِدَادًا مِنْ عَيْشٍ وَرَجُلٍ أَصَابَتْهُ فَاقَةٌ حَتَّى يَقُومَ ثَلَاثَةٌ مِنْ ذَوِي الْحِجَا مِنْ قَرَابَةِ قَوْمِهِ فَيَقُولُونَ: لَقَدْ أَصَابَتْ فُلَانًا فَاقَةٌ فَحَلَّتْ لَهُ الْمَسْأَلَةُ، حَتَّى يُصِيبَ قِوَامًا مِنْ عَيْشٍ أَوْ قَالَ: سِدَادًا مِنْ عَيْشٍ فَمَا سِوَاهُنَّ مِنَ الْمَسْأَلَةِ سُحْتٌ يَأْكُلُهَا صَاحِبُهَا سُحْتًا»

(O Qabisah! Begging is only allowed for three: a man who incurred debts solving disputes, so he is allowed to beg until he collects its amount and then stops. A man who was inflicted by a disaster that consumed his wealth, he is allowed to beg until he collects what suffices for his livelihood. And a man who was overcome by poverty, that three wise relatives of his stand up and proclaim, `So-and-so was overcome by poverty.' This man is allowed to beg until he collects what sustains his livelihood. Other than these cases, begging is an unlawful amount that one illegally devours.) Muslim collected this Hadith. Abu Sa`id said, "During the time of the Messenger of Allah , a man was struck by disaster because of fruits that he bought, causing him extensive debts. The Prophet said,

«تَصَدَّقُوا عَلَيْهِ»

(Give him charity.) The people did that but the amount collected did not cover his debts. The Prophet said to the man's debtors,

«خُذُوا مَا وَجَدْتُمْ وَلَيْسَ لَكُمْ إِلَّا ذَلِكَ»

(Take what was collected, you will have nothing beyond that.)" Muslim collected this Hadith.

In the Cause of Allah

In the cause of Allah is exclusive for the benefit of the fighters in Jihad, who do not receive compensation from the Muslim Treasury.

Ibn As-Sabil (Wayfarer)

Ibn As-Sabil is a term used for the needy traveler in a land, where he does not have what helps him continue his trip. This type has a share in the Zakah for what suffices him to reach his destination, even if he had money there. The same is true for whoever intends to travel from his area but does not have enough money. This type also has a share in the Zakah money to suffice for his trip and back. This is proven in the Ayah as well as the following Hadith. Imams Abu Dawud and Ibn Majah recorded that Ma`mar said that Zayd bin Aslam said that `Ata' bin Yasar said that Abu Sa`id Al-Khudri said that the Messenger of Allah said,

«لَا تَحِلُّ الصَّدَقَةُ لِغَنِيٍّ إِلَّا لِخَمْسَةٍ: لِعَامِلٍ عَلَيْهَا، أَوْ رَجُلٍ اشْتَرَاهَا بِمَالِهِ، أَوْ غَارِمٍ، أَوْ غَازٍ فِي سَبِيلِ اللَّهِ، أَوْ مِسْكِينٍ تُصُدِّقَ عَلَيْهِ مِنْهَا فَأَهْدَى لِغَنِيٍّ»

(Sadaqah is not rightful for a wealthy person except in five cases: those employed to collect it, one who bought a charity item with his money, a Gharim (debtor), a fighter in the cause of Allah, or a poor man who gets a part of the Zakah so he gives it as a gift to a rich man.) Allah's statement,

(a duty imposed by Allah), means, a decision, decree and division ordained by Allah,

(And Allah is All-Knower, All-Wise), knowledgeable of all things outwardly and inwardly and what benefits His servants,

(All-Wise), in all what he declares, does, legislates and decides, there is no true deity or lord except Him.

Surah: 9 Ayah: 61

﴿ وَمِنْهُمُ ٱلَّذِينَ يُؤْذُونَ ٱلنَّبِىَّ وَيَقُولُونَ هُوَ أُذُنٌ قُلْ أُذُنُ خَيْرٍ لَّكُمْ يُؤْمِنُ بِٱللَّهِ وَيُؤْمِنُ لِلْمُؤْمِنِينَ وَرَحْمَةٌ لِّلَّذِينَ ءَامَنُواْ مِنكُمْ وَٱلَّذِينَ يُؤْذُونَ رَسُولَ ٱللَّهِ لَهُمْ عَذَابٌ أَلِيمٌ ﴾

61. And among them are men who annoy the Prophet (Muhammad (peace be upon him)) and say: "He is (lending his) ear (to every news)." Say: "He listens to what is best for you; he believes in Allâh, has faith in the believers, and is a mercy to those of you who believe." But those who hurt Allâh's Messenger (Muhammad (peace be upon him)) will have a painful torment.

Transliteration

61. Waminhumu allatheena yu/thoona alnnabiyya wayaqooloona huwa othunun qul othunu khayrin lakum yu/minu biAllahi wayu/minu lilmu/mineena warahmatun lillatheena amanoo minkum waallatheena yu/thoona rasoola Allahi lahum AAathabun aleemun

Tafsir Ibn Kathir

Hypocrites annoy the Prophet

Allah says, some hypocrites bother the Messenger of Allah by questioning his character, saying,

(he is (lending his) ear), to those who say anything about us; he believes whoever talks to him. Therefore, if we went to him and swore, he would believe us. Similar was reported from Ibn `Abbas, Mujahid and Qatadah. Allah said,

(Say: "He listens to what is best for you"), he knows who's saying the truth and who is lying,

(he believes in Allah; has faith in the believers), he believes the believers,

(and is a mercy to those of you who believe"), and a proof against the disbelievers,

(But those who annoy Allah's Messenger, will have a painful torment.)

Surah: 9 Ayah: 62 & Ayah: 63

﴿ يَحْلِفُونَ بِٱللَّهِ لَكُمْ لِيُرْضُوكُمْ وَٱللَّهُ وَرَسُولُهُ أَحَقُّ أَن يُرْضُوهُ إِن كَانُواْ مُؤْمِنِينَ ﴾

62. They swear by Allâh to you (Muslims) in order to please you, but it is more fitting that they should please Allâh and His Messenger (Muhammad (peace be upon him)) if they are believers.

$$\text{﴿ أَلَمْ يَعْلَمُوٓا۟ أَنَّهُۥ مَن يُحَادِدِ ٱللَّهَ وَرَسُولَهُۥ فَأَنَّ لَهُۥ نَارَ جَهَنَّمَ خَٰلِدًا فِيهَا ۚ ذَٰلِكَ ٱلْخِزْىُ ٱلْعَظِيمُ ۝ ﴾}$$

63. Know they not that whoever opposes and shows hostility to Allâh (glorified and exalted be He) and His Messenger (peace be upon him), certainly for him will be the Fire of Hell to abide therein. That is the extreme disgrace.

Transliteration

62. Yahlifoona biAllahi lakum liyurdookum waAllahu warasooluhu ahaqqu an yurdoohu in kanoo mu/mineena   63. Alam yaAAlamoo annahu man yuhadidi Allaha warasoolahu faanna lahu nara jahannama khalidan feeha thalika alkhizyu alAAatheemu

Tafsir Ibn Kathir

Hypocrites revert to Lies to please People

Qatadah said about Allah's statement,

(They swear by Allah to you (Muslims) in order to please you) "A hypocrite man said, `By Allah! They (hypocrites) are our chiefs and masters. If what Muhammad says is true, they are worse than donkeys.' A Muslim man heard him and declared, `By Allah! What Muhammad says is true and you are worse than a donkey!' The Muslim man conveyed what happened to the Prophet who summoned the hypocrite and asked him,

$$\text{«مَا حَمَلَكَ عَلَى الَّذِي قُلْتَ؟»}$$

(What made you say what you said) That man invoked curses on himself and swore by Allah that he never said that. Meanwhile, the Muslim man said, `O Allah! Assert the truth of the truthful and expose the lies of the liar.' Allah revealed this Verse.''' Allah's statement,

(Know they not that whoever opposes and shows hostility to Allah and His Messenger,) means, have they not come to know and realize that those who defy, oppose, wage war and reject Allah, thus becoming on one side while Allah and His Messenger on another side,

(certainly for him will be the fire of Hell to abide therein), in a humiliating torment,

(That is the extreme disgrace)(9:63), that is the greatest disgrace and the tremendous misery.

Surah: 9 Ayah: 64

﴿ تَحْذَرُ ٱلْمُنَـٰفِقُونَ أَن تُنَزَّلَ عَلَيْهِمْ سُورَةٌ تُنَبِّئُهُم بِمَا فِى قُلُوبِهِمْ ۚ قُلِ ٱسْتَهْزِءُوٓا۟ إِنَّ ٱللَّهَ مُخْرِجٌ مَّا تَحْذَرُونَ ﴿٦٤﴾ ﴾

64. The hypocrites fear lest a Sûrah (chapter of the Qur'ân) should be revealed about them, showing them what is in their hearts. Say: "(Go ahead and) mock! But certainly Allâh will bring to light all that you fear."

Transliteration

64. Yahtharu almunafiqoona an tunazzala AAalayhim sooratun tunabbi-ohum bima fee quloobihim quli istahzi-oo inna Allaha mukhrijun ma tahtharoona

Tafsir Ibn Kathir

The Hypocrites fear Public Exposure of Their Secrets

Mujahid said, "The hypocrites would say something to each other then declare, `We wish that Allah does not expose this secret of ours," There is a similar Ayah to this one, that is, Allah's statement,

(And when they come to you, they greet you with a greeting wherewith Allah greets you not, and say within themselves: "Why should Allah punish us not for what we say" Hell will be sufficient for them; they will burn therein. And worst indeed is that destination!) (58:8). Allah said in this Ayah,

(Say: "(Go ahead and) mock! But certainly Allah will bring to light all that you fear."), He will expose and explain your reality to His Messenger through revelation. Allah said in other Ayat,

(Or do those in whose hearts is a disease (of hypocrisy), think that Allah will not bring to light all their hidden ill-wills) (47:29), until,

(but surely, you will know them by the tone of their speech!)(47:30). This is why, according to Qatadah, this Surah is called `Al-Fadihah' (the Exposing), because it exposed the hypocrites.

Surah: 9 Ayah: 65 & Ayah: 66

﴿ وَلَئِن سَأَلْتَهُمْ لَيَقُولُنَّ إِنَّمَا كُنَّا نَخُوضُ وَنَلْعَبُ ۚ قُلْ أَبِٱللَّهِ وَءَايَـٰتِهِۦ وَرَسُولِهِۦ كُنتُمْ تَسْتَهْزِءُونَ ﴿٦٥﴾ ﴾

65. If you ask them (about this), they declare: "We were only talking idly and joking." Say: "Was it at Allâh (glorified and exalted be He), and His Ayât (proofs, evidences, verses, lessons, signs, revelations, etc.) and His Messenger (peace be upon him) that you were mocking?"

Chapter 9: At-Tawba (Repentance), Verses 001-092

﴿ لَا تَعْتَذِرُواْ قَدْ كَفَرْتُم بَعْدَ إِيمَـٰنِكُمْ إِن نَّعْفُ عَن طَآئِفَةٍ مِّنكُمْ نُعَذِّبْ طَآئِفَةً بِأَنَّهُمْ كَانُواْ مُجْرِمِينَ ۝ ﴾

66. Make no excuse; you disbelieved after you had believed. If We pardon some of you, We will punish others amongst you because they were Mujrimûn (disbelievers, polytheists, sinners, criminals.).

Transliteration

65. Wala-in saaltahum layaqoolunna innama kunna nakhoodu wanalAAabu qul abiAllahi waayatihi warasoolihi kuntum tastahzi-oona 66. La taAAtathiroo qad kafartum baAAda eemanikum in naAAfu AAan ta-ifatin minkum nuAAaththib ta-ifatan bi-annahum kanoo mujrimeena

Tafsir Ibn Kathir

The Hypocrites rely on False, Misguided Excuses

`Abdullah bin `Umar said, "During the battle of Tabuk, a man was sitting in a gathering and said, `I have never seen like these reciters of ours! They have the hungriest stomachs, the most lying tongues and are the most cowardice in battle.' A man in the Masjid said, `You lie. You are a hypocrite, and I will surely inform the Messenger of Allah. ' This statement was conveyed to the Messenger of Allah and also a part of the Qur'an was revealed about it.'" `Abdullah bin `Umar said, "I have seen that man afterwards holding onto the shoulders of the Messenger's camel while stones were falling on him, declaring, `O Allah's Messenger! We were only engaged in idle talk and jesting,' while the Messenger of Allah was reciting,

("Was it at Allah, and His Ayat and His Messenger that you were mocking") (9:65).'" Allah said,

(Make no excuse; you disbelieved after you had believed.) on account of your statement and mocking,

(If We pardon some of you, We will punish others among you) for not all of you will be forgiven, some will have to taste the torment,

(because they were criminals), they were criminals because of this terrible, sinful statement.

Surah: 9 Ayah: 67 & Ayah: 68

﴿ ٱلْمُنَـٰفِقُونَ وَٱلْمُنَـٰفِقَـٰتُ بَعْضُهُم مِّنۢ بَعْضٍ يَأْمُرُونَ بِٱلْمُنكَرِ وَيَنْهَوْنَ عَنِ ٱلْمَعْرُوفِ وَيَقْبِضُونَ أَيْدِيَهُمْ ۚ نَسُواْ ٱللَّهَ فَنَسِيَهُمْ ۗ إِنَّ ٱلْمُنَـٰفِقِينَ هُمُ ٱلْفَـٰسِقُونَ ۝ ﴾

67. The hypocrites, men and women, are from one another; they enjoin (on the people) Al-Munkar (i.e. disbelief and polytheism of all kinds and all that Islâm has forbidden), and forbid (people) from Al-Ma'rûf (i.e. Islâmic Monotheism and all that Islâm orders one to do), and they close their hands (from giving (spending in Allâh's Cause) alms.). They have forgotten Allâh, so He has forgotten them. Verily, the hypocrites are the Fâsiqûn (rebellious, disobedient to Allâh).

﴿ وَعَدَ ٱللَّهُ ٱلْمُنَـٰفِقِينَ وَٱلْمُنَـٰفِقَـٰتِ وَٱلْكُفَّارَ نَارَ جَهَنَّمَ خَـٰلِدِينَ فِيهَا ۚ هِىَ حَسْبُهُمْ ۚ وَلَعَنَهُمُ ٱللَّهُ ۖ وَلَهُمْ عَذَابٌ مُّقِيمٌ ﴾

68. Allâh has promised the hypocrites; men and women, and the disbelievers, the Fire of Hell, therein shall they abide. It will suffice them. Allâh has cursed them and for them is the lasting torment.

Transliteration

67. Almunafiqoona waalmunafiqatu baAAduhum min baAAdin ya/muroona bialmunkari wayanhawna AAani almaAAroofi wayaqbidoona aydiyahum nasoo Allaha fanasiyahum inna almunafiqeena humu alfasiqoona 68. WaAAada Allahu almunafiqeena waalmunafiqati waalkuffara nara jahannama khalideena feeha hiya hasbuhum walaAAanahumu Allahu walahum AAathabun muqeemun

Tafsir Ibn Kathir

Other Characteristics of Hypocrites

Allah admonishes the hypocrites who, unlike the believers, who enjoin righteousness and forbid evil,

(they enjoin evil, and forbid the good, and they close their hands), from spending in Allah's cause,

(They have forgotten Allah), they have forgotten the remembrance of Allah,

(so He has forgotten them.), by treating them as if He has forgotten them. Allah also,

(And it will be said: "This Day We will forget you as you forgot the meeting of this Day of yours) (45:34). Allah said,

(Verily, the hypocrites are the rebellious) the rebellious from the way of truth who embrace the wicked way,

(Allah has promised the hypocrites -- men and women -- and the disbelievers, the fire of Hell), on account of their evildoing mentioned here,

(therein shall they abide.), for eternity, they and the disbelievers,

(It will suffice them.), as a torment,

(Allah has cursed them), He expelled and banished them (from His mercy),

(and for them is the lasting torment.)

Surah: 9 Ayah: 69

﴿ كَالَّذِينَ مِن قَبْلِكُمْ كَانُوٓاْ أَشَدَّ مِنكُمْ قُوَّةً وَأَكْثَرَ أَمْوَٰلاً وَأَوْلَٰداً فَٱسْتَمْتَعُواْ بِخَلَٰقِهِمْ فَٱسْتَمْتَعْتُم بِخَلَٰقِكُمْ كَمَا ٱسْتَمْتَعَ ٱلَّذِينَ مِن قَبْلِكُم بِخَلَٰقِهِمْ وَخُضْتُمْ كَٱلَّذِى خَاضُوٓاْ أُوْلَٰٓئِكَ حَبِطَتْ أَعْمَٰلُهُمْ فِى ٱلدُّنْيَا وَٱلْءَاخِرَةِ وَأُوْلَٰٓئِكَ هُمُ ٱلْخَٰسِرُونَ ﴾

69. Like those before you: they were mightier than you in power, and more abundant in wealth and children. They had enjoyed their portion (awhile), so enjoy your portion (awhile) as those before you enjoyed their portion (awhile); and you indulged in play and pastime (and in telling lies against Allâh and His Messenger Muhammad (peace be upon him)) as they indulged in play and pastime. Such are they whose deeds are in vain in this world and in the Hereafter. Such are they who are the losers.

Transliteration

69. Kaallatheena min qablikum kanoo ashadda minkum quwwatan waakthara amwalan waawladan faistamtaAAoo bikhalaqihim faistamtaAAtum bikhalaqikum kama istamtaAAa allatheena min qablikum bikhalaqihim wakhudtum kaallathee khadoo olaika habitat aAAmaluhum fee alddunya waal-akhirati waola-ika humu alkhasiroona

Tafsir Ibn Kathir

Allah says, these people were touched by torment in this life and the Hereafter, just as those before them. Allah's statement,

(their portion), means, (they mocked) their religion, according to Al-Hasan Al-Basri. Allah's statement,

(and you indulged in play and pastime as they indulged in play and pastime), indulged in lies and falsehood,

(Such are they whose deeds are in vain), their deeds are annulled; they will not acquire any rewards for them because they are invalid,

(in this world and in the Hereafter. Such are they who are the losers.) because they will not acquire any rewards for their actions. Ibn `Abbas commented, "How similar is this night to the last night,

(Like those before you...) These are the Children of Israel, with whom we were compared. The Prophet said,

«وَالَّذِي نَفْسِي بِيَدِهِ لَتَتَّبِعُنَّهُمْ حَتَّى لَوْ دَخَلَ الرَّجُلُ مِنْهُمْ جُحْرَ ضَبٍّ لَدَخَلْتُمُوهُ»

(By He in Whose Hand is my life! You will imitate them, and even if a man of them entered the den of a lizard, you will enter it likewise!)" Abu Hurayrah narrated that the Messenger of Allah said,

«وَالَّذِي نَفْسِي بِيَدِهِ لَتَتَّبِعُنَّ سَنَنَ الَّذِينَ مِنْ قَبْلِكُمْ شِبْرًا بِشِبْرٍ وَذِرَاعًا بِذِرَاعٍ، وَبَاعًا بِبَاعٍ حَتَّى لَوْ دَخَلُوا جُحْرَ ضَبٍّ لَدَخَلْتُمُوهُ»

(By He in Whose Hand is my soul! You will follow the traditions of those who were before you a hand span for a hand-span and forearm's length for forearm's length, and an arm's length for an arm's length. And even if they enter the den of a lizard, you will also enter it.) They asked, "Who, O Allah's Messenger, the People of the Book" He said,

«فَمَنْ؟»

(Who else)" This Hadith is similar to another Hadith collected in the Sahih.

Surah: 9 Ayah: 70

﴿ أَلَمْ يَأْتِهِمْ نَبَأُ الَّذِينَ مِن قَبْلِهِمْ قَوْمِ نُوحٍ وَعَادٍ وَثَمُودَ وَقَوْمِ إِبْرَاهِيمَ وَأَصْحَابِ مَدْيَنَ وَالْمُؤْتَفِكَاتِ أَتَتْهُمْ رُسُلُهُم بِالْبَيِّنَاتِ فَمَا كَانَ اللَّهُ لِيَظْلِمَهُمْ وَلَـكِن كَانُوا أَنفُسَهُمْ يَظْلِمُونَ ﴾ (٧٠)

70. Has not the story reached them of those before them? - The people of Nûh (Noah), 'Ad, and Thamûd, the people of Ibrahîm (Abraham), the dwellers of Madyan (Midian) and the cities overthrown (i.e. the people to whom Lût (Lot) preached), to them came their Messengers with clear proofs. So it was not Allâh Who wronged them, but they used to wrong themselves.

Transliteration

70. Alam ya/tihim nabao allatheena min qablihim qawmi noohin waAAadin wathamooda waqawmi ibraheema waas-habi madyana waalmu/tafikati atat-hum rusuluhum bialbayyinati fama kana Allahu liyathlimahum walakin kanoo anfusahum yathlimoona

Tafsir Ibn Kathir

Advising the Hypocrites to learn a Lesson from Those before Them

Allah advises the hypocrites who reject the Messengers,

(Has not the story reached them of those before them) have you (hypocrites) not learned the end of the nations before you who rejected the Messengers,

(The people of Nuh), and the flood that drowned the entire population of the earth, except those who believed in Allah's servant and Messenger Nuh, peace be upon him,

(and `Ad), who perished with the barren wind when they rejected Hud, peace be upon him,

(and Thamud), who were overtaken by the Sayhah (awful cry) when they denied Salih, peace be upon him, and killed the camel,

(and the people of Ibrahim), over whom He gave Ibrahim victory and the aid of clear miracles. Allah destroyed their king Nimrod, son of Canaan, son of Koch from Canaan, may Allah curse him,

(and the dwellers of Madyan), the people of Shu`ayb, peace be upon him, who were destroyed by the earthquake and the torment of the day of the Shade,

(and the overturned cities), the people of Lut who used to live in Madyan. Allah said in another Ayah,

(And He destroyed the overturned cities) (53:53), meaning the people of the overturned cities in reference to Sadum (Sodom), their major city. Allah destroyed them all because they rejected Allah's Prophet Lut, peace be upon him, and because they committed the sin that none before them had committed (homosexuality).

(to them came their Messengers with clear proofs.), and unequivocal evidence,

(So it was not Allah Who wronged them), when He destroyed them, for He established the proofs against them by sending the Messengers and dissipating the doubts,

(but they used to wrong themselves), on account of their denying the Messengers and defying the Truth; this is why they earned the end, torment and punishment, that they did.

Surah: 9 Ayah: 71

﴿ وَٱلْمُؤْمِنُونَ وَٱلْمُؤْمِنَٰتُ بَعْضُهُمْ أَوْلِيَآءُ بَعْضٍ يَأْمُرُونَ بِٱلْمَعْرُوفِ وَيَنْهَوْنَ عَنِ ٱلْمُنكَرِ وَيُقِيمُونَ ٱلصَّلَوٰةَ وَيُؤْتُونَ ٱلزَّكَوٰةَ وَيُطِيعُونَ ٱللَّهَ وَرَسُولَهُۥٓ أُو۟لَٰٓئِكَ سَيَرْحَمُهُمُ ٱللَّهُ إِنَّ ٱللَّهَ عَزِيزٌ حَكِيمٌ ۝ ﴾

71. The believers, men and women, are Auliyâ' (helpers, supporters, friends, protectors) of one another; they enjoin (on the people) Al-Ma'rûf (i.e. Islâmic Monotheism and all that Islâm orders one to do), and forbid (people) from Al-Munkar (i.e. polytheism and disbelief of all kinds, and all that Islâm has forbidden); they perform As-Salât (Iqâmat-as-Salât) and give the Zakât, and obey Allâh and His Messenger. Allâh will have His Mercy on them. Surely Allâh is All-Mighty, All-Wise.

Transliteration

71. Waalmu/minoona waalmu/minatu baAAduhum awliyao baAAdin ya/muroona bialmaAAroofi wayanhawna AAani almunkari wayuqeemoona alssalata wayu/toona alzzakata wayuteeAAoona Allaha warasoolahu ola-ika sayarhamuhumu Allahu inna Allaha AAazeezun hakeemun

Tafsir Ibn Kathir

Qualities of Faithful Believers

After Allah mentioned the evil characteristics of the hypocrites, He then mentioned the good qualities of the believers,

(The believers, men and women, are supporters of one another;) they help and aid each other. Surely, an authentic Hadith states,

«الْمُؤْمِنُ لِلْمُؤْمِنِ كَالْبُنْيَانِ يَشُدُّ بَعْضُهُ بَعْضًا»

(The believer to the believer is just like a building, its parts support each other.) and the Prophet crossed his fingers together. In the Sahih it is recorded,

«مَثَلُ الْمُؤْمِنِينَ فِي تَوَادِّهِمْ وَتَرَاحُمِهِمْ كَمَثَلِ الْجَسَدِ الْوَاحِدِ، إِذَا اشْتَكَى مِنْهُ عُضْوٌ تَدَاعَى لَهُ سَائِرُ الْجَسَدِ بِالْحُمَّى وَالسَّهَرِ»

(The example of the believers in the compassion and mercy they have for each other, is the example of one body: if a part of it falls ill, the rest of the body suffers with fever and sleeplessness.) Allah's statement,

(...they enjoin good, and forbid evil), this is similar to,

(Let there arise out of you a group of people inviting to all that is good, enjoining Al-Ma`ruf and forbidding the Munkar...) (3:104). Allah said next,

(they perform the Salah, and give the Zakah), they obey Allah and are kind to His creation,

(and obey Allah and His Messenger), concerning what he commands and refraining from what he prohibits,

(Allah will have mercy on them.) Therefore, Allah will give mercy to those who have these qualities,

(Surely, Allah is All-Mighty), He grants glory to those who obey Him, for indeed, might and glory is from Allah Who gives it to His Messenger and the believers,

(All-Wise), in granting these qualities to the believers, while giving evil characteristics to hypocrites. Surely, Allah's wisdom is perfect in all His actions; praise and glory be to Him.

Surah: 9 Ayah: 72

﴿ وَعَدَ ٱللَّهُ ٱلْمُؤْمِنِينَ وَٱلْمُؤْمِنَـٰتِ جَنَّـٰتٍ تَجْرِى مِن تَحْتِهَا ٱلْأَنْهَـٰرُ خَـٰلِدِينَ فِيهَا وَمَسَـٰكِنَ طَيِّبَةً فِى جَنَّـٰتِ عَدْنٍ وَرِضْوَٰنٌ مِّنَ ٱللَّهِ أَكْبَرُ ذَٰلِكَ هُوَ ٱلْفَوْزُ ٱلْعَظِيمُ ۞ ﴾

72. Allâh has promised to the believers - men and women, - Gardens under which rivers flow to dwell therein forever, and beautiful mansions in Gardens of 'Adn (Eden Paradise). But the greatest bliss is the Good Pleasure of Allâh. That is the supreme success.

Transliteration

72. WaAAada Allahu almu/mineena waalmu/minati jannatin tajree min tahtiha al-anharu khalideena feeha wamasakina tayyibatan fee jannati AAadnin waridwanun mina Allahi akbaru thalika huwa alfawzu alAAatheemu

Tafsir Ibn Kathir

Good News for the Believers of Eternal Delight

Allah describes the joys and eternal delight He has prepared for the believers, men and women in,

(Gardens under which rivers flow to dwell therein forever) for eternity,

(and beautiful mansions), built beautifully in good surroundings. In the Two Sahihs, it is recorded that Abu Musa, `Abdullah bin Qays Al-Ash`ari said that the Messenger of Allah said,

«جَنَّتَانِ مِنْ ذَهَبٍ آنِيَتُهُمَا وَمَا فِيهِمَا، وَجَنَّتَانِ مِنْ فِضَّةٍ آنِيَتُهُمَا وَمَا فِيهِمَا، وَمَا بَيْنَ الْقَوْمِ وَبَيْنَ أَنْ يَنْظُرُوا إِلَى رَبِّهِمْ إِلَّا رِدَاءُ الْكِبْرِيَاءِ عَلَى وَجْهِهِ فِي جَنَّةِ عَدْنٍ»

(Two gardens, their pots and whatever is in them are made of gold, and two gardens, their pots and whatever is in them are made of silver. Only the Veil of Pride of Allah's Face separates the people from gazing at Him, in the garden of Eden.) He also narrated that the Messenger of Allah said,

«إِنَّ لِلْمُؤْمِنِ فِي الْجَنَّةِ لَخَيْمَةً مِنْ لُؤْلُؤَةٍ وَاحِدَةٍ مُجَوَّفَةٍ، طُولُهَا سِتُّونَ مِيلًا فِي السَّمَاءِ لِلْمُؤْمِنِ فِيهَا أَهْلُونَ يَطُوفُ عَلَيْهِمْ لَا يَرَى بَعْضُهُمْ بَعْضًا»

(For the believer in Paradise there is a tent like a hollow pearl which is sixty miles high in the sky, and in the tent the believer will have (so large) a family that he visits them all and some of them would not be able to see the others.) The Two Sahihs collected this Hadith. It is recorded in the Two Sahihs that Abu Hurayrah said that the Messenger of Allah said,

«مَنْ آمَنَ بِاللهِ وَرَسُولِهِ وَأَقَامَ الصَّلَاةَ وَصَامَ رَمَضَانَ، فَإِنَّ حَقًّا عَلَى اللهِ أَنْ يُدْخِلَهُ الْجَنَّةَ هَاجَرَ فِي سَبِيلِ اللهِ، أَوْ (جَلَسَ) فِي أَرْضِهِ الَّتِي وُلِدَ فِيهَا»

(Whoever believes in Allah and His Messenger, offers prayer perfectly and fasts the month of Ramadan, will rightfully be granted Paradise by Allah, no matter whether he emigrates in Allah's cause, or remains in the land where he is born.) The people said, "O Allah's Messenger! Shall we acquaint the people with this good news" He said,

«إِنَّ فِي الْجَنَّةِ مِائَةَ دَرَجَةٍ أَعَدَّهَا اللهُ لِلْمُجَاهِدِينَ فِي سَبِيلِهِ بَيْنَ كُلِّ دَرَجَتَيْنِ كَمَا بَيْنَ السَّمَاءِ وَالْأَرْضِ، فَإِذَا سَأَلْتُمُ اللهَ فَاسْأَلُوهُ الْفِرْدَوْسَ فَإِنَّهُ أَعْلَى الْجَنَّةِ وَأَوْسَطُ الْجَنَّةِ، وَمِنْهُ تَفَجَّرُ أَنْهَارُ الْجَنَّةِ، وَفَوْقَهُ عَرْشُ الرَّحْمَنِ»

(Paradise has one-hundred grades which Allah has prepared for the Mujahidin who fight in His cause, the distance between each two grades is like the distance between the heaven and the earth. So, when you ask Allah, ask Him for Al-Firdaws which is the best and highest part of Paradise, from it gush forth the rivers of Paradise and above it is the `Arsh (Throne) of the Beneficent.) Imam Ahmad recorded that Abu Hurayrah said, that the Messenger of Allah said,

«إِذَا صَلَّيْتُمْ عَلَيَّ فَسَلُوا اللهَ لِيَ الْوَسِيلَةَ»

(If you invoke Allah for Salah (blessings) on me, then also invoke Him to grant me Al-Wasilah.) He was asked, "What is Al-Wasilah, O Allah's Messenger" He said,

Chapter 9: At-Tawba (Repentance), Verses 001-092

«أَعْلَى دَرَجَةٍ فِي الْجَنَّةِ لَا يَنَالُهَا إِلَّا رَجُلٌ وَاحِدٌ وَأَرْجُو أَنْ أَكُونَ أَنَا هُوَ»

(The highest grade in Paradise, it will be for only one man, and I hope I am that man.) The Musnad contains a Hadith from Sa`d bin Mujahid At-Ta'i, that Abu Al-Mudillah said, that Abu Hurayrah said, "We said, `O Allah's Messenger! Talk to us about Paradise, what is it built of' He said,

«لِبَنَةُ ذَهَبٍ وَلِبَنَةُ فِضَّةٍ، وَمِلَاطُهَا الْمِسْكُ وَحَصْبَاؤُهَا اللُّؤْلُؤُ وَالْيَاقُوتُ، وَتُرَابُهَا الزَّعْفَرَانُ. مَنْ يَدْخُلُهَا يَنْعَمْ لَا يَبْأَسْ وَيَخْلُدْ لَايَمُوتُ، لَا تَبْلَى ثِيَابُهُ وَلَا يَفْنَى شَبَابُهُ»

(A brick of gold and a brick of silver. Its mortar is from musk, its gravel is pearls and rubies. Its sand is saffron. Whoever enters it will enjoy the delights, will never be hopeless, and will live forever and will not die. His clothes will never decay nor will his youth ever end.)" Allah said next,

(But the greatest bliss is the good pleasure of Allah)(9:72), meaning, Allah's pleasure is more grand, greater and better than the delight the believers will be enjoying (in Paradise). Imam Malik narrated, that Zayd bin Aslam said that `Ata' bin Yasar said that Abu Sa`id Al-Khudri said that the Messenger of Allah said,

«إِنَّ اللهَ عَزَّ وَجَلَّ يَقُولُ لِأَهْلِ الْجَنَّةِ: يَا أَهْلَ الْجَنَّةِ فَيَقُولُونَ: لَبَّيْكَ رَبَّنَا وَسَعْدَيْكَ وَالْخَيْرُ فِي يَدَيْكَ. فَيَقُولُ: هَلْ رَضِيتُمْ؟ فَيَقُولُونَ: وَمَا لَنَا لَا نَرْضَى يَا رَبِّ وَقَدْ أَعْطَيْتَنَا مَا لَمْ تُعْطِ أَحَدًا مِنْ خَلْقِكَ، فَيَقُولُ: أَلَا أُعْطِيكُمْ أَفْضَلَ مِنْ ذَلِكَ؟ فَيَقُولُونَ: يَا رَبِّ وَأَيُّ شَيْءٍ أَفْضَلُ مِنْ ذَلِكَ؟ فَيَقُولُ: أُحِلُّ عَلَيْكُمْ رِضْوَانِي فَلَا أَسْخَطُ عَلَيْكُمْ بَعْدَهُ أَبَدًا»

(Allah, the Exalted and Ever High, will say to the people of Paradise, `O residents of Paradise!' They will say, `Labbayka (here we are!), our Lord, and Sa`dayk (we are happy at your service!) and all the good is in Your Hand.' He will ask them, `Are you pleased' They will say, `Why would not we be pleased, O Lord, while You have given us what You have not given any other of your creation' He will say, `Should I give you what is better than all this' They will say, `O Lord! What is better than all this' He will say, `I will grant you My pleasure and will never afterwards be angry with you.') The Two Sahihs collected the Hadith of Malik.

Surah: 9 Ayah: 73 & Ayah: 74

﴿ يَٰٓأَيُّهَا ٱلنَّبِىُّ جَٰهِدِ ٱلْكُفَّارَ وَٱلْمُنَٰفِقِينَ وَٱغْلُظْ عَلَيْهِمْ ۚ وَمَأْوَىٰهُمْ جَهَنَّمُ ۖ وَبِئْسَ ٱلْمَصِيرُ ﴾ ۞

73. O Prophet (Muhammad (peace be upon him))! Strive hard against the disbelievers and the hypocrites, and be harsh against them, their abode is Hell, - and worst indeed is that destination.

﴿ يَحْلِفُونَ بِٱللَّهِ مَا قَالُوا۟ وَلَقَدْ قَالُوا۟ كَلِمَةَ ٱلْكُفْرِ وَكَفَرُوا۟ بَعْدَ إِسْلَٰمِهِمْ وَهَمُّوا۟ بِمَا لَمْ يَنَالُوا۟ ۚ وَمَا نَقَمُوٓا۟ إِلَّآ أَنْ أَغْنَىٰهُمُ ٱللَّهُ وَرَسُولُهُۥ مِن فَضْلِهِۦ ۚ فَإِن يَتُوبُوا۟ يَكُ خَيْرًا لَّهُمْ ۖ وَإِن يَتَوَلَّوْا۟ يُعَذِّبْهُمُ ٱللَّهُ عَذَابًا أَلِيمًا فِى ٱلدُّنْيَا وَٱلْءَاخِرَةِ ۚ وَمَا لَهُمْ فِى ٱلْأَرْضِ مِن وَلِىٍّ وَلَا نَصِيرٍ ﴾ ۞

74. They swear by Allâh that they said nothing (bad), but really they said the word of disbelief, and they disbelieved after accepting Islâm, and they resolved that (plot to murder Prophet Muhammad (peace be upon him)) which they were unable to carry out, and they could not find any cause to do so except that Allâh and His Messenger had enriched them of His Bounty. If then they repent, it will be better for them, but if they turn away, Allâh will punish them with a painful torment in this worldly life and in the Hereafter. And there is none for them on earth as a Walî (supporter, protector) or a helper.

Transliteration

73. Ya ayyuha alnnabiyyu jahidi alkuffara waalmunafiqeena waoghluth AAalayhim wama/wahum jahannamu wabi/sa almaseeru   74. Yahlifoona biAllahi ma qaloo walaqad qaloo kalimata alkufri wakafaroo baAAda islamihim wahammoo bima lam yanaloo wama naqamoo illa an aghnahumu Allahu warasooluhu min fadlihi fa-in yatooboo yaku khayran lahum wa-in yatawallaw yuAAaththibhumu Allahu AAathaban aleeman fee alddunya waal-akhirati wama lahum fee al-ardi min waliyyin wala naseerin

Tafsir Ibn Kathir

The Order for Jihad against the Disbelievers and Hypocrites

Allah commanded His Messenger to strive hard against the disbelievers and the hypocrites and to be harsh against them. Allah also commanded him to be merciful with the believers who followed him, informing him that the destination of the disbelievers and hypocrites is the Fire in the Hereafter. Ibn Mas`ud commented on Allah's statement,

(Strive hard against the disbelievers and the hypocrites) "With the hand, or at least have a stern face with them." Ibn `Abbas said, "Allah commanded the Prophet to fight the disbelievers with the sword, to strive against the hypocrites with the tongue and annulled lenient treatment of them." Ad-Dahhak commented, "Perform Jihad against the disbelievers with the sword and be harsh with the hypocrites with words, and this is the Jihad performed against them." Similar was said by Muqatil and Ar-Rabi`. Al-Hasan and Qatadah said, "Striving against them includes establishing the (Islamic Penal) Law of equality against them." In combining these statements, we could say that Allah causes punishment of the disbelievers and hypocrites with all of these methods in various conditions and situations, and Allah knows best.

Reason behind revealing Ayah 9:74

Al-Amawi said in his Book on Battles, "Muhammad bin Ishaq narrated that Az-Zuhri said that `Abdur-Rahman bin `Abdullah bin Ka`b bin Malik narrated from his father, from his grandfather that he said, `Among the hypocrites who lagged behind (from battle) and concerning whom the Qur'an was revealed, was Al-Julas bin Suwayd bin As-Samit, who was married to the mother of `Umayr bin Sa`d. `Umayr was under the care of Al-Julas. When the Qur'an was revealed about the hypocrites, exposing their practices, Al-Julas said, `By Allah! If this man (Muhammad) is saying the truth, then we are worse than donkeys.' `Umayr bin Sa`d heard him and said, `By Allah, O Julas! You are the dearest person to me, has the most favor on me and I would hate that harm should touch you, more than I do concerning anyone else! You have uttered a statement that if I exposed, will expose you, but if I hide, it will destroy me. One of them is a lesser evil than the other.' So `Umayr went to the Messenger of Allah and told him what Al-Julas said. On realizing this, Al-Julas went to the Prophet and swore by Allah that he did not say what `Umayr bin Sa`d conveyed he said. `He lied on me,' Al-Julas said. Allah sent in his case this verse,

(They swear by Allah that they said nothing (bad), but really they said the word of disbelief, and they disbelieved after accepting Islam) until the end of Ayah. The Messenger of Allah conveyed this Ayah to Al-Julas, who, they claim, repented and his repentance was sincere, prompting him to refrain from hypocrisy.'" Imam Abu Ja`far Ibn Jarir recorded that Ibn `Abbas said, "The Messenger of Allah was sitting under the shade of a tree when he said,

«إِنَّهُ سَيَأْتِيكُمْ إِنْسَانٌ فَيَنْظُرُ إِلَيْكُمْ بِعَيْنَيِ الشَّيْطَانِ فَإِذَا جَاءَ فَلَا تُكَلِّمُوهُ»

(A man will now come and will look to you through the eyes of a devil. When he comes, do not talk to him.)' A man who looked as if he was blue (so dark) came and the Messenger of Allah summoned him and said,

«عَلَامَ تَشْتُمُنِي أَنْتَ وَأَصْحَابُكَ»

(Why do you curse me, you and your companions) That man went and brought his friends and they swore by Allah that they did nothing of the sort, and the Prophet pardoned them. Allah, the Exalted and Most Honored revealed this verse,

(They swear by Allah that they said nothing (bad)...)

Hypocrites try to kill the Prophet

Allah said next,

(and they resolved that which they were unable to carry out) It was said that this Ayah was revealed about Al-Julas bin Suwayd, who tried to kill his wife's son when he said he would inform the Messenger of Allah (about Al-Julas' statement we mentioned earlier). It was also said that it was revealed in the case of `Abdullah bin Ubayy who plotted to kill the Messenger of Allah . As-Suddi said, "This verse was revealed about some men who wanted to crown `Abdullah bin Ubayy even if the Messenger of Allah did not agree. It was reported that some hypocrites plotted to kill the Prophet , while he was at the battle of Tabuk, riding one night. They were a group of more than ten men. Ad-Dahhak said, "This Ayah was revealed about them." In his book, Dala'il An-Nubuwah, Al-Hafiz Abu Bakr Al-Bayhaqi recorded that Hudhayfah bin Al-Yaman said, "I was holding the bridle of the Messenger's camel while `Ammar was leading it, or vise versa. When we reached Al-`Aqabah, twelve riders intercepted the Prophet. When I alerted the Messenger, he shouted at them and they all ran away. The Messenger of Allah asked us,

«هَلْ عَرَفْتُمُ الْقَوْمَ؟»

(Did you know who they were) We said, `No, O Allah's Messenger! They had masks. However, we know their horses.' He said,

«هؤُلَاءِ الْمُنَافِقُونَ إِلَى يَوْمِ الْقِيَامَةِ وَهَلْ تَدْرُونَ مَا أَرَادُوا؟»

(They are the hypocrites until the Day of Resurrection. Do you know what they intended) We said, `No.' He said,

«أَرَادُوا أَنْ يُزَاحِمُوا رَسُولَ اللهِ فِي الْعَقَبَةِ فَيُلْقُوهُ مِنْهَا»

(They wanted to mingle with the Messenger of Allah and throw him from the `Aqabah (to the valley).) We said, `O Allah's Messenger! Should you ask their tribes to send the head of each one of them to you' He said,

«لَا. أَكْرَهُ أَنْ تَتَحَدَّثَ الْعَرَبُ بَيْنَهَا أَنَّ مُحَمَّدًا قَاتَلَ بِقَوْمٍ حَتَّى إِذَا أَظْهَرَهُ اللهُ بِهِمْ أَقْبَلَ عَلَيْهِمْ بِقَتْلِهِمْ ثُمَّ قَالَ اللَّهُمَّ ارْمِهِمْ بِالدُّبَيْلَةِ»

(No, for I hate that the Arabs should say that Muhammad used some people in fighting and when Allah gave him victory with their help, he commanded that they be killed.) He then said, (O Allah! Throw the Dubaylah at them.) We asked, `What is the Dubaylah, O Allah's Messenger' He said,

Chapter 9: At-Tawba (Repentance), Verses 001-092

«شِهَابٌ مِنْ نَارٍ يَقَعُ عَلَى نِيَاطِ قَلْبِ أَحَدِهِمْ فَيُهْلِكُ»

(A missile of fire that falls on the heart of one of them and brings about his demise.)" Abu At-Tufayl said, "Once, there was a dispute between Hudhayfah and another man, who asked him, `I ask you by Allah, how many were the Companions of Al-`Aqabah' The people said to Hudhayfah, `Tell him, for he asked you.' Hudhayfah said, `We were told that they were fourteen men, unless you were one of them, then the number is fifteen! I testify by Allah that twelve of them are at war with Allah and His Messenger in this life and when the witness comes forth for witness. Three of them were pardoned, for they said, `We did not hear the person whom the Messenger sent to announce something, and we did not know what the people had plotted,' for the Prophet had been walking when he said,

«إِنَّ الْمَاءَ قَلِيلٌ فَلَا يَسْبِقَنِي إِلَيْهِ أَحَدٌ»

(Water is scarce, so none among you should reach it before me.) When he found that some people had reached it before him, he cursed them.''' `Ammar bin Yasir narrated in a Hadith collected by Muslim, that Hudhayfah said to him that the Prophet said,

«فِي أَصْحَابِي اثْنَا عَشَرَ مُنَافِقًا لَا يَدْخُلُونَ الْجَنَّةَ وَلَا يَجِدُونَ رِيحَهَا حَتَّى يَلِجَ الْجَمَلُ فِي سَمِّ الْخِيَاطِ: ثَمَانِيَةٌ مِنْهُمْ تَكْفِيكَهُمُ الدُّبَيْلَةُ سِرَاجٌ مِنْ نَارٍ يَظْهَرُ بَيْنَ أَكْتَافِهِمْ حَتَّى يَنْجُمَ فِي صُدُورِهِم»

(Among my Companions are twelve hypocrites who will never enter Paradise or find its scent, until the camel enters the thread of the needle. Eight of them will be struck by the Dubaylah, which is a missile made of fire that appears between their shoulders and pierces their chest.) This is why Hudhayfah was called the holder of the secret, for he knew who these hypocrites were, since the Messenger of Allah gave their names to him and none else. Allah said next,

(and they could not find any cause to do so except that Allah and His Messenger had enriched them of His bounty.) This Ayah means, the Messenger did not commit an error against them, other than that Allah has enriched them on account of the Prophet's blessed and honorable mission! And had Allah guided them to what the Prophet came with, they would have experienced its delight completely. The Prophet once said to the Ansar,

«أَلَمْ أَجِدْكُمْ ضُلَّالًا فَهَدَاكُمُ اللهُ بِي، وَكُنْتُمْ مُتَفَرِّقِينَ فَأَلَّفَكُمُ اللهُ بِي، وَعَالَةً فَأَغْنَاكُمُ اللهُ بِي»

(Have I not found you misguided and Allah guided you through me, divided and Allah united you through me, and poor and Allah enriched you through me) Whenever the Messenger asked them a question, they replied, "Allah and His Messenger have granted the favor." This type of statement,

(And they had no fault except that they believed in Allah...), is uttered when there is no wrong committed. Allah called the hypocrites to repent,

(If then they repent, it will be better for them, but if they turn away; Allah will punish them with a painful torment in this worldly life and in the Hereafter.) The Ayah says, if they persist on their ways, Allah will inflict a painful torment on them in this life, by killing, sadness and depression, and in the Hereafter with torment, punishment, disgrace and humiliation,

(And there is none for them on earth as a protector or a helper.) who will bring happiness to them, aid them, bring about benefit or fend off harm.

Surah: 9 Ayah: 75, Ayah: 76, Ayah: 77 & Ayah: 78

﴿ وَمِنْهُم مَّنْ عَـٰهَدَ ٱللَّهَ لَئِنْ ءَاتَىٰنَا مِن فَضْلِهِۦ لَنَصَّدَّقَنَّ وَلَنَكُونَنَّ مِنَ ٱلصَّـٰلِحِينَ ﴾

75. And of them are some who made a covenant with Allâh (saying): "If He bestowed on us of His Bounty, we will verily give Sadaqâh (Zakât and voluntary charity in Allâh's Cause) and will be certainly among those who are righteous."

﴿ فَلَمَّآ ءَاتَىٰهُم مِّن فَضْلِهِۦ بَخِلُوا۟ بِهِۦ وَتَوَلَّوا۟ وَّهُم مُّعْرِضُونَ ﴾

76. Then when He gave them of His Bounty, they became niggardly (refused to pay the Sadaqâh (Zakât or voluntary charity)) and turned away, averse.

﴿ فَأَعْقَبَهُمْ نِفَاقًا فِى قُلُوبِهِمْ إِلَىٰ يَوْمِ يَلْقَوْنَهُۥ بِمَآ أَخْلَفُوا۟ ٱللَّهَ مَا وَعَدُوهُ وَبِمَا كَانُوا۟ يَكْذِبُونَ ﴾

77. So He punished them by putting hypocrisy into their hearts till the Day whereon they shall meet Him, because they broke that (covenant with Allâh) which they had promised Him and because they used to tell lies.

﴿ أَلَمْ يَعْلَمُوٓا۟ أَنَّ ٱللَّهَ يَعْلَمُ سِرَّهُمْ وَنَجْوَىٰهُمْ وَأَنَّ ٱللَّهَ عَلَّـٰمُ ٱلْغُيُوبِ ﴾

78. Know they not that Allâh knows their secret ideas, and their Najwa (secret counsels), and that Allâh is the All-Knower of the unseen.

Transliteration

75. Waminhum man AAahada Allaha la-in atana min fadlihi lanassaddaqanna walanakoonanna mina alssaliheena 76. Falamma atahum min fadlihi bakhiloo bihi

watawallaw wahum muAAridoona   77. FaaAAqabahum nifaqan fee quloobihim ila yawmi yalqawnahu bima akhlafoo Allaha ma waAAadoohu wabima kanoo yakthiboona
78. Alam yaAAlamoo anna Allaha yaAAlamu sirrahum wanajwahum waanna Allaha AAallamu alghuyoobi

Tafsir Ibn Kathir

Hypocrites seek Wealth but are Stingy with Alms

Allah says, some hypocrites give Allah their strongest oaths that if He enriches them from His bounty, they will give away alms and be among the righteous. However, they did not fulfill their vows or say the truth with their words. The consequence of this action is that hypocrisy was placed in their hearts until the Day they meet Allah the Exalted, on the Day of Resurrection. We seek refuge with Allah from such an end. Allah said,

(...because they broke that (covenant) with Allah which they had promised to Him) He placed hypocrisy in their hearts because they broke their promise and lied. In the Two Sahihs, it is recorded that the Messenger of Allah said,

«آيَةُ الْمُنَافِقِ ثَلَاثٌ: إِذَا حَدَّثَ كَذَبَ، وَإِذَا وَعَدَ أَخْلَفَ، وَإِذَا ائْتُمِنَ خَانَ»

(There are three signs for a hypocrite: if he speaks, he lies; if he promises, he breaks the promise; and if he is entrusted, he betrays the trust.) Allah said,

(Know they not that Allah knows their secret ideas, and their Najwa,) Allah states that He knows the secret and what is more hidden than the secret. He has full knowledge of what is in their hearts, even when they pretend that they will give away alms, if they acquire wealth, and will be grateful to Allah for it. Truly, Allah knows them better than they know themselves, for He is the All-Knower of all unseen and apparent things, every secret, every session of counsel, and all that is seen and hidden.

Surah: 9 Ayah: 79

﴿ ٱلَّذِينَ يَلْمِزُونَ ٱلْمُطَّوِّعِينَ مِنَ ٱلْمُؤْمِنِينَ فِى ٱلصَّدَقَٰتِ وَٱلَّذِينَ لَا يَجِدُونَ إِلَّا جُهْدَهُمْ فَيَسْخَرُونَ مِنْهُمْ سَخِرَ ٱللَّهُ مِنْهُمْ وَلَهُمْ عَذَابٌ أَلِيمٌ ۝ ﴾

79. Those who defame such of the believers who give charity (in Allâh's Cause) voluntarily, and those who could not find to give charity (in Allâh's Cause) except what is available to them - so they mock at them (believers); Allâh will throw back their mockery on them, and they shall have a painful torment.

Transliteration

79. Allatheena yalmizoona almuttawwiAAeena mina almu/mineena fee alssadaqati waallatheena la yajidoona illa juhdahum fayaskharoona minhum sakhira Allahu minhum walahum AAathabun aleemun

Tafsir Ibn Kathir

Hypocrites defame Believers Who give the Little Charity They can afford

Among the traits of the hypocrites is that they will not leave anyone without defaming and ridiculing him in all circumstances even those who give away charity. If, for instance, someone gives away a large amount, the hypocrites say that he is showing off. If someone gives away a small amount they say that Allah stands not in need of this man's charity. Al-Bukhari recorded that `Ubaydullah bin Sa`id said that Abu An-Nu`man Al-Basri said that Shu`bah narrated that Sulayman said that Abu Wa'il said that Abu Mas`ud said, "When the verses of charity were revealed, we used to work as porters. A man came and distributed objects of charity in abundance and they (hypocrites) said, `He is showing off.' Another man came and gave a Sa` (a small measure of food grains); they said, `Allah is not in need of this small amount of charity.' Then the Ayah was revealed;

(Those who defame the volunteers...)" Muslim collected this Hadith in the Sahih. Al-`Awfi narrated that Ibn `Abbas said, "One day, the Messenger of Allah went out to the people and called them to bring forth their charity, and they started bringing their charity. Among the last to come forth was a man who brought a Sa` of dates, saying, `O Allah's Messenger! This is a Sa` of dates. I spent the night bringing water and earned two Sa` of dates for my work. I kept one Sa` and brought you the other Sa`.' The Messenger of Allah ordered him to add it to the charity. Some men mocked that man, saying, `Allah and His Messenger are not in need of this charity. What benefit would this Sa` of yours bring' `Abdur-Rahman bin `Awf asked Allah's Messenger , `Are there any more people who give charity' The Messenger of Allah said,

《لَمْ يَبْقَ أَحَدٌ غَيْرُكَ》

(None besides you!) `Abdur-Rahman bin `Awf said, `I will give a hundred Uqiyah of gold as a charity.' `Umar bin Al-Khattab said to him, `Are you crazy' `Abdur-Rahman said, `I am not crazy.' `Umar said, `Have you given what you said would give' `Abdur-Rahman said, `Yes. I have eight thousand (Dirhams), four thousand I give as a loan to my Lord and four thousand I keep for myself.' The Messenger of Allah said,

《بَارَكَ اللهُ لَكَ فِيمَا أَمْسَكْتَ وَفِيمَا أَعْطَيْتَ》

(May Allah bless you for what you kept and what you gave away). However, the hypocrites defamed him, `By Allah! `Abdur-Rahman gave what he gave just to show off.' They lied, for `Abdur-Rahman willingly gave that money, and Allah revealed about his innocence and the innocence of the fellow who was poor and brought only a Sa` of dates. Allah said in His Book,

(Those who defame such of the believers who give charity voluntarily) (9:79).'" A similar story was narrated from Mujahid and several others. Ibn Ishaq said, "Among the believers who gave away charity were `Abdur-Rahman bin `Awf who gave four thousand Dirhams and `Asim bin `Adi from Bani `Ajlan. This occurred after the

Messenger of Allah encouraged and called for paying charity. `Abdur-Rahman bin `Awf stood and gave away four thousand Dirhams. `Asim bin `Adi also stood and gave a hundred Wasaq of dates, but some people defamed them, saying, `They are showing off.' As for the person who gave the little that he could afford, he was Abu `Aqil, from Bani Anif Al-Arashi, who was an ally of Bani `Amr bin `Awf. He brought a Sa` of dates and added it to the charity. They laughed at him, saying, `Allah does not need the Sa` of Abu `Aqil.'" Allah said,

(so they mock at them (believers); Allah will throw back their mockery on them) rebuking them for their evil actions and defaming the believers. Truly, the reward, or punishment, is equitable to the action. Allah treated them the way mocked people are treated, to aid the believers in this life. Allah has prepared a painful torment in the Hereafter for the hypocrites, for the recompense is similar to the deed.

Surah: 9 Ayah: 80

﴿ اسْتَغْفِرْ لَهُمْ أَوْ لَا تَسْتَغْفِرْ لَهُمْ إِن تَسْتَغْفِرْ لَهُمْ سَبْعِينَ مَرَّةً فَلَن يَغْفِرَ ٱللَّهُ لَهُمْ ذَٰلِكَ بِأَنَّهُمْ كَفَرُوا۟ بِٱللَّهِ وَرَسُولِهِۦ ۗ وَٱللَّهُ لَا يَهْدِى ٱلْقَوْمَ ٱلْفَـٰسِقِينَ ﴾

80. Whether you (O Muhammad (peace be upon him)) ask forgiveness for them (hypocrites) or ask not forgiveness for them - (and even) if you ask seventy times for their forgiveness - Allâh will not forgive them because they have disbelieved in Allâh and His Messenger (Muhammad (peace be upon him)) And Allâh guides not those people who are Fâsiqûn (rebellious, disobedient to Allâh).

Transliteration

80. Istaghfir lahum aw la tastaghfir lahum in tastaghfir lahum sabAAeena marratan falan yaghfira Allahu lahum thalika bi-annahum kafaroo biAllahi warasoolihi waAllahu la yahdee alqawma alfasiqeena

Tafsir Ibn Kathir

The Prohibition of asking for Forgiveness for Hypocrites

Allah says to His Prophet that hypocrites are not worthy of seeking forgiveness for them and that if he asks Allah to forgive them seventy times, Allah will not forgive them. The number seventy here was mentioned to close the door on this subject, for Arabs use this number when they exaggerate, not that they actually mean seventy or more than seventy. Ash-Sha`bi said that when `Abdullah bin Ubayy was dying, his son went to the Prophet and said to him, "My father has died, I wish you could attend him and pray the funeral prayer for him." The Prophet said,

《 مَا اسْمُكَ 》

("What is you name) He said, "Al-Hubab bin `Abdullah." The Prophet said,

«بَلْ أَنْتَ عَبْدُاللهِ بْنُ عَبْدِاللهِ إِنَّ الْحُبَابَ اسْمَ شَيْطَان»

(Rather, you are `Abdullah bin `Abdullah, for Al-Hubab is a devil's name.) The Prophet went along with him, attended his father's funeral, gave him his shirt as a shroud and prayed the funeral prayer for him. He was asked, "Would you pray on him, when he is a hypocrite'' He said,

«إِنَّ اللهَ قَالَ:

(إِن تَسْتَغْفِرْ لَهُمْ سَبْعِينَ مَرَّةً)

وَلَأَسْتَغْفِرَنَّ لَهُمْ سَبْعِينَ وَسَبْعِينَ وَسَبْعِين»

(Allah said,(...(and even) if you ask seventy times for their forgiveness...) Verily, I will ask Allah to forgive them seventy times and seventy more and seventy more.)'' Similar narrations were collected from `Urwah bin Az-Zubayr, Mujahid, Qatadah bin Di`amah and Ibn Jarir.

Surah: 9 Ayah: 81 & Ayah: 82

﴿ فَرِحَ ٱلْمُخَلَّفُونَ بِمَقْعَدِهِمْ خِلَـٰفَ رَسُولِ ٱللَّهِ وَكَرِهُوٓاْ أَن يُجَـٰهِدُواْ بِأَمْوَٰلِهِمْ وَأَنفُسِهِمْ فِى سَبِيلِ ٱللَّهِ وَقَالُواْ لَا تَنفِرُواْ فِى ٱلْحَرِّ ۗ قُلْ نَارُ جَهَنَّمَ أَشَدُّ حَرًّا ۚ لَّوْ كَانُواْ يَفْقَهُونَ ﴾

81. Those who stayed away (from Tabuk expedition) rejoiced in their staying behind the Messenger of Allâh; they hated to strive and fight with their properties and their lives in the Cause of Allâh, and they said: "March not forth in the heat." Say: "The Fire of Hell is more intense in heat", if only they could understand!

﴿ فَلْيَضْحَكُواْ قَلِيلًا وَلْيَبْكُواْ كَثِيرًا جَزَآءًۢ بِمَا كَانُواْ يَكْسِبُونَ ﴾

82. So let them laugh a little and (they will) cry much as a recompense of what they used to earn (by committing sins).

Transliteration

81. Fariha almukhallafoona bimaqAAadihim khilafa rasooli Allahi wakarihoo an yujahidoo bi-amwalihim waanfusihim fee sabeeli Allahi waqaloo la tanfiroo fee alharri qul naru jahannamaashaddu harran law kanoo yafqahoona 82. Falyadhakoo qaleelan walyabkoo katheeran jazaan bima kanoo yaksiboona

Tafsir Ibn Kathir

Hypocrites rejoice because They remained behind from Tabuk!

Allah admonishes the hypocrites who lagged behind from the battle of Tabuk with the Companions of the Messenger of Allah, rejoicing that they remained behind after the Messenger departed for the battle,

(they hated to strive and fight), along with the Messenger,

(with their properties and their lives in the cause of Allah, and they said), to each other,

("March not forth in the heat.") Tabuk occurred at a time when the heat was intense and the fruits and shades became delightful. This is why they said,

("March not forth in the heat") Allah said to His Messenger,

(Say) to them,

("The fire of Hell..."), which will be your destination because of your disobedience,

("...is more intense in heat;"), than the heat that you sought to avoid; it is even more intense than fire. Imam Malik narrated that Abu Az-Zinad said that Al-A`raj narrated that Abu Hurayrah said that the Messenger of Allah said,

«نَارُ بَنِي آدَمَ الَّتِي تُوقِدُونَهَا جُزْءٌ مِنْ سَبْعِينَ جُزْءًا مِنْ نَارِ جَهَنَّمَ»

(The fire that the son of Adam kindles is but one part of seventy parts of the Fire of Jahannam.) They said, "O Allah's Messenger! This fire alone is enough." He said,

«فُضِّلَتْ عَلَيْهَا بِتِسْعَةٍ وَسِتِّينَ جُزْءًا»

((Hellfire) was favored by sixty-nine parts.) The Two Sahihs collected this Hadith. Al-A`mash narrated that Abu Ishaq said that An-Nu`man bin Bashir said that the Messenger of Allah said,

«إِنَّ أَهْوَنَ أَهْلِ النَّارِ عَذَابًا يَوْمَ الْقِيَامَةِ لِمَنْ لَهُ نَعْلَانِ وَشِرَاكَانِ مِنْ نَارِ جَهَنَّمَ يَغْلِي مِنْهُمَا دِمَاغُهُ كَمَا يَغْلِي الْمِرْجَلُ، لَا يَرَى أَنَّ أَحَدًا مِنْ أَهْلِ النَّارِ أَشَدُّ عَذَابًا مِنْهُ وَإِنَّهُ أَهْوَنُهُمْ عَذَابًا»

(On the Day of Resurrection, the person who will receive the least punishment among the people of the Fire, wears two slippers made from the Fire of Jahannam causing his brain to boil, just as a pot boils. He thinks that none in the Fire is receiving a more severe torment than he, when in fact he is receiving the least torment.) The Two Sahihs collected this Hadith. There are many other Ayat and Prophetic Hadiths on this subject. Allah said in His Glorious Book,

(By no means! Verily, it will be the Fire of Hell. Taking away (burning completely) the scalp!) (70:15-16),

(Al-Hamim (boiling water) will be poured down over their heads. With it will melt (or vanish away) what is within their bellies, as well as (their) skins. And for them are hooked rods of iron (to punish them). Every time they seek to get away therefrom, from anguish, they will be driven back therein, and (it will be said to them): "Taste the torment of burning!") (22:19-22), and,

(Surely, those who disbelieved in Our Ayat, We shall burn them in Fire. As often as their skins are roasted through, We shall change them for other skins that they may taste the punishment.)(4:56) Allah said here,

(Say: "The fire of Hell is more intense in heat;" if only they could understand!) meaning, if they have any comprehension or understanding, they would have marched with the Messenger of Allah during the heat, so as to save themselves from the Fire of Jahannam, which is much more severe. Allah, the Exalted, then warns the hypocrites against their conduct,

(So let them laugh a little...) Ibn Abi Talhah reported that Ibn `Abbas commented, "Life is short, so let them laugh as much as they like in it. But when life ends and they are returned to Allah, the Exalted and Most Honored, they will start crying forever without end."

Surah: 9 Ayah: 83

﴿ فَإِن رَّجَعَكَ ٱللَّهُ إِلَىٰ طَآئِفَةٍ مِّنْهُمْ فَٱسْتَـْٔذَنُوكَ لِلْخُرُوجِ فَقُل لَّن تَخْرُجُوا۟ مَعِىَ أَبَدًا وَلَن تُقَـٰتِلُوا۟ مَعِىَ عَدُوًّا ۖ إِنَّكُمْ رَضِيتُم بِٱلْقُعُودِ أَوَّلَ مَرَّةٍ فَٱقْعُدُوا۟ مَعَ ٱلْخَـٰلِفِينَ ﴾

83. If Allâh brings you back to a party of them (the hypocrites), and they ask your permission to go out (to fight), say: "Never shall you go out with me, nor fight an enemy with me; you were pleased to sit (inactive) on the first occasion, then you sit (now) with those who lag behind."

Transliteration

83. Fa-in rajaAAaka Allahu ila ta-ifatin minhum faista/thanooka lilkhurooji faqul lan takhrujoo maAAiya abadan walan tuqatiloo maAAiya AAaduwwan innakum radeetum bialquAAoodi awwala marratin faoqAAudoo maAAa alkhalifeena

Tafsir Ibn Kathir

Hypocrites are barred from participating in Jihad

Allah commands His Messenger, peace be upon him,

(If Allah brings you back), from this battle,

(to a party of them) in reference to the twelve (hypocrite) men, according to Qatadah,

(and they ask your permission to go out), with you to another battle,

(say: "Never shall you go out with me nor fight an enemy with me...") as an admonishment and punishment for them. Allah mentioned the reason for this decision,

("You were pleased to sit (inactive) on the first occasion...") Allah said in a similar Ayah,

(And We shall turn their hearts and their eyes away (from guidance), as they refused to believe therein for the first time.) (6:110) The recompense of an evil deed includes being directed to follow it with another evil deed, while the reward of a good deed includes being directed to another good deed after it. For instance, Allah said concerning the `Umrah of Hudaybiyyah,

(Those who lagged behind will say, when you set forth to take the spoils.)(48:15) Allah said next,

("...then you sit (now) with those who lag behind.") in reference to the men who lagged behind from (Tabuk) battle, according to Ibn `Abbas.

Surah: 9 Ayah: 84

﴿ وَلَا تُصَلِّ عَلَىٰ أَحَدٍ مِّنْهُم مَّاتَ أَبَدًا وَلَا تَقُمْ عَلَىٰ قَبْرِهِ ۖ إِنَّهُمْ كَفَرُوا بِاللَّهِ وَرَسُولِهِ وَمَاتُوا وَهُمْ فَاسِقُونَ ﴾

84. And never (O Muhammad (peace be upon him)) pray (funeral prayer) for any of them (hypocrites) who dies, nor stand at his grave. Certainly they disbelieved in Allâh and His Messenger, and died while they were Fâsiqûn (rebellious, - disobedient to Allâh and His Messenger (peace be upon him))

Transliteration

84. Wala tusalli AAala ahadin minhum mata abadan wala taqum AAala qabrihi innahum kafaroo biAllahi warasoolihi wamatoo wahum fasiqoona

Tafsir Ibn Kathir

The Prohibition of Prayer for the Funeral of Hypocrites

Allah commands His Messenger to disown the hypocrites, to abstain from praying the funeral prayer when any of them dies, from standing next to his grave to seek Allah's forgiveness for him, or to invoke Allah for his benefit. This is because hypocrites disbelieved in Allah and His Messenger and died as such. This ruling applies to all those who are known to be hypocrites, even though it was revealed about the specific case of `Abdullah bin Ubayy bin Salul, the chief hypocrite. Al-Bukhari recorded that Ibn `Umar said, "When `Abdullah bin Ubayy died, his son, `Abdullah bin `Abdullah, came to the Messenger of Allah and asked him to give him his shirt to shroud his father in, and the Messenger did that. He also asked that the Prophet offer his father's funeral prayer, and Allah's Messenger stood up to offer the funeral prayer. `Umar took hold of the Prophet's robe and said, `O Allah's Messenger! Are you going to offer his funeral prayer even though your Lord has forbidden you to do so' Allah's Messenger said,

《إِنَّمَا خَيَّرَنِي اللهُ فَقَالَ:

(I have been given the choice, for Allah says:

(اسْتَغْفِرْ لَهُمْ أَوْ لاَ تَسْتَغْفِرْ لَهُمْ إِن تَسْتَغْفِرْ لَهُمْ سَبْعِينَ مَرَّةً فَلَن يَغْفِرَ اللَّهُ لَهُمْ)

(Whether you ask forgiveness for them (hypocrites), or do not ask for forgiveness for them. Even though you ask for their forgiveness seventy times, Allah will not forgive them.)

وَسَأَزِيدُهُ عَلَى السَّبْعِينَ》

(Verily, I will ask (for forgiveness for him) more than seventy times).' `Umar said, `He is a hypocrite!' So Allah's Messenger offered the funeral prayer and on that Allah revealed this Verse,

(And never (O Muhammad) pray (funeral prayer) for any of them (hypocrites) who dies, nor stand at his grave.)" `Umar bin Al-Khattab narrated a similar narration. In this narration, `Umar said, "The Prophet offered his funeral prayer, walked with the funeral procession and stood on his grave until he was buried. I was amazed at my daring to talk like this to the Messenger of Allah, while Allah and His Messenger have better knowledge. By Allah, soon afterwards, these two Ayat were revealed,

(And never (O Muhammad) pray (funeral prayer) for any of them (hypocrites) who dies.) Ever since this revelation came, the Prophet never offered the funeral prayer for any hypocrite nor stood on his grave until Allah, the Exalted and Most Honored, brought death to him." At-Tirmidhi collected this Hadith in his Tafsir (section of his Sunan) and said, "Hasan Sahih". Al-Bukhari also recorded it.

Surah: 9 Ayah: 85

﴿ وَلَا تُعْجِبْكَ أَمْوَالُهُمْ وَأَوْلَادُهُمْ إِنَّمَا يُرِيدُ ٱللَّهُ أَن يُعَذِّبَهُم بِهَا فِى ٱلدُّنْيَا وَتَزْهَقَ أَنفُسُهُمْ وَهُمْ كَـٰفِرُونَ ۝ ﴾

85. And let not their wealth or their children amaze you. Allâh's Plan is to punish them with these things in this world, and that their souls shall depart (die) while they are disbelievers.

Transliteration

85. Wala tuAAjibka amwaluhum waawladuhum innama yureedu Allahu an yuAAaththibahum biha fee alddunya watazhaqa anfusuhum wahum kafiroona

Tafsir Ibn Kathir

We mentioned before the explanation of a similar Ayah, all the thanks and praises are due to Allah.

Surah: 9 Ayah: 86 & Ayah: 87

﴿ وَإِذَا أُنزِلَتْ سُورَةٌ أَنْ ءَامِنُوا۟ بِٱللَّهِ وَجَـٰهِدُوا۟ مَعَ رَسُولِهِ ٱسْتَـْٔذَنَكَ أُو۟لُوا۟ ٱلطَّوْلِ مِنْهُمْ وَقَالُوا۟ ذَرْنَا نَكُن مَّعَ ٱلْقَـٰعِدِينَ ۝ ﴾

86. And when a Sûrah (chapter from the Qur'ân) is revealed, enjoining them to believe in Allâh and to strive hard and fight along with His Messenger, the wealthy among them ask your leave to exempt them (from Jihâd) and say, "Leave us (behind), we would be with those who sit (at home)."

﴿ رَضُوا۟ بِأَن يَكُونُوا۟ مَعَ ٱلْخَوَالِفِ وَطُبِعَ عَلَىٰ قُلُوبِهِمْ فَهُمْ لَا يَفْقَهُونَ ۝ ﴾

87. They are content to be with those (the women) who sit behind (at home). Their hearts are sealed up (from all kinds of goodness and right guidance), so they understand not.

Transliteration

86. Wa-itha onzilat sooratun an aminoo biAllahi wajahidoo maAAa rasoolihi ista/thanaka oloo alttawli minhum waqaloo tharna nakun maAAa alqaAAideena 87. Radoo bi-an yakoonoo maAAa alkhawalifi watubiAAa AAala quloobihim fahum la yafqahoona

Tafsir Ibn Kathir

Admonishing Those Who did not join the Jihad

Allah chastises and admonishes those who stayed away from Jihad and refrained from performing it, even though they had the supplies, means and ability to join it. They asked the Messenger for permission to stay behind, saying,

("Leave us (behind), we would be with those who sit (at home)") thus accepting for themselves the shame of lagging behind with women, after the army had left. If war starts, such people are the most cowardice, but when it is safe, they are the most boastful among men. Allah described them in another Ayah,

(Then when fear comes, you will see them looking to you, their eyes revolving like (those of) one over whom hovers death; but when the fear departs, they will smite you with sharp tongues.)(33:19) their tongues direct their harsh words against you, when it is safe to do so. In battle, however, they are the most cowardice among men. Allah said in another Ayah,

(Those who believe say: "Why is not a Surah sent down (for us) But when a decisive Surah (explaining and ordering things) is sent down, and fighting is mentioned therein, you will see those in whose hearts is a disease looking at you with a look of one fainting to death. But it was better for them. Obedience (to Allah) and good words (were better for them). And when the matter is resolved on, then if they had been true to Allah, it would have been better for them.) (47:20-21) sAllah said next,

(Their hearts are sealed up) because of their staying away from Jihad and from accompanying the Messenger in Allah's cause,

(so they understand not.) they neither understand what benefits them so that they perform it nor what hurts them so that they avoid it.

Surah: 9 Ayah: 88 & Ayah: 89

﴿ لَـٰكِنِ ٱلرَّسُولُ وَٱلَّذِينَ ءَامَنُوا۟ مَعَهُۥ جَـٰهَدُوا۟ بِأَمْوَٰلِهِمْ وَأَنفُسِهِمْ ۚ وَأُو۟لَـٰٓئِكَ لَهُمُ ٱلْخَيْرَٰتُ ۖ وَأُو۟لَـٰٓئِكَ هُمُ ٱلْمُفْلِحُونَ ۝ ﴾

88. But the Messenger (Muhammad (peace be upon him)) and those who believed with him (in Islâmic Monotheism) strove hard and fought with their wealth and their lives (in Allâh's Cause). Such are they for whom are the good things, and it is they who will be successful.

﴿ أَعَدَّ ٱللَّهُ لَهُمْ جَنَّـٰتٍ تَجْرِى مِن تَحْتِهَا ٱلْأَنْهَـٰرُ خَـٰلِدِينَ فِيهَا ۚ ذَٰلِكَ ٱلْفَوْزُ ٱلْعَظِيمُ ﴾

89. For them Allâh has got ready Gardens (Paradise) under which rivers flow, to dwell therein forever. That is the supreme success.

Transliteration

88. Lakini alrrasoolu waallatheena amanoo maAAahu jahadoo bi-amwalihim waanfusihim waola-ika lahumu alkhayratu waola-ika humu almuflihoona 89. aAAadda Allahu lahum jannatin tajree min tahtiha al-anharu khalideena feeha thalika alfawzu alAAatheemu

Tafsir Ibn Kathir

After Allah mentioned the sins of the hypocrites, He praised the faithful believers and described their reward in the Hereafter,

(But the Messenger and those who believed with him strove hard and fought) until the end of these two Ayat (9:88-89). This describes the qualities, as well as, the reward of faithful believers. Allah said,

(Such are they for whom are the good things), in the Hereafter, in the gardens of Al-Firdaws and the high grades.

Surah: 9 Ayah: 90

﴿ وَجَاءَ ٱلْمُعَذِّرُونَ مِنَ ٱلْأَعْرَابِ لِيُؤْذَنَ لَهُمْ وَقَعَدَ ٱلَّذِينَ كَذَبُواْ ٱللَّهَ وَرَسُولَهُۥ سَيُصِيبُ ٱلَّذِينَ كَفَرُواْ مِنْهُمْ عَذَابٌ أَلِيمٌ ﴾

90. And those who made excuses from the bedouins came (to you, O Prophet (peace be upon him)) asking your permission to exempt them (from the battle), and those who had lied to Allâh and His Messenger sat at home (without asking the permission for it); a painful torment will seize those of them who disbelieve.

Transliteration

90. Wajaa almuAAaththiroona mina al-aAArabi liyu/thana lahum waqaAAada allatheena kathaboo Allaha warasoolahu sayuseebu allatheena kafaroo minhum AAathabun aleemun

Tafsir Ibn Kathir

Allah describes here the condition of the bedouins who lived around Al-Madinah, who asked for permission to remain behind from Jihad when they came to the Messenger to explain to him their weakness and inability to join the fighting. Ad-Dahhak said that Ibn `Abbas said that they were those who had valid excuses, for Allah said next, (and those who had lied to Allah and His Messenger sat at home), and did not ask for permission for it; and Allah warned them of painful punishment, (a painful torment will seize those of them who disbelieve.)

Surah: 9 Ayah: 91, Ayah: 92 (end of Part 10) & Ayah: 93

﴿ لَّيْسَ عَلَى ٱلضُّعَفَاءِ وَلَا عَلَى ٱلْمَرْضَىٰ وَلَا عَلَى ٱلَّذِينَ لَا يَجِدُونَ مَا يُنفِقُونَ حَرَجٌ إِذَا نَصَحُواْ لِلَّهِ وَرَسُولِهِۦ مَا عَلَى ٱلْمُحْسِنِينَ مِن سَبِيلٍ وَٱللَّهُ غَفُورٌ رَّحِيمٌ ﴾

91. There is no blame on those who are weak or ill or who find no resources to spend (in holy fighting (Jihâd)) if they are sincere and true (in duty) to Allâh and

His Messenger. No ground (of complaint) can there be against the Muhsinûn (good-doers). And Allâh is Oft-Forgiving, Most Merciful.

﴿ وَلَا عَلَى ٱلَّذِينَ إِذَا مَآ أَتَوْكَ لِتَحْمِلَهُمْ قُلْتَ لَآ أَجِدُ مَآ أَحْمِلُكُمْ عَلَيْهِ تَوَلَّوْا۟ وَّأَعْيُنُهُمْ تَفِيضُ مِنَ ٱلدَّمْعِ حَزَنًا أَلَّا يَجِدُوا۟ مَا يُنفِقُونَ ﴾ ۝

92. Nor (is there blame) on those who came to you to be provided with mounts, when you said: "I can find no mounts for you," they turned back, while their eyes overflowing with tears of grief that they could not find anything to spend (for Jihâd).

﴿ ۞ إِنَّمَا ٱلسَّبِيلُ عَلَى ٱلَّذِينَ يَسْتَـْٔذِنُونَكَ وَهُمْ أَغْنِيَآءُ رَضُوا۟ بِأَن يَكُونُوا۟ مَعَ ٱلْخَوَالِفِ وَطَبَعَ ٱللَّهُ عَلَىٰ قُلُوبِهِمْ فَهُمْ لَا يَعْلَمُونَ ﴾ ۝

93. The ground (of complaint) is only against those who are rich, and yet ask exemption. They are content to be with (the women) who sit behind (at home) and Allâh has sealed up their hearts (from all kinds of goodness and right guidance) so that they know not (what they are losing).

Transliteration

91. Laysa AAala aldduAAafa-i wala AAala almarda wala AAala allatheena la yajidoona ma yunfiqoona harajun itha nasahoo lillahi warasoolihi ma AAala almuhsineena min sabeelin waAllahu ghafoorun raheemun 92. Wala AAala allatheena itha ma atawka litahmilahum qulta la ajidu ma ahmilukum AAalayhi tawallaw waaAAyunuhum tafeedu mina alddamAAi hazanan alla yajidoo ma yunfiqoona 93. Innama alssabeelu AAala allatheena yasta/thinoonaka wahum aghniyao radoo bi-an yakoonoo maAAa alkhawalifi watabaAAa Allahu AAala quloobihim fahum la yaAAlamoona

Tafsir Ibn Kathir

Legitimate Excuses for staying away from Jihad

Allah mentions here the valid excuses that permit one to stay away from fighting. He first mentions the excuses that remain with a person, the weakness in the body that disallows one from Jihad, such as blindness, limping, and so forth. He then mentions the excuses that are not permanent, such as an illness that would prevent one from fighting in the cause of Allah, or poverty that prevents preparing for Jihad. There is no sin in these cases if they remain behind, providing that when they remain behind, they do not spread malice or try to discourage Muslims from fighting, but all the while observing good behavior in this state, just as Allah said,

(No means (of complaint) can there be against the doers of good. And Allah is Oft-Forgiving, Most Merciful.) Al-Awza`i said, "The people went out for the Istisqa' (rain) prayer. Bilal bin Sa`d stood up, praised Allah and thanked Him then said, `O those who are present! Do you concur that wrong has been done' They said, `Yes, by Allah!' He said, `O Allah! We hear your statement,

(No means (of complaint) can there be against the doers of good.) O Allah! We admit our errors, so forgive us and give us mercy and rain.' He then raised his hands and the people also raised their hands, and rain was sent down on them." Mujahid said about Allah's statement,

(Nor (is there blame) on those who came to you to be provided with mounts) Mujahid said; "It was revealed about Bani Muqarrin from the tribe of Muzaynah. " Ibn Abi Hatim recorded that Al-Hasan said that the Messenger of Allah said,

«لَقَدْ خَلَّفْتُمْ بِالْمَدِينَةِ أَقْوَامًا مَا أَنْفَقْتُمْ مِنْ نَفَقَةٍ وَلَا قَطَعْتُمْ وَادِيًا وَلَا نِلْتُمْ مِنْ عَدُوَ نَيْلًا إِلَّا وَقَدْ شَرَكُوكُمْ فِي الْأَجْرِ»

(Some people have remained behind you in Al-Madinah; and you never spent anything, crossed a valley, or afflicted hardship on an enemy, but they were sharing the reward with you.) He then recited the Ayah,

(Nor (is there blame) on those who came to you to be provided with mounts, when you said: "I can find no mounts for you.") This Hadith has a basis in the Two Sahihs from Anas, the Messenger of Allah said,

«إِنَّ بِالْمَدِينَةِ أَقْوَامًا مَا قَطَعْتُمْ وَادِيًا وَلَا سِرْتُمْ سَيْرًا إِلَّا وَهُمْ مَعَكُم»

(Some people have remained behind in Al-Madinah and you never crossed a valley or marched forth, but they were with you.) They said, "While they are still at Al-Madinah" He said,

«نَعَمْ حَبَسَهُمُ الْعُذْرِ»

(Yes, as they have been held back by a (legal) excuse.) Then, Allah criticized those who seek permission to remain behind while they are rich, admonishing them for wanting to stay behind with women who remained in their homes,

(and Allah has sealed up their hearts, so that they know not (what they are losing).)

www.ingramcontent.com/pod-product-compliance
Lightning Source LLC
Chambersburg PA
CBHW081112080526
44587CB00021B/3559